Tort Law in Portugal

Tort Law in Portugal

Second Edition

Nuno Manuel Pinto Oliveira
André Gonçalo Dias Pereira

This book was originally published as a monograph in the International Encyclopaedia of Laws/Tort Law.

Founding Editor: Roger Blanpain
General Editor: Frank Hendrickx
Volume Editor: Britt Weyts

Wolters Kluwer

Published by:
Kluwer Law International B.V.
PO Box 316
2400 AH Alphen aan den Rijn
The Netherlands
E-mail: lrs-sales@wolterskluwer.com
Website: www.wolterskluwer.com/en/solutions/kluwerlawinternational

Sold and distributed by:
Wolters Kluwer Legal & Regulatory U.S.
920 Links Avenue
Landisville, PA 17538
United States of America
E-mail: customer.service@wolterskluwer.com

ISBN 978-94-035-3749-8

e-Book: ISBN 978-94-035-3759-7
web-PDF: ISBN 978-94-035-3769-6

This title is available on www.kluwerlawonline.com

The Authors

Nuno Manuel Pinto Oliveira took his first degree ('licenciatura') at the Coimbra Law School, Portugal, in 1995, with average marks of 17/20. He was then awarded the Azeredo Perdigão Prize for the best student at Coimbra Law School in 1995. In 2000, he took his PhD at the European University Institute, Florence. In 2008, he took his 'agregação' (roughly equivalent to the French 'aggrégation') at the University of Minho, Braga, Portugal. In 2011, he was tenured as a full-time associate professor, and in 2016, he was tenured as a full professor of Civil Law (Contracts, Torts, Restitution). In November 2018, he was nominated as Justice at the Portuguese Supreme Court.

André Gonçalo Dias Pereira is Associate Professor of Private Law at the University of Coimbra, where he completed his legal education (LLB (1998, Manuel de Andrade Prize for Best Student in 1997), LLM (2003, Manuel de Andrade Prize for Best Master Student in 2003) and PhD (2014, *summa cum laude*)), and in 2023, he became Associate Professor; he is Director of the Centre for Biomedical Law and Researcher at University of Coimbra Institute for Legal Research. He is an active member of the editorial board of several journals, and he is President of the Institutional Review Board of AIBILI. He is also a member of the Ethics Committee of the National Institute of Legal Medicine and Forensic Sciences and the Ethics Committee of the University of Coimbra and Vice-President of the National Council of Ethics for Life Sciences. At the international level, Pereira is Chair of the Education Committee of the World Association for Medical Law (2023–present), and he is Fellow of the European Centre of Tort and Insurance Law, a member of the Brazilian Institute for Tort Law (IBERC), a member of the Iberoamerican Law Institute (IDIBE), Vice-President and Founder of the Portuguese Speaking Association for Health Law (ALDIS), and a member of the Luso-Brazilian Institute for Comparative Law and the International Academy of Comparative Law (Ciencia ID: 951E-7E45-3E7F).

The Authors

Table of Contents

List of Abbreviations

AAFDL	Associação Académica da Faculdade de Direito de Lisboa
Art.	Article
BGB	Bürgerliches Gesetzbuch
BMJ	Boletim do Ministério da Justiça
CC	Civil Code
CEDOUA	Centro de Estudos do Direito do Ordenamento, do Urbanismo e do Ambiente
CJEU	Court of Justice of the European Union
Coord.	Coordinator
e.g.	*exempli gratia*
EC	European Community
ed.	Edition
eds	Editors
EEC	European Economic Community
etc.	*et cetera*
EU	European Union
ff.	and the following
GDP	Gross Domestic Product
GNR	National Republican Guard
GRERCA	Groupe de Recherche Européen sur la Responsabilité Civile et l'Assurance
Hrsg.	Herausgeber/in
i.e.	*id est*
INE	Instituto Nacional de Estatística
IRJS	Institut de Recherche Juridique de la Sorbonne
n.	Note
No.	Number
PhD	Philosophiae Doctor
Proc.	Process
RFDUC	Revista da Faculdade de Direito da Universidade Católica

List of Abbreviations

RFDUP	Revista da Faculdade de Direito da Universidade Porto
RLJ	Revista de Legislação e Jurisprudência
STJ	Supremo Tribunal de Justiça
T.	Tome
v.	Versus
vol.	Volume

General Introduction

§1. General Background of the Country

I. Geography

1. The Portuguese Republic, situated in the European Continent and in the Iberian Peninsula, has a territory of 92,152 square kilometres, which encompasses its continental and insular territory. Its continental borders are in the North and East with Spain and South and West with the Atlantic Ocean. It has two archipelagos, Madeira and Azores, in the Atlantic Ocean, which have a territory of 741 and 2333 square kilometres, respectively. Its capital and largest city is Lisbon.

Madeira is situated merely 500 kilometres from the African coast and circa 1000 kilometres from the European continent. It is formed by Madeira and Porto Santo Islands and by the uninhabited Desertas and Selvagens Islands, as well as by several islets.

Located between North America and the European continent, the Azores is at an approximate distance of 1600 kilometres from the main land. It has nine islands – Corvo, Flores, Faial, Pico, São Jorge, Graciosa, Terceira, São Miguel and Santa Maria – and the Formigas Islets, which are classified as a Natural Reserve. The highest point within the Portuguese territory is on Pico Island at Mount Pico at 2351 metres above sea level, making it also the highest point of the Mid-Atlantic Ridge.

The main land is divided into eighteen districts – Viana do Castelo; Braga; Vila Real; Bragança; Oporto; Aveiro; Viseu; Guarda; Coimbra; Castelo Branco; Leiria; Santarém; Portalegre; Lisbon; Évora; Setúbal; Beja and Faro – and has its highest point at Serra da Estrela, 1993 metres above sea level.

Portugal has one of the world's largest Exclusive Economic Zones, with a territory of 1,727,408 square kilometres.

II. History

2. Portugal was founded on 5 October 1143 with the signature of the Treaty of Zamora, which recognized its independence from the Kingdom of León and King Alfonso VII, and, simultaneously, Afonso Henriques as its first King – starting the Afonsine Dynasty of the House of Burgundy, which ruled Portugal until 1383 and had nine kings. It stands out as a time mainly dedicated to expanding the country's territory towards the South (which was dubbed Recapture). In 1383, John I of Castile and son-in-law of King Ferdinand I, the last King of the Afonsine Dynasty, claimed the Portuguese throne. That triggered John of Aviz, the illegitimate son of Ferdinand's father, King Peter I, together with other nobles and General Nuno Álvares Pereira, to battle against what they saw as future incorporation of Portugal into Castile. Between 1383 and 1385, Portugal had no crown King, but ultimately John I of Castile was defeated in the Battle of Aljubarrota and John of Aviz was acclaimed King in the Portuguese Cortes of Coimbra in 1385. That was the start of the second Portuguese dynasty, the Joanine Dynasty or Dynasty of Aviz, which also had nine kings and ruled Portugal between 1385 and 1580. It was marked for being not only the Age of Discovery and maritime trade – Madeira and Azores were discovered, as well as, among others, Cape Verde, an eastern route to India and later Brazil – but also of colonization and slavery, all of which made Portugal an economic superpower in the fifteenth and sixteenth centuries.

In 1580, the Portuguese succession crisis started when King Ferdinand died in battle and had no heir to the throne and neither did his uncle, King-Cardinal Henry of Portugal. It is discussed among historians if Henry was followed by António I, who would have ruled for a little over a month, since, in 1580, Philip II of Spain was crowned King Philip I of Portugal in Tomar beginning the third era of Kings, the Phillippine Dynasty. It lasted from 1581 to 1640 and had three Kings. Portugal remained an independent country but shared its Kings with the Spanish Empire in what was called the Iberian Union.

In 1640, John IV led a rebellion with other nobles and started the Portuguese Restoration War. He was acclaimed King in 1640, determining the beginning of the last Portuguese dynasty, the Dynasty of Braganza. It had twelve Kings and two Queens and lasted between 1640 and 1910. During this time, a significant number of Portuguese settled in Brazil in what was called 'The Gold Rush'. The main figure of that era was Marquis of Pombal, who was nominated Secretary of State of Internal Affairs and later Secretary of State of Foreign Affairs and War during the reign of King Joseph I. He is mainly known for the abolition of slavery, his economic policies, the reformation of the University of Coimbra and the rebuilding of Lisbon after the earthquake of 1755, developing what is now called the Pombaline city centre. In the years after, especially after an alleged assassination attempt on the King, the Marquis of Pombal became ruthless, expelling the Jesuits and killing the Távora Family and the Duke of Aveiro. Nevertheless, he became powerless, by order of Queen Maria I, after King Joseph's death.

In 1908, both King Carlos I and his heir apparent, Prince Luis Filipe, died in what has become known as The Regicide. He was followed by King Manuel II, but in 1910, a revolution ended the Monarchy and proclaimed Portugal as a Republic. Until this day, Portugal has a national holiday on 5 October to celebrate the implementation of the Republic.

The First Republic years are remembered for their instability, since it only lasted sixteen years but had forty-five governments. It is remembered as a time of separation between State and Church and the emerging of a secularist era, giving ground, e.g., to the legalization of divorce.

In 1926, however, a coup d'état had overthrown the First Republic and initiated what would be the Second Republic. From 1926 to 1933, Portugal lived in a Military Dictatorship, marked by the dissolution of the Parliament and of political parties, first led by Mendes Cabeçadas, but quickly passed on to General Costa Gomes and next to General Óscar Carmona. Carmona created the National Dictatorship and, in 1928, made António Oliveira Salazar, a law professor, his Finance Minister. Salazar's power continued to grow, and in 1932, he became Prime Minister. In 1933, a new Constitution was approved and began a long-lasting dictatorship called Estado Novo. From 1932 to 1968, Salazar had an authoritarian, nationalist, corporativist and fascist regime, worried about keeping the Portuguese colonies and silencing the opposition. There was a secret police (PIDE), and political prisoners were kept and tortured in several prisons from Tarrafal in Cape Verde to Aljube in Lisbon. Starting in 1961, the regime fought the Colonial War in Africa, which resulted from the insurgence of several nationalist movements in the colonies. When Salazar became ill in 1968, he was substituted by Marcello Caetano. Nevertheless, on 25 April 1974, a military coup by the Armed Forces Movement was made with popular support on the streets, what is now known as the Carnation Revolution – so dubbed by the shortage of shots fired and because carnations were distributed on the streets and put into the soldier's rifles. To this day, 25 April is annually celebrated as a national holiday, being regarded as Freedom Day. Some of their main promises were to end the Colonial War and grant independence to the colonized countries. After some initial troubled times, democracy was installed, censorship was abolished, political prisoners were freed, and, among other achievements, a new Constitution was made in 1976.

Since then, Portugal has lived in what is called the Third Republic, with a total of, for now, twenty-one governments. In 1986, together with Spain, Portugal joined the European Economic Community, now the European Union, and, in 1999, adopted the Euro as its official currency and entered the Eurozone.

III. Political System

3. Since 1976, Portugal has been a mixed presidential and parliamentary Republic,[1] characterized by its variable architecture contingent on each election's political power attainment – e.g., if a party or coalition in government has a parliamentary majority, the system's presidential side is less noticeable and vice versa.

As signs of being partially a parliamentary system, the Portuguese political system has government autonomy; governmental accountability to the Parliament and government counter-signature. The government's autonomy is enshrined in Articles 110 and 182 of the Constitution of the Portuguese Republic. The first norm acknowledges it as a sovereign body, and the second as the top body within the Public Administration's hierarchy with the power to conduct the general policy of the country. According to the Constitution's Article 190, the Government is accountable, not only to the President of the Republic (revealing some presidential tendencies) but also to the Parliament. In accordance, Article 191 establishes the Prime Minister's accountability, within the government's political responsibilities, to the Parliament, and, at the same time, the government's Minister's accountability not

1. For a more comprehensive reading, *see* J.J. Gomes Canotilho, *Direito Constitucional e Teoria da Constituição*, 7 ed., Almedina, 2003, 597–610.

only to the Prime Minister but also to the Parliament. The Government can, therefore, suffer a motion of censure (which leads to its removal) or propose a confidence motion (whose failure also leads to its removal), according to Articles 193 and 195. Lastly, the government has the power to counter-signature some of the President's acts, as established in Article 140.

Complementarily, the Portuguese system also has some presidential traces. First, the President of the Republic is elected in a universal, secret and direct suffrage (Article 121), having, therefore, direct legitimacy. The President does not have legislative initiative, but he has, according to Article 136 of the Constitution veto power, for political and constitutional reasons. Lastly, as enshrined in Articles 133 and 134, the President has several ways of directing policy and a number of personal responsibilities (being, for example, the Commander-in-Chief of the Armed Forces), which adds to the fact of the Government's power to counter-signature being an exemption and not a rule.

IV. Economic and Social Values

A. *Economic and Social Values*

4. Portugal is a country with an estimated population of, as of 2022, 10,444,242 people,[2] with 7.5% of its residents being foreign and a gross domestic product (GDP) of approximately EUR 265,508.000 in 2023.[3] It has an active population of 5,325.2 million people, and 78.7% of people are of active age (15–64 years old). As the majority of the developed countries, Portugal has an ageing society, with a fertility rate of 1.43, consisting of only 13% of people under age 14 and 24% of people 65 years old or more – which culminates in an ageing index of 185.6.

Accompanying the trendlines, the number of marriages is at ca. 37,000, when in 1960, it was 69,457, and 59.5% of children were born out of wedlock. The percentage of civil marriages was 78.1% (in 2023), and there were 1,009 same-sex marriages.

Education-wise, Portugal's literacy rate for 2021 was 96.78%. In 2021, 2,92,809 individuals aged 10 years old or more could not read or write, which corresponds to an illiteracy rate of 3.1% – a decrease of 2.1 p.p. from 2011 when the rate was 5.2%.

At the moment, 92% of children of matching schooling age are enrolled in preschool; 96% in the first cycle; and 87% both in the second and third cycles.

In 2021, according to the Census, 17.2% of the resident population had completed higher education, and 52,627 people had a PhD.

An average Portuguese household income is EUR 21.537, and 17% of the population is at the at-risk-of-poverty rate, 21% of whom are under 18 years old and 17% are 65 years old or older. As of 2022, 78.7% of the Portuguese population of active age was considered active, 80.9% male and 76.6% being female. 42.7% of the total

2. *See* INE (Instituto Nacional de Estatística) https://www.ine.pt.
3. More data can be found at Pordata. *See*, https://www.pordata.pt/Portugal.

Portuguese population is considered inactive – with 739.9 thousand being students, 2,032 million retirees, 343.9 thousand people being stay-at-home spouses and 637.1 thousand for other reasons.

According to recent data, 54% of the Portuguese population is employed, 3% in the primary sector, 25% in the secondary and 72% in the tertiary sector. Only 11% of the working population is considered part-time employed. Approximately 21% of the working mainland population works for the national minimum wage (EUR 820), and the unemployment rate is ca. 7% in 2024.

§2. Legal Systems

I. Primacy of Legislation and Codification

5. The Portuguese legal system belongs to the commonly denominated Civil Law system, relying, therefore, mainly on codified law rather than, as in Common Law systems, the authority of precedent and custom.[4] The first Book of the Civil Code, entitled General Part, has, in its Title I, a Chapter dedicated to the Sources of Law. This subject matter is kept on the Civil Code as a result of tradition and is evidence of the central role played by Civil Law[5] and the Civil Code within the Portuguese legal system.[6] Article 1 of the Civil Code cites, as immediate sources of law, laws and corporative rules. The reference to 'laws' should be interpreted in a broader sense, in line with Article 1(2) of the Civil Code, as in all generic and mandatory statutes emitted by the State competent bodies, which encompasses a plurality of legal acts, from the Constitution to Ordinances.

Corporative rules were to be understood, in keeping with Article 1(2), as the rules prescribed by representative bodies, mainly, as stated, 'moral, cultural, economic or professional, within their field of competence, as well as their respective statutes and internal rules'. It is a reference to corporative bodies, enshrined in the 1933 Portuguese Constitution and eliminated in the Constitution of 1976, making them, therefore, nowadays, not sources of law.[7]

Article 3 refers to local practices or habits, indicating that they can only be relevant if their value is recognized by law and they are not contrary to good faith (bona fides). They are alluded to, e.g., in Article 234 of the Civil Code, deeming the acceptance of a deal unnecessary for its conclusion, alongside the deal's nature and circumstances and its proposal if the counterpart's behaviour shows an intention towards acceptance. The fact that local practices or habits are only relevant when

4. For a broader reading on this matter, F.J. Pinto Bronze, *Lições de Introdução ao Direito*, 2 ed., Coimbra Editora, 690–700.
5. *See*, C.A. da Mota Pinto, *Teoria Geral do Direito Civil*, 4 ed., Coimbra Editora, 2012, 63–64.
6. Nevertheless, considering their significance to the legal system as whole, some authors argue they should belong on the Constitution. *See*, F.J. Pinto Bronze, *Lições de Introdução ao Direito*, 2 ed., Coimbra Editora, 687.
7. C.A. da Mota Pinto, *Teoria Geral do Direito Civil*, 4 ed., Coimbra Editora, 2012, 64.

stipulated by law is a departure from considering custom as a source of law. If there is no sense of enforceability per se, without an underlying law, then custom cannot be held as a source of law.[8]

Lastly, the Civil Code makes a reference to equity, enshrining that the Court can only resort to an equitable decision in three situations: when a specific norm so indicates; when both parties agree, and the legal matter is not unavailable to negotiation; and when the parties have previously stipulated the resort to equity in an arbitration clause.

Up to 1995, Portugal had another source of law called *Assentos*, revoked by the Decree-Law No. 329A/95, 12 December 1995, and challenged by the Constitutional Court 1993.[9] Those were regulated by Article 2 of the Civil Code and were regarded as an instrument to overcome the alleged existence of loopholes and to ascertain, among several possible interpretations, which should be the shared understanding of a certain norm. The achieved solution would have general and mandatory enforceability, i.e., act as a legal norm instead of being only applicable to a specific case. They emanated from the full configuration of the Supreme Court of Justice and were prompted by the existence of two conflicting, on the same subject matter, Supreme Court decisions, or, exceptionally, from decisions of second instance courts. They were widely controversial among some authors, and their constitutionality was questioned since they converted case law and legal opinions into legislation, jeopardizing the fundamental principle of separation of powers.[10]

II. Position of the Judiciary

6. In line with the principle of separation of powers, the judiciary is separate and independent from the legislative and executive powers, being enshrined in Article 203 of the Constitution that 'The Courts are independent and subjected only to the law.' They are, according to Article 202, 'entities that exercise sovereignty with the competence to administer justice in the name of the people'. Court decisions are, if not of a mere expedient nature, according to Article 205(1), necessarily reasoned. As established in (2) of the same Article 205, 'Court decisions are binding on all public and private entities and prevail over the decisions of any other authorities.'

The Constitution also regulates the organization of the judiciary, aided by Law No. 62/2013, 26 August 2013 and the Decree-Law No. 49/2014, 27 March 2014. It contemplates, in Article 209, several court categories, such as the Constitutional Court (regulated by Law No. 28/82, 15 November of 1982); the Supreme Court of Justice and the other judicial courts of first and second instance; the Supreme Administrative Court and the other administrative and tax courts; the Court of Auditors (ruled by Law No. 98/97, 26 August 1997). It envisions, on Article 209(2), the existence of maritime courts; arbitration courts (mainly regulated by Law No. 63/2011 of 14 December 2011); and Justices of the Peace (regulated by Law No. 78/2001, 13 July 2001). Lastly, during the time of war, Article 213 gives ground to

8. C.A. da Mota Pinto, *Teoria Geral do Direito Civil*, 4 ed., Coimbra Editora, 2012, 66.
9. Decision 810/93.
10. *See*, F.J. Pinto Bronze, *Lições de Introdução ao Direito*, 2 ed., Coimbra Editora, 703–713.

the formation of Military Courts, with merely military jurisdiction – an exception to the constitutional prohibition in Article 209(4) of certain crimes being solely judged in certain courts.

According to Article 204 of the Portuguese Constitution, all Courts are considered Constitutional Courts, being a diffused judicial review model, but, nonetheless, the Constitutional Court also has concentrated powers, as enshrined in Articles 277 to 283, making the system as a whole of mixed nature.[11]

There are two jurisdictional orders, one pertaining to judicial courts and one to administrative and tax courts; the first ones are regarded as the common courts for civil and criminal matters, as stated in Article 211(1) of the Constitution, whereas the second ones are focused on administrative and tax cases.

The highest court of the judicial order is the Supreme Court of Justice based in Lisbon and with a national purview. It has a total of sixty judges plus four military judges, one for each branch of the Armed Forces and one for the National Republican Guard (GNR).

Portugal has five second instance courts, called Tribunais da Relação, located in Guimarães, Oporto, Coimbra, Lisbon and Évora. Their jurisdiction is established on Map II, annexed to the Decree-Law No. 49/2014. Each Court has a variable number of judges, between 57 and 66 in Guimarães; 103 and 119 in Oporto; 53 and 61 in Coimbra; 133 and 153 in Lisbon; and between 53 and 61 in Évora. In addition, the Lisbon and Oporto Courts also have four military judges each, just as the Supreme Court of Justice.

The first instance courts encompass, as laid down in Article 33 of Law No. 62/2013, District Courts and Courts of Broad Territorial Jurisdiction.[12] There are twenty-three district courts; there is one in each Administrative District of the country, but in Lisbon, there are three, and in Oporto, there are two. Each District Court is divided into different specializations and generic competence. Also contemplated as a first instance court are the Courts of Broad Territorial Jurisdiction, differentiated because of their areas of expertise. Article 83 of Law No. 62/2013 catalogues as possible Courts of Broad Territorial Jurisdiction, for example, the Court of Intellectual Property, the Court of Competition, Regulation and Oversight and the Maritime Court. Although these are courts of first instance, they have broader jurisdiction than the District courts, and some even have nationwide authority.

The administrative jurisdictional order also has three court instances. They are also regulated by Law No. 62/2013, by Law No. 13/2002, 19 February 2002, and Decree-Law No. 325/2003, 29 December 2003. The highest court is the Supreme Administrative Court, located in Lisbon, but with nationwide jurisdiction. The second instance courts are the Central Administrative Court North and Central Administrative Court South, whose jurisdictions are contemplated in Article 2 of the Decree-Law No. 325/2003. The lower courts are Tax Courts and Administrative courts, and their jurisdiction is established on the annexed map to the Decree-Law No. 325/2003.

---

11. J.J. Gomes Canotilho, *Direito Constitucional e Teoria da Constituição*, 7 ed., Almedina, 2003, 917.
12. Nevertheless, in some matters, both higher courts act as courts of first instance, e.g., when governmental or judiciary authorities are implicated. *See*, Arts 55 and 73 of Law No. 62/2013.

III. Distinction Between Public and Private Law

7. The distinction between public and private law can be drawn in several ways, depending on the chosen approach. Overall, the traditional Portuguese legal doctrine embraces the so-called subject's theory, focusing on the nature of the individuals or entities governed by the law in hand. The emphasis is not merely on their nature per se, but rather, in case-by-case, analysing the role they play in each given moment – since an entity generally classified as a public entity can act as any other private individual and vice versa. Consequently, a case would be a matter of Private Law whenever the involved parties acted amidst sovereign power and, in contrast, would be considered a Public Law issue if there was any such power.[13]

Other traditional perspectives to which an allusion is due are the *interest theory* and the *hierarchy theory*. The first one makes a distinction by examining the norm and searching for the protected interest's nature: if it is unveiled as a public interest, the issue would be deemed of Public Law; if it reveals a private interest, the issue would be classified as Private Law. This perspective has several problems, making it just partially true, since the distinction between what should be categorized as a public or a private interest is not always clear, and various norms assure both at the same time – as is the case, for example, with contracts formal requirements.[14]

The second perspective accentuates the existence of a power relationship, in which case we would be in the face of Public Law or, if the contrary were true, Private Law. However, that disregards the fact that sometimes Public Law matters lack any dominant intervenient (as in-between two equivalent public authorities) and that there are private law relationships that entail some kind of authority and subordination (as an employment relationship).[15]

Alternatively, some authors suggest a less rigid understanding, viewing it as a spectrum where the marked distinctions would appear within its range – on one side would rest communitarian concerns, with a social component, and on the other, individual and private interests, allowing each specific case to flow between them, either nearing one or another.[16]

Normally, Private Law encompasses the study of the Law of Obligations, Property Law, Family and Succession Law, Commercial Law, Labour Law and Private International Law. However, Public Law is commonly thought of as comprising Constitutional Law, Criminal Law and Criminal Procedure, Administrative and Administrative Procedure, Tax Law and Criminal Procedure, and, lastly, Civil Procedure Law.

13. C.A. da Mota Pinto, *Teoria Geral do Direito Civil*, Coimbra Editora, 4 ed., 2012, 39–40.
14. *See*, C.A. da Mota Pinto, *Teoria Geral do Direito Civil*, Coimbra Editora, 4 ed., 2012, 36–38.
15. *See*, C.A. da Mota Pinto, *Teoria Geral do Direito Civil*, Coimbra Editora, 4 ed., 2012, 39.
16. P. Pais de Vasconcelos, *Teoria Geral do Direito Civil*, 8 ed., Almedina, 2017, 6–9.

IV. Sources of Private Law, in General, and of Tort Law, in Particular

A. The Civil Codes of 1867 and 1966

8. The modern codification movement started in Portugal in the nineteenth century, and it was most influenced at that time by French law. In spite of the fact that Commercial Law was the first branch of private law to be codified,[17] Civil Law followed shortly.

In 1867, the first Portuguese Civil Code was enacted. António Luiz de Seabra, influenced by the *Code Napoleon,* wrote the whole Code alone. It adopted a very peculiar style – its systematization is different from the one adopted by the French Code.[18] The Civil Code, as the 'code of the person', should follow 'the personal biography' of the citizen.

It goes without saying that, at the time, this meant 'the personal biography' of the citizen of the nineteenth century. It was a Code meant for the bourgeois and the landowner.

In 1966, after more than twenty years of preparation, the new *Código Civil* was enacted. It entered into force on 1 June 1967. Zweigert/Kötz commented that this Code '*is remarkable for the intelligent attention it pays to foreign legislation* – especially German, Swiss, and Italian – *to the point where one may wonder whether Portuguese private law ought still to be included in the Romanistic legal family*'.[19] In fact, Portuguese Civil law, over the last century, has jumped over the Rhine and the Alps and established a fruitful dialogue with German, Austrian and Swiss, as well as with Italian Law.

It is submitted that the distinction between a Romanistic legal family, a Germanistic legal family and a Nordic legal family should no longer be accepted.[20]

In fact, all these systems belong to the *continental legal family*. In distinguishing them, legal systems like the Italian and the Portuguese, which have many common features with both French law and German law, would be difficult, if not impossible, to classify.

In spite of the fact that the distinction between a Romanistic and a Germanistic legal family is no longer to be accepted, it is apparent that the external, formal structure of the German Civil Code clearly inspired the formal structure of the Portuguese Civil Code.[21]

In the first place, the Portuguese legislature opted for the solution of keeping Commercial Law and Labour Law out of the scope of the Portuguese Civil Code.

---

17. The first Commercial Code dates back from 1833; Ferreira Borges was its main mentor and it had a particularly national character; it codified the national customs of the *lex mercatoria* and previous legislation. In 1888, it was replaced by a new one, which took account of the Commercial Codes of Italy and Spain, which had regard for the Code de Commerce.
18. *See* L. Menezes Leitão, *O Ensino do Direito das Obrigações* (2001).
19. Zweigert/Kötz, *An Introduction to Comparative Law*, 3rd edition (1998), 108 (emphasis added).
20. J.M. Rainer, *Europäisches Privatrecht: Die Rechtsvergleichung* (2002), 57.
21. Jorge Sinde Monteiro, 'Manuel de Andrade e a influência do BGB sobre o Código Civil português de 1966', Boletim da Faculdade de Direito – Volume Comemorativo, 2003, 181–207. There is a German version in Eric Jayme/Heinnz-Peter Mansel (Hrsg.), Auf dem Wege zu einem gemeineuropäischen Privatrecht – 100 Jahre BGB und die lusophonen Länder (Symposium in Heidelberg, 19–30.11.1996), Nomos Verlagsgesellschft, Baden-Baden, 1997, 29–49.

Thus, only 'classical' private law will be found in its 2334 articles. In this respect, the German model of 1900 (Bürgerliches Gesetzbuch (BGB)) was followed, rather than the Italian *Codice Civile* of 1942.

Second, the Portuguese Civil Code adheres to the system of the German Civil Code (the so-called *Pandektensystem*).[22] It is divided into five parts (in five Books).

Book I addresses the so-called General Part. Books II to V address the special parts of Civil Law. Book II tackles the Law of Obligations – including contracts, torts and restitution; Book III regulates Property Law and other rights in rem; Family Law is consecrated in Book IV; concerning Successions Law, there is Book V.[23,24]

Finally, when analysing a legal system, one shall look not only at the legal texts but also at the law in action, as developed by the courts and legal scholars.

The influence of German speaking countries has been important, especially in what concerns advanced academic works. In fact, academics pay attention to the doctrine in those countries and sooner or later, this trend has some influence in the courts.

B. *The Place for the Law of Civil Liability Within the System of the Portuguese Civil Code*

9. In keeping with the structure of the Portuguese Civil Code, the core principles and rules on non-contractual, tortious liability form a part of Book II.

Book II is divided into Title I, on the *Law of Obligations in General* (i.e., on creditor-debtor relationships in general) and Title II, on *Special Types of Contract*.

Chapter II of Title I deals with five sources of obligations – contracts, defined as bilateral or reciprocal legal acts – Section I of Chapter II, Articles 405 to 456; unilateral legal acts (*einseitiges Rechtsgeschäft*) – Section II, Articles 457 to 463;

---

22. For an analysis of the system of the German Civil Code, *see* A.B. Schwarze, 'Zur Entstehung des modernen Pandektensystems', in: 42 *Zeitschrift der Savigny-Stiftung für Rechtsgeschicthe. Romanistische Abteilung* (1921) 578–610; R. Zimmermann, *The Law of Obligations. Roman Foundations of the Civilian Tradition* 29–31; F. Ranieri, *Europäisches Obligationenrecht*, 3rd edition (Wien/New York: Springer 2009) 51–61; Ch. Baldus/Th. Raff, 'La capacité du "Système des Padectes"', in: 2008 *Studia Universitates Babes Bolyal. Iurisprudentia* 101–114; H. Dedek, 'Border Control: Some Comparative Remarks on the Cartography of Obligations', in: J.W. Neyers/R. Bronaugh/S.G.A. Pitel (coord.), *Exploring Contract Law* (Oxford/Portland: 2009) 25–49, especially at 35–42; J.-P. Schmidt, 'Pandektensystem', in: J. Basedow/K.J. Hopt/R. Zimmermann/A. Stier (eds), *The Max Planck Encyclopedia of European Private Law*, vol. I (Hamburg/Oxford: Max-Planck Gesellschaft/Oxford University Press 2012) 774–777.

23. For a critique of the German system, *see, for example*, O. de Carvalho, *A teoria geral da relação jurídica. Seu sentido e limites* (Coimbra: Centelha 1981) and A. Menezes Cordeiro, *Tratado de direito civil*, vol. I (Coimbra: Livraria Almedina 2012) 83 ff., especially 83–87 and 170–178; for a defence, *see, for example*, C.A. da Mota Pinto/A. Pinto Monteiro/P. Mota Pinto, *Teoria geral do direito civil*, 4th edition (Coimbra: Coimbra Editora 2005) 17–22, and J.M. Antunes Varela, Das obrigações em geral, vol. I, at 35–47.

24. For a comparison between the systems of both German and Portuguese Civil Codes, *see* A.G. Dias Pereira, 'Portuguese Tort Law: A Comparison with the Principles of European Tort Law', in H. Koziol/B.C. Steininger (eds), *European Tort Law 2004* (Wien/New York: Springer 2005) 623–648, at 623–627.

benevolent intervention in another's affairs (*negotiorum gestio*) – Section III, Articles 464 to 472; unjust enrichment – Section IV, Articles 473 to 482; and, finally, it deals with non-contractual, tortious liability – Section V of Chapter II, Articles 483 to 510.[25]

Within Section V, the Portuguese Civil Code distinguishes between *liability for wrongful acts,* that is to say, *fault-based, subjective liability* (Subsection I of section V, Articles 483 to 498) from *strict, objective liability* (Subsection II, Articles 499 to 510).

Article 483(1) sets a general principle of fault-based, subjective liability for one's own acts: 'Whoever, whether by wilful misconduct (dolus) or by negligence unlawfully infringes the rights of another person or any legal provision intended to safeguard the interests of others must compensate the injured party for damage arising from such violation.'

It is to be supplemented by Article 486 on liability for one's own omissions.

In addition to the general principle in Article 483, there are two particular, specific clauses: the first applies to cases of offence against consideration and credit – Article 484 – and the second to damages caused by advice and recommendations – Article 485.[26]

Articles 487 to 489 specify the concept of fault. Articles 495 and 496 specify the concept of damages relevant to non-contractual, tortious liability by stating the general principle that non-pecuniary losses are to be compensated – Article 496 – and by setting the specific rules on compensation for death or physical injury – Article 495.

Articles 490 and 497 refer to the case of multiple tortfeasors. Article 490 holds all authors – all joint-doers – accomplices and instigators liable for the damage resulting from a common, tortious act, and Article 497 supplements Article 490 by holding all of them jointly and severally liable (= by holding all of them liable *in solidum*). Article 498 refers to limitation by setting a three-year limitation for claims resulting from torts.

Articles 491 to 493 and 499 to 510 deviate from the general principle in Article 483(1).

In fact, in cases of liability for others, liability for dangerous activities, as well as liability for dangerous things, the requirement of fault does not hold to its fuller extent.

---

25. *See, for example,* Ch. von Bar, *The Common European Law of Torts, vol. I – The Core Areas of Tort Law, the Approximation in Europe and Its Accommodation in the System* (Oxford: Oxford University Press 1998) 33 ff. 'The new law of delict of the Portuguese Código Civil was chiefly developed by Vaz Serra. Like the more modern code of other European nations, it is marked by a certain "legal eclecticism" (Markeisnis). (…) The concept and design of the Portuguese basic delictual provision (Art. 483(1) CC) reveals a strong German influence'.
26. Recent special torts are related with the certification service providers and online service providers (the Directive 2000/31/EC: Directive on electronic commerce). Decree-Law No. 62/2003, 3 April implements EC Directive EC/1993/93 on Digital Signature. Article 26 establishes civil liability of the certifying entity towards the certificate titular and third parties for non-accomplishment of legal duties. *See* J. Sinde Monteiro, 'Assinatura electrónica e certificação (A Directiva 1999/93/CE e o Decreto-Lei n.º 290–D/99, de 2 de Agosto)', in Revista de Legislação e de Jurisprudência (2001), 261–272.

In the case of Articles 491 to 493, the requirement of fault still holds, even though in a milder form, for the burden of proof is reversed. In the case of Articles 499 to 510, the requirement of fault does not hold anymore – Articles 499 to 510 refer to strict liability.

It follows from the general principle in Article 483(1) that fault liability is the rule and strict liability is (but) an exception. Furthermore, it follows from such a relationship between rule and exception that cases of no-fault, strict liability for others, liability for dangerous activities and liability for dangerous things are to be specified by the law.[27]

The norms in Articles 483 to 510 are to be supplemented by two sets of norms.[28]

First, norms regulating defences are to be found in Book I – and, within Book I, on the General part, they are to be found in Articles 334 ff., especially in Article 336 (on self-help), in Article 337 (self-defence), in Article 339 (necessity) and in Article 340 (consent).

Second, norms regulating the obligation to compensate are to be found in Book II, Chapter III – on the '*Types of obligations*' – and, within Chapter III, in Section VIII.

The reason why they are to be found in Chapter III, Section VIII, lies in the fact that principles and rules concerning the general principle of *restitutio in natura* – Article 562 – causation – Article 563 – damages – Articles 564 to 568 – and contributory negligence – Articles 570 to 572 – apply both to liability in contract and to liability in tort.

1. References to Contractual and Non-contractual: Liability

10. It follows from the German system, adopted by the Portuguese Civil Code, that civil liability, both contractual and tortious, is referred to in Book II. It also follows from such a system that contractual and tortious liability is referred to in different chapters of Book II.

The Portuguese legislator takes non-contractual, non-obligational, tortious liability as the cause of new relationships of obligation and contractual, obligational liability as a response to the non-performance of old, pre-existing relationships. Whenever the debtor causes performance to be impossible, either by wilful or negligent misconduct, the duty to perform would transform itself into the duty to compensate the creditor for all damages caused by non-performance – it is argued that the duty to perform and the duty to compensate are two moments of one, and the same, obligation. It is argued, therefore, that both duties are identical.[29] In spite of

27. Article 483(2) confirms this idea by stating that 'an obligation to pay compensation when there is no fault shall arise only in cases specified by law'.

28. *See*, in German language, J. Sinde Monteiro/R. Moura Ramos/H. Hörster, 'Portugal', in *Christian v. Bar* (Hrsg.), Deliktsrecht in Europa (1994).

29. *See, for example*, G. Moreira, Instituições de direito civil português (Coimbra: Imprensa da Universidade 1907) 591/'Estudo sobre a responsabilidade civil', in: 37 Revista de Legislação e de Jurisprudência (1904–1905) 561–564; M. de Andrade, Teoria geral da relação jurídica (Coimbra: Livrara Almedina 1974, reprint) at 21; C.A. da Mota Pinto/A. Pinto Monteiro/P. Mota Pinto, Teoria Geral do Direito Civil, at 372.

the fact that such a theory is far from consensual – there is a divide between the so-called *School of Coimbra* and the so-called *School of Lisbon*, the former accepting[30] and the latter rejecting the identity of the obligation[31] – it clearly corresponds to the formal, external structure of the Civil Code.[32]

In case of non-obligational liability, the cause of new obligation is the tort itself;[33] liability in tort is a part of the chapter dealing with the *Sources of obligations*. Fundamental principles and rules referring to non-contractual, non-obligational, tortious liability are to be found in Articles 483 ff. of the Portuguese Civil Code. Because contractual, obligational liability is supposed to be the cause of no new relationships of obligation at all, liability in contract is a part of the chapter dealing with *Performance and non-performance of obligations* – fundamental principles and rules referring to contractual, obligational liability are to be found in Articles 798 ff.

Finally, there is a set of provisions applying to the duty to compensate. They are to be found in Articles 562 ff, for they are included in the Chapter on the *Types of obligations* (in Portuguese, '*Modalidades das obrigações*'). It follows from the fact that the duty to compensate is a common effect of both contract and tort that Articles 562 ff. are to be applied to all types of liability.

§3. Function of the Law of Torts (Indemnification; Prevention; Sanction?)

11. It is generally assumed that tort law aims at two different purposes. First, tort law aims at compensating losses, and second, it aims at preventing and – whenever prevention fails – at repressing the very unlawful, wrongful conduct that caused that very loss that is at stake.[34]

30. *See* especially C.A. da Mota Pinto, Cessão da posição contratual (Coimbra: Livraria Almedina 1982) 428–429, footnote 2.
31. *See* especially M.D. Gomes da Silva, O dever de prestar e o dever de indemnizar (Lisboa 1944) 331–361; A. Menezes Cordeiro, Direito das obrigações, vol. I (Lisboa: AAFDUL 1980) 225–226; L. Menezes Leitão, Direito das obrigações, vol. I – Introdução. Da constituição das obrigações, 285–288.
32. For an intermediate perspective, *see* A. Menezes Cordeiro, Tratado de direito civil português, vol. II – Direito das obrigações, I. – Introdução. Sistemas e direito europeu das obrigações. Dogmática geral (Coimbra: Livraria Almedina 2010) 305 ff.; C. Serra, A falência no quadro da tutela jurisdicional dos direitos de crédito. O problema da natureza do processo de liquidação aplicável à insolvência no direito português (Coimbra: Coimbra Editora 2009) 51–54; N.M. Pinto Oliveira, Princípios de direito dos contratos (Coimbra: Combra Editora 2011) 549–562; A. Menezes Cordeiro, Tratado de direito civil, vol. VI – Direito das obrigações. Introdução. Sistemas e direito europeu das obrigações. Dogmática geral (Coimbra: Livraria Almedina 2012).
33. Strictly speaking, liability is never a cause – is never a causative event. Whereas acts – whether lawful or unlawful – may be causes, liabilities may not. They are always responses.
34. *See*, for instance, J.M. Antunes Varela, Das obrigações em geral, vol. I, 542–544; M.J. Almeida Costa, Direito das obrigações, 521, fn. 3; F. Pessoa Jorge, Ensaio sobre os pressupostos da responsabilidade civil, 47–52J. Ribeiro de Faria, Direito das obrigações, vol. I, 425–428; M. Carneiro da Frada, Direito civil. Responsabilidade civil. O método do caso (Coimbra: Livraria Almedina 2006) 64–72.

It is also generally assumed that the purpose of compensating losses is to have, at least, some precedence – i.e., some priority – over the purpose of preventing and repressing unlawful, wrongful conducts.

Compensation would be essential. Prevention and repression would not.[35] Compensation would perform the basic, fundamental function. Prevention and repression would not – they would play an accessory, subordinate role.[36]

The priority of compensation over prevention and repression results from the principle according to which Tort Law depends on damages. Tort law shall only apply if the victim sustains a loss. Furthermore – in the case he did – the priority of compensation over prevention and repression results from the rule, implicit in Articles 562 and 566 of the Portuguese Civil Code, that the amount awarded to the victim shall not exceed the amount of the loss he sustained.

In accordance with the basic principle of duty to compensate, enshrined in Article 562 of the Portuguese Civil Code, '[t]he person who is bound to make compensation must restore the situation which would exist if the circumstance making him liable to compensate had not occurred'. The principle in Article 562 is developed by the rules in Articles 564 ff., especially by the rule on the amount of damages for pecuniary loss in Article 566(3):

> Whenever damages [for pecuniary loss] are to be awarded in money, they shall correspond to the difference between the actual situation of the defendant's assets, at the most recent date that could be taken into account by the court, and the hypothetical situation of the defendant's assets in the absence of damaging event.[37]

Even though prevention and repression perform an accessory, subordinate function, they have a place in the law of torts, at least in the following:

First, damages depend on the tortfeasors' unlawfulness and fault. Article 483(1) requires unlawfulness, by referring to an infringement of either the rights or of any legal provision aimed at protecting the interests of another person. Furthermore, Article 483(1) requires fault, by referring to wilful misconduct (*dolus*) and to negligence, and Article 483(2) stresses that '[a]n obligation to pay compensation where there is no fault shall arise only in cases specified by law'.[38]

Second, in what concerns damages for non-pecuniary loss, the amount of damages to be awarded always depends on the tortfeasor's degree of fault.

It follows from Article 496(4) that 'the amount of compensation [to be awarded to the victim of non-pecuniary loss] shall be fixed equitably by the court, having

35. *See*, for instance, J.M. Antunes Varela, Das obrigações em geral, vol. I, 542.
36. *See*, for instance, J.M. Antunes Varela, Das obrigações em geral, vol. I, 542.
37. For a balanced assessment of the importance of Arts 562 and 563 of the Portuguese Civil Code, for the purpose of determining the functions of tort law, *see* J. Gomes, 'Uma função preventiva para a responsabilidade civil e uma função reparatória para a responsabilidade penal?', in: Revista de direito e economia 15 (1989) 105–144; M. Carneiro da Frada, Direito civil. Responsabilidade civil. O método do caso, 65–66.
38. *See* J.M. Antunes Varela, Das obrigações em geral, vol. I, at 542–543; J. Ribeiro de Faria, Direito das obrigações, vol. I, 427; P. Meira Lourenço, A função punitiva da responsabilidade civil (Coimbra: Coimbra Editora 2006) 247–250.

regard in any event to the circumstances mentioned in Article 494', and it follows from Article 494 that the relevant circumstances of the case include the tortfeasor's degree of fault.[39]

Third, (even) in what concerns damages for pecuniary loss, the amount of damages sometimes depends on the tortfeasor's degree of fault.[40,41]

Fourth, in the event of contributory negligence, the amount of damages depends on the comparison of the gravity of each party's fault.[42]

Fifth, and finally, in the event there are multiple tortfeasors, Article 497(2) reads that '[i]n internal relations, liability is apportioned taking into account the degree of fault of each tortfeasor and his contribution to damage'.[43,44]

Professor Menezes Cordeiro proposed a revision of the classic doctrine on the functions of tort law by distinguishing the purposes of non-contractual, tortious liability in the case of pecuniary and non-pecuniary losses.

Liability for pecuniary losses should aim primarily at compensating damages. In the case the damaging event caused pecuniary loss – and no more than a pecuniary loss – to the injured party, the courts should respect the limits resulting from Article 483 of the Portuguese Civil Code. Liability for non-pecuniary losses should aim, first, at preventing any unlawful contribution to the risk and, second, at repressing the contribution to the risk that materialized in an actual, concrete, and effective loss.

Non-pecuniary losses normally result from the infringement of ethical or moral values relating to the human person and to their dignity; non-contractual, tortious

---

39. *See* P. Meira Lourenço, A função punitiva da responsabilidade civil, 278–297.
40. In keeping with Art. 494 of the Portuguese Civil Code, '[w]here liability is based on mere fault, compensation may be fixed equitably at as amount lower than that corresponding to the damage caused, provided that the degree of fault of the wrongdoer, the financial situation of the wrongdoer and of the injured party, as well as the other circumstances of the case so justify'.
41. *See* J.M. Antunes Varela, *Das obrigações em geral*, vol. I, at 542–543; J. Ribeiro de Faria, *Direito das obrigações*, vol. I, 427; P. Meira Lourenço, A função punitiva da responsabilidade civil, 250–258 and 267–272.
42. In keeping with Art. 570 of the Portuguese Civil Code, '[i]f any faulty conduct of the injured party has contributed either to the occurrence of the damage or to its aggravation, the court shall determine, on the basis of comparison of the gravity of each party's fault, as well as on the basis of the consequences of their consequences, whether compensation is to be fully awarded [to the injured party], fixed equitably at an amount lower than that of damage, or fully excluded'.
43. *See* J.M. Antunes Varela, Das obrigações em geral, vol. I, 543; J. Ribeiro de Faria, Direito das obrigações, vol. I, 427; P. Meira Lourenço, A função punitiva da responsabilidade civil, 259–267.
44. P. Meira Lourenço finds additional argument in the following: in the first place, and in some circumstances the court may determine damages according to fairness – *see* Art. 566(3) – second, it is commonly held there is a general principle of irrelevance of merely potential, virtual causes; third, in accordance with Art. 496(1) of the Portuguese Civil Code, non-pecuniary damage is to be compensated and, frequently, it is compensated with the intention of punishing the wrongdoer; and, fourth, Portuguese private law provides for 'punishment' in the areas of property law (e.g., Art. 1320), copyright law, labour law and environmental law. Meira Lourenço, thus, upholds the thesis that tort law performs a punitive function, and that it should perform such a punitive function, notably in the event the wrongdoer acted with intention and received profits superior to the damage – to the loss of the injured person (A função punitiva da responsabilidade civil, passim).

liability was to restore trust in social and political institutions – including legal institutions – designed to protect the human person from injury.[45]

It is submitted that Professor Menezes Cordeiro's distinction fits the classic concepts and structures of tort law. In fact, it has always been acknowledged that liability for pecuniary losses and for non-pecuniary losses are fundamentally different. Professor Menezes Cordeiro emphasizes the difference by stressing that compensation for pecuniary losses and satisfaction for non-pecuniary losses are to perform different functions.

In the case of pecuniary losses, full compensation is always possible. In the case of non-pecuniary losses, it is not – by definition, it is never possible.

Whereas, in the case of pecuniary losses, the precedence of compensation over prevention and repression is fully warranted, in the case of non-pecuniary losses, it is not – the precedence of compensation over prevention and repression is to be replaced by a complex system.[46]

In articulating the complex relationship between compensation, prevention and repression, the Portuguese legal system seems to draw from two basic, fundamental ideas: from the idea that prevention should have some precedence over compensation for the losses the injured party has already sustained[47,48,49] and from the idea that punishment and repression of the – tortfeasor and wrongdoer – should have no autonomy in private law.[50,51] Honsell rightly pointed out that the renaissance of punitive and repressive elements in private law clashes with the idea of compensation and the principle of proportionality, which are – and should remain – basic,

---

45. A. Menezes Cordeiro, Tratado de Direito Civil Português, vol. II – Direito das obrigações, III. – Gestão de negócios. Enriquecimento sem causa. Responsabilidade civil, 419–422.
46. *See, for example*, P. Meira Lourenço, A função punitiva da responsabilidade civil, 380–388.
47. For an expression of the precedence of prevention over compensation, *see* Art. 70(2) of the Portuguese Civil Code: 'Regardless of any civil liability, the person threatened or offended may apply to measures adequate to the circumstances of the case to prevent the threat from being realized or to attenuate the effects of an offence already committed' [for the translation of Art. 70(2) *see* G. Brüggemeier/A. Colombi-Ciacchi/P. O'Callaghan, *Personality Rights in European Tort Law* (Cambridge: Cambridge University Press 2010) 122]. The terms 'regardless of any civil liability' suggest that preventive measures appropriate to the circumstances of the case should be preferred to compensatory and repressive measures, such as damages for the infringement of the victim's personality rights.
48. *See, for example*, M. Carneiro da Frada, Direito civil. Responsabilidade civil. O método do caso, 65–66.
49. For a comparative account, *see* G. Brüggemeier, Haftungsrecht. Struktur, Prinzipien, Schutzbereich (Berlin/Heidelberg: Springer 2006) 9: 'Von einer gesellschaftspolitischen Standpunkt aus ist die Verhütung von Schadensfällen grundsätzlich das vorrangige Ziel'.
50. *See, for example*, M. Carneiro da Frada, Direito civil. Responsabilidade civil. O método do caso, 67 – arguing that, within the framework of Portuguese private law, civil liability performs no punitive or repressive function whatsoever.
51. For a comparative account, *see* H. Koziol/V. Wilcox (eds), *Punitive Damages. Common Law and Civil Law Perspectives* (Wien/New York: Springer 2009). – It should be stressed that, in tort law systems comparable to the Portuguese, such as the German, the Austrian, and the Swiss, there is some consensus on the exclusion of punishment and repression from the functions of civil liability, contractual and non-contractual – *see, for example*, N. Jansen/L. Rademacher, 'Punitive Damages in Germany', in: H. Koziol/V. Wilcox (eds), *Punitive Damages. Common Law and Civil Law Perspectives* (Wien/New York: Springer 2009) 75–86; H. Koziol, *Basic Questions of Tort Law from a Germanic Perspective* (Wien: Sramek 2012), 83–84.

fundamental principles of the legal system.[52] Even if he was concentrating on German and Swiss law, Honsell's argument in this matter fully applies to Portugal.[53]

I. Disgorgement Damages, Restitution Law and Tort Law

12. In keeping with the idea that private law should perform no punitive, repressive function, tort law should concentrate on compensation and prevention of unlawful, wrongful conduct. There is some consensus as to the idea that effective prevention requires disgorgement of the profits that the tortfeasor derived from his unlawful, wrongful conduct.[54],[55] There is no consensus at all as to whether disgorgement of profits is to result from the law of damages – i.e., from tort law – or from the law of restitution.

It could be argued that the causative event of the duty to disgorge profits lies in the defendant's civil wrong. Disgorgement should thus depend on the principles and rules of the law of torts. It could be argued that the causative event of the duty to disgorge profits lies in the defendant's enrichment and in the assessment that such enrichment is unfair or unjust. Disgorgement should thus depend on the principles and rules of the law of restitution.

In a doctoral dissertation,[56] Professor H. Sousa Antunes argued that disgorgement of gains or profits arising from unlawful, wrongful conduct could – and indeed should – result from tort law.

Private law would aim at establishing a fair patrimonial relationship between individuals.[57] In the case of unlawful conduct, there would be a 'rupture in the fair

52. H. Honsell, 'Die Erosion des Privatrechts durch das Europarecht' *ZIP – Zeitschrift für Wirtschaftsrecht* 29 (2008) 621–630, at 626–629; for a fully developed presentation of the reasons for rejecting punitive damages, *see, for example*, H. Honsell, 'Der Strafgedanke im Zivilrecht – ein juristischer Atavismus', in: L. Aderold/B. Grunewald/D. Klingberg/W.G. Paefgen (eds), *Festschrift für Harm-Peter Westermann zum 70. Geburtstag* (Köln: Otto Schmidt 2008) 315–336; and H. Honsell, '100 Jahre Schweizerisches Obligationenrecht', in: *Zeitschrift für Schweizerisches Recht/Revue de droit suisse* 130 (2011) 5–115, at 47–52.
53. For a philosophical discussion to the compensatory and punitive functions of tort law, *see* M. Miranda Barbosa, 'Reflexões em torno da responsabilidade civil: teleologia e telonomologia em debate', in: 81 Boletim da Faculdade de Direito [da Universidade de Coimbra] (2005) 511–600.
54. *See*, for instance, M. Carneiro da Frada, Direito civil. Responsabilidade civil. O método do caso, 65–66; P. Meira Lourenço, A função punitiva da responsabilidade civil, 388–390 and 400–405; H. Sousa Antunes, Da inclusão do lucro ilícito entre as consequências da responsabilidade civil extracontratual: a sua legitimação pelo dano (Coimbra: Coimbra Editora 2011); H. Sousa Antunes, 'Disgorgement of Profits in Portugal: A Journey Between the Present and the Future', in: E. Hondius/A. Janssen (eds), Disgorgement of Profits. Gain-Based Remedies Throughout the World, Cham/Heidelberg/New York/Dordrecht/London: Springer 2015) 75–86.
55. For a comparative account, *see* H. Sousa Antunes, *Da inclusão do lucro ilícito entre as consequências da responsabilidade civil extracontratual: a sua legitimação pelo dano*, 247–278; E. Hondius/A. Janssen (eds), *Disgorgement of Profits. Gain-Based Remedies Throughout the World*, Cham/Heidelberg/New York/Dordrecht/London: Springer 2015).
56. H. Sousa Antunes, Da inclusão do lucro ilícito entre as consequências da responsabilidade civil extracontratual: a sua legitimação pelo dano, especially from 205 ff.
57. H. Sousa Antunes, H. Sousa Antunes, Da inclusão do lucro ilícito entre as consequências da responsabilidade civil extracontratual: a sua legitimação pelo dano, 278–292; H. Sousa Antunes, 'Disgorgement of Profits in Portugal: A Journey Between the Present and the Future', 178.

patrimonial relationship between individuals'.[58] Because the rupture results from unlawful conduct, tort law should apply. The general purpose of private law should specify in the particular, specific purpose of tort law: if private law aims at establishing a fair patrimonial relationship between individuals, tort law will aim at restoring such a fair relationship.

The concept of fairness applying to private law, in general, and to tort law, in particular, is a relational concept; the relevant rupture could be assessed from both the perspective of the tortfeasor and the perspective of the victim.

From the perspective of the tortfeasor, the rupture in the fair patrimonial relationship between the parties could be assessed by referring to the gains the tortfeasor derived from his unlawful, wrongful conduct. From the perspective of the victim, the rupture in the fair patrimonial relationship could be assessed by referring to two things: first, it could be assessed by referring to the losses in the victim's assets; second, it could be assessed by referring to the gains – to the profits – in the wrongdoer's assets.

Professor Sousa Antunes suggests there is a damage in the fact that the tortfeasor derived gains, or profits, from unlawful, wrongful conduct against the victim. In spite of the fact it refers to the tortfeasor's assets, it should be conceptualized as non-patrimonial damage, for it would result from an injury to the victim's sense of justice.[59] The principle according to which '[n]obody may benefit from unlawful and wrongful behaviour'[60] would form a part of the general and objective sense of justice of the community and of the individual and subjective sense of justice of each one of its members. In case the victim, as a member of a community supporting such a principle, found out that the tortfeasor benefited from his unlawful and wrongful conduct by deriving a gain or a profit from the interference in the victim's interests, he would sustain non-patrimonial damage, for his sense of justice would be offended.[61]

'The culpable enrichment of a third party', Professor Sousa Antunes writes, 'wounds the injured party's sense of justice'.[62] Article 496(1) of the Portuguese Civil Code requires the judge to compensate 'non-pecuniary damage that, due to its seriousness, deserves protection by the law'. It would follow from the rule in Article 496(1) that, in restoring fairness, Portuguese tort law should compensate the victim of both his patrimonial and his non-patrimonial loss by disgorging the wrongdoer of all gains or profits.

---

58. H. Sousa Antunes, 'Disgorgement of Profits in Portugal: A Journey Between the Present and the Future', 178.
59. H. Sousa Antunes, 'Disgorgement of Profits in Portugal: A Journey Between the Present and the Future', 178 and 179.
60. H. Sousa Antunes, 'Disgorgement of Profits in Portugal: A Journey Between the Present and the Future', 179.
61. H. Sousa Antunes, Da inclusão do lucro ilícito entre as consequências da responsabilidade civil extracontratual: a sua legitimação pelo dano, 292–324.
62. H. Sousa Antunes, 'Disgorgement of Profits in Portugal: A Journey Between the Present and the Future', 179.

'Compensation for this damage [could] only, naturally, be achieved by passing into the sphere of the injured party the advantages that the third party obtained unlawfully.'[63]

Whereas the idea according to which '[n]obody may benefit from unlawful and wrongful behaviour' can be considered the expression of a common sense of justice, the inference that all injuries to such an expression of the common sense of justice are being represented as damage – thus requiring compensation or satisfaction – is, at the very least, highly doubtful.

It can be accepted that private law aims at establishing a fair patrimonial relationship between the parties. It can also be accepted that whenever there is a rupture in the patrimonial relationship between the parties, private law aims at restoring fairness. In doing so, private law divides itself into two branches – the law of restitution and the law of torts. Even though '[t]he distinction between the two [branches of private law] will be difficult to establish in some cases', it is submitted that 'it is important to respect it'.[64]

If the rupture in the fair relationship between the parties results from unjust losses, it should be up to the law of torts to tackle the issue by compensating the victim. If, however, the rupture in the fair relationship between the parties results from unjust gains and profits, it should be up to the law of restitution to tackle the issue by disgorging the wrongdoer. That is to say that disgorgement should be a problem for the law of restitution and that, conversely, disgorgement should be no problem at all for the law of torts.[65]

It should be openly recognized that the law of restitution for unjust enrichment faces a few problems in addressing the disgorgement of profits.

Professor F.M. Pereira Coelho advanced the thesis that the duty to disgorge for intervention in another's rights and interests should be submitted to two cumulative limits: the first limit would depend on the subjective value of the tortfeasor's enrichment, and the second limit would depend on the objective value of the victim's loss (on the so-called *dano real*).[66]

Professors L. Menezes Leitão[67] and J. Gomes[68] concurred with Professor F.M. Pereira Coelho in supporting the thesis that restitution refers to the objective value of the victim's rights and interests.[69]

---

63. H. Sousa Antunes, 'Disgorgement of Profits in Portugal: A Journey Between the Present and the Future', 178.
64. M. Carneiro da Frada, Direito civil. Responsabilidade civil. O método do caso, 67.
65. *See*, for instance, M. Carneiro da Frada, Direito civil. Responsabilidade civil. O método do caso, 67: 'Since what is at issue is the interference by the party committing the harm with rights which grant a reserved sphere of action to their holder (rights of exclusivity), the doctrine of allocation (Zuweisungsgehalt) will be charged with justifying, according to the principles of unjust enrichment […], the obligation to disgorge the profits obtained as a result of the harm'.
66. F.M. Pereira Coelho, O enriquecimento e o dano (Coimbra: Livraria Almedina 1970).
67. L.M. Menezes Leitão, O enriquecimento sem causa no direito civil. Estudo dogmático sobre a viabilidade da configuração unitária do instituto, face à contraposição entre as diferentes categorias de enriquecimento sem causa (Cadernos de Ciência e Técnica Fiscal: Lisboa 1996) 910 ff.
68. J. Gomes, O conceito de enriquecimento, o enriquecimento forçado e os vários paradigmas do enriquecimento sem causa (Porto: Universidade Católica 1998) 801.
69. For a discussion on the relationship between the preventive and repressive functions of the law of restitution and of the law of torts, *see* L. Menezes Leitão, O enriquecimento sem causa no direito

It follows that, in referring to the objective value of the victim's rights and interest, they allow the tortfeasor to benefit from his unlawful and wrongful conduct by retaining the difference between the subjective, patrimonial value of the enrichment and the objective value of the victim's loss.[70]

In spite of that, even recognizing that the law of restitution for unjust enrichment faces a few problems in addressing disgorgement of profits, it is submitted that the problems within the law of restitution are to be resolved within the law of restitution – not by transferring them to the law of torts.

§4. Relationship Between Torts and Criminal Law

13. Criminal Law is the maximum exponent of the public law system since it conveys the punitive powers of the State (ius puniendi), imposing penalties and security measures. Each legal order can have different goals and different framings to justify the State's intervention under Criminal Law. The Portuguese Constitution lays the ground for a Penal system solely rooted in the idea of prevention, not retribution. Since the death penalty was abolished in the nineteenth century, the harsher possible penalty still in place is a prison sentence. Nevertheless, human dignity is enshrined as a guiding principle of the Portuguese legal system, and the Constitution of the Portuguese Republic states in its Article 1 that 'Portugal is a sovereign Republic, based on the dignity of the human person and the will of the people and committed to building a free, just and solidary society.' With regard to Criminal Law, human dignity acts as an underlying justification for other constitutional legislative options.

First, Article 18(2) of the Constitution states, 'The law may only restrict rights, freedoms and guarantees in cases expressly provided for in the Constitution, and such restrictions must be limited to those needed to safeguard other constitutionally protected rights and interests.' It gives justification for the above-cited preventive scope of criminal law penalties.[71] Accordingly, Article 40(1) of the Portuguese Penal Code states that 'The enforcement of penalties and security measures aims the protection of legal goods and the agent's reintegration in society.' In the same line, Article 70 of the Penal Code states that 'The penalty quantum, within the limits imposed by law, is determined according to the agent's fault and the required need for prevention.'

Consequently, only the need to safeguard legal goods, mainly constitutionally protected ones, allows for the restriction of rights, freedoms and guarantees that a penalty represents – be it freedom-depriving or not.

The understanding of prevention can be positive or negative, both in a general and particular way. A positive general prevention perspective intends to reinforce

---

civil, 707 ff.; J. Gomes, O conceito de enriquecimento, o enriquecimento forçado e os vários paradigmas do enriquecimento sem causa, 429 ff., 759 ff. and 801 ff.

70. For a critique on the limits resulting from the objective value of the victim's loss, or from the objective value of the victim's rights and interests, *see, for example*, J.M. Antunes Varela, Das obrigações em geral, vol. I, 512–516.

71. *See*, J. de Figueiredo Dias, *Direito Penal Parte Geral*, 2.ª ed., T. I Coimbra Editora, Coimbra, 2012, 79.

the violated norm's validity and ensure the public that, despite the commitment of crimes, the rule of law prevails. In contrast, the negative general prevention perspective aims to intimidate and cause fear of the consequences of perpetrating a crime. Conversely, a positive particular/ or individual angle on prevention aims at the rehabilitation or resocialization of an agent of a crime into society, whereas the negative approach intends either to intimidate the agent or to isolate him/her from society.

The first group – general prevention – envisions that criminal measures act upon the community, whereas the second group – particular prevention – has a focus on its impact on the perpetrator of the crime. The Portuguese legal system has a place for both of them, since, as we saw above, Article 40 of the Penal Code enshrines, as the scope of penalties and security measures, both the protection of legal goods – resounding the general perspective – and the agent's reintegration into society – also showing a focus on the individual.[72]

That being said, Article 18(2) of the Constitution only accommodates a positive general prevention approach, which serves as the optimal measurement of the expectations of the community. Below its minimal limit, confidence in the rule of law would be in jeopardy, but a penalty that outweighs its maximal cap, e.g., for considerations of particular prevention – would be deemed unconstitutional. From this framework, the particular prevention perspective comes into play and, depending on the agent's resocialization needs, will help to determine a specific quantum. In line with the norms above-cited, the angle is mainly positive since resocialization contemplates inclusion and not isolation. If the socialization needs are spare, the penalty amount will be closer to the minimal limit of the general prevention scheme; on the contrary, if the agent unveils a socialization shortfall, the penalty amount will be closer to the maximal point of the general prevention border. At last, the agent's fault has a role to play. Since the system is grounded on the protection of human dignity, a penalty can never surpass the proven degree of fault and can only be imposed if the existence of fault is proven.[73]

As was briefly recounted above, the State acts through Criminal Law to ensure well-defined goals, which are different from the ones in pursuit with Tort Law, where the main objective is to compensate an injured party and restore a present hypothetical situation.[74]

Nevertheless, the same action can trigger both a criminal and a tort law response, mainly for the commitment of a crime, also causing damages. In that case, Article 129 of the Penal Code forwards its applicable regime to the civil law camp. Even so, Article 130 anticipates the chance of simultaneously the agent and tortfeasor not having the means to compensate the victim. In its (1), it gives space to the existence of special regimes, but in (2), it allows the Court to, if the injured party so claims, compensate the caused damages by bestowing upon the said party the instruments,

---

72. For further developments, *see* J. de Figueiredo Dias, *Direito Penal Parte Geral*, 2.ª ed., T. I Coimbra Editora, Coimbra, 2012, 49–58.
73. About the penalty's quantum determination, *see* J. de Figueiredo Dias, *Direito Penal Parte Geral*, 2.ª ed., T. I Coimbra Editora, Coimbra, 2012, 78–85.
74. *See*, Functions of tort law.

results or advantages declared as lost in favour of the State because of their connection to the crime, in line with Articles 109 and following of the Penal Code. Likewise, if the damage caused is of such a serious nature that the injured party's livelihood is in peril and there's no indication that the agent can fulfil its duties, the Court can, if the victim so requires, assign the amount of an imposed fine by way of compensation. In both cases, as stated by Article 130(4) of the Penal Code, the State becomes subrogated, up to the advanced amount, on the injured party's right to compensation.

The Code of Criminal Procedure sets in its Articles 71 to 84 the norms pertinent to the so-called civil participants in criminal proceedings. Article 71 enshrines the *principle of adherence,* which means that if a tort law claim is based on an act that also constitutes a crime, the claim should be made in a criminal procedure rather than in a civil one, except if otherwise is stipulated by law. Article 72 establishes some cases where a separated civil claim is allowed, as in, e.g., when, eight months after the crime's communication to public authorities, still no charges were made; if proceedings are suspended or terminated; if the totality of damages cannot be assessed at that moment; when criminal proceedings rely upon a complaint or private prosecution, etc. It is worth noting that, as enshrined in Article 72(2) of the Code of Criminal Procedure, in the case of criminal proceedings depending on a complaint or private prosecution, a prior civil claim in a civil court represents a waiver of the right to take legal action on a Criminal Court.

Lastly, a clear connection between torts and criminal law is shown when a criminal law norm has, as a precondition, the fulfilment of a duty to compensate, as is the case with Article 51 of the Penal Code concerning the range of possibly imposed duties in order for staying the enforcement of a prison sentence.

§5. Relationship Between Contractual and Delictual or Tortious Responsibility (Is There a Rule of Non-Cumul; What about Pre-contractual Liability?)

14. In Portugal, as in France, Italy, or Spain, the branch of the law referring to damages and the duty to compensate them is usually labelled as the law of civil liability ('responsabilidade civil').[75] The concept of civil liability is intertwined with

75. *See, for example,* J.M. Antunes Varela, Das obrigações em geral, vol. I, 10th edition (Coimbra: Livraria Almedina 2000) 518 ff.; I. Galvão Telles, Direito das obrigações, 7th edition (Coimbra: Coimbra Editora 1997) 208 ff.; M.J. Almeida Costa, Direito das obrigações, 10th edition (Coimbra: Livraria Almedina 2006) 517 ff.; F. Pessoa Jorge, Direito das obrigações (Lisboa: AAFDUL 1966–1967) 496 ff; F. Pessoa Jorge, Ensaio sobre os pressupostos da responsabilidade civil (Coimbra: Livraria Almedina 1999, reprint); R. Alarcão, Direito das obrigações (Texto elaborado pelos Drs. J. Sousa Ribeiro, J.F. Sinde Monteiro, Almeno de Sá e J.C. Proença, com base nas lições do Prof. Doutor Rui de Alarcão ao 3.º ano jurídico) (Coimbra 1983) 205 ff.; A. Menezes Cordeiro, Direito das obrigações, vol. II (Lisboa: AAFDUL 1994, reprint) 257 ff.; J. Ribeiro de Faria, Direito das obrigações, vol. I (Coimbra: Livraria Almedina 2001, reprint) 410 ff; J.F. Sinde Monteiro, 'Responsabilidade civil – I. Introdução', in: Revista de direito e economia 4 (1978) 312–405; L. Menezes Leitão, Direito das obrigações, vol. I – Introdução. Da constituição das obrigações, 7th edition (Coimbra: Livraria Almedina 2008) 285 ff.; A. Menezes Cordeiro, Tratado de direito civil português, vol. II – Direito das obrigações, III. – Gestão de negócios. Enriquecimento sem causa.

the concept of a duty to compensate. 'Civil liability is the duty to compensate damages someone sustained.'[76] It is all about indemnifying the person who sustained damage.

There is a difference, by no means immaterial, between the concept of a law of *civil liability* and the concept of a law of *civil wrongs* – i.e., of a law of *torts*. In keeping with the distinction between *causative events* and *responses*,[77] it shall be emphasized that the concept of a *law of torts*, as well as the concept of a *law of wrongs*, refer to the cause – to the *causative event* – and the concept of a *law of civil liability* refers to the *response* to such an event. Whereas *torts* are *causes* (causative events), *liabilities* are *responses*.

It follows from such a distinction that *civil liability* is a *response*.[78]

Furthermore, civil liability is a multi-causal response.[79]

It may be the response to the breach of duty, as it may be the response to no breach. Strict *liability*, for example, is the response to no tort – to no wrong. In the case civil liability is the response to the breach of duty – to a *civil wrong* – it may result either from the breach of a *contract* or from the breach of an *obligation*, irrespective of whether such an *obligation* is *contractual* or *non-contractual*; it may result either from pre-contractual or from post-contractual liability – from *culpa in contrahendo* or from *culpa post factum finitum*; it may result from a *tort*, in the strictest sense of the word.

The distinction between the concepts of contractual, obligational liability and non-contractual, non-obligational, or tortious liability is far from clear.

In the first place, there are significant divergences as to *words*. Second, and more importantly, such significant divergences as to *words* reflect significant – even more significant – divergences as to *concepts*.

It should be recognized that both the term *contractual liability* and the term *non-contractual liability* are less than satisfactory. On the one hand, the term *contractual liability* seems to be too narrow in scope. It seems to include only liability resulting from the breach of a contract.[80,81] It seems, therefore, to exclude liability resulting from the breach of a unilateral legal transaction,[82] for instance, from the breach of a unilateral, binding promise. In accordance with the concepts and the structures of the Portuguese Civil Code, the principles and rules on *contractual*

Responsabilidade civil (Coimbra: Livraria Almedina 2010) 387 ff; J.F. Sinde Monteiro, 'Rudimentos da responsabilidade civil', in: Revista da Faculdade de Direito da Universidade do Porto 2 (2005), 349–390.

76. I. Galvão Telles, Direito das obrigações, 208.
77. *See* P. Birks, *Unjust Enrichment*, 2nd edition (Oxford: Oxford University Press 2004) 3–5 and 9–11.
78. In a sense, the expression law of civil liability could be better translated as law of damages, for damages, like liabilities, are responses.
79. *See* P. Birks, Unjust Enrichment, at 9–11.
80. Contracts must consist of an agreement. They are, by definition, bilateral or multilateral legal transactions.
81. *See*, for instance, J.M. Antunes Varela, Das obrigações em geral, vol. I, 519, fn. 1.
82. On the concept of a legal transaction, or juridical act, *see* Art. II – 1:101 of the (Draft) Common Frame of Reference: 'A juridical act is any statement or agreement, whether express or implied from conduct, which is intended to have legal effect as such. It may be unilateral, bilateral or multilateral' (Ch. von Bar/E. Clive (eds), *Principles, Definitions and Model Rules of European Private Law. Draft Common Frame of Reference* (Munich: Sellier 2009) 183).

liability are to apply, however, to the liability resulting from the breach of any legal transaction – this means from the breach of any legally binding promise – be it *bilateral* or *unilateral*. On the other hand, the term *non-contractual liability* seems to be much too wide. It seems to include any liability resulting from any event different from *breach of a contract*.

For the terms *contractual* and *non-contractual liability* are less than satisfactory, it has been suggested that *contractual liability* should be replaced by *obligational liability*,[83,84] and that *non-contractual liability* should be replaced by *aquilian*,[85] *delictual*[86] or *non-obligational liability*.[87]

The problem with both *aquilian* and *delictual liability* is a matter of words.

It is rather doubtful whether modern civil liability should be named by referring to its ancient predecessor.[88] It is even more doubtful whether modern civil liability, encompassing *no-fault, objective* or *strict liability*, should be named by referring to *civil delicts, civil wrongs* or *torts*.[89]

The problem with *non-obligational liability* is a matter of concepts.

The concept of an *obligational liability* could be positively determined:

> From the perspective of the creditor, obligations liability would refer to all types of liability resulting from the breach of the creditor's right, defined as a relative right and as a right to the debtor's performance; and, from the perspective of the debtor, obligational liability would refer to all types of liability resulting from the breach of the debtor's duty, defined as a special or specific duty and as a duty to perform – because the creditor's right and the debtor's

---

83. *See, for example*, M. de Andrade, Teoria geral das obrigações, 3rd. edition (Coimbra: Livraria Almedina 1966) 337; I. Galvão Telles, Direito das obrigações, 211–213; F. Pessoa Jorge, Direito das obrigações, 257 and 500–501; F. Pessoa Jorge, Ensaio sobre os pressupostos da responsabilidade civil, 37–42; A. Menezes Cordeiro, Direito das obrigações, vol. II, 273, fn. 47; A. Menezes Cordeiro, Tratado de direito civil português, vol. II – Direito das obrigações, III. – Gestão de negócios. Enriquecimento sem causa. Responsabilidade civil, 387–388.
84. For a suggestion that replacing contractual liability for obligational liability is not necessary, for the term contractus were to be taken in the sense it had in the classic Roman law, referring to all obligations distinct from liability ex delicto, *see, for example*, L. Mengoni, 'Responsabilità contrattuale (diritto vigente)', in: Enciclopedia del diritto, vol. XXXiX (Milano: Giuffrè) 1072–1099, at 1072.
85. *See*, for instance, A. Menezes Cordeiro, Tratado de direito civil português, vol. II – Direito das obrigações, III. – Gestão de negócios. Enriquecimento sem causa. Responsabilidade civil, 387–388.
86. *See*, for instance, F. Pessoa Jorge, Ensaio sobre os pressupostos da responsabilidade civil, 37–42.
87. *See*, for instance, I. Galvão Telles, *Direito das obrigações*.
88. *See, for example*, R. Zimmermann, 'Usus modernus legis Aquiliae and Delictual Liability Today', Stellenbosch Law Review, vol. 1 (1990), 67–93 (67); *The Law of Obligations. Roman Foundations of the Civilian Tradition* (Cape Town/Wetton/Johannesburg: Juta & Co. 1990) 1017–1018: 'Even in Roman law, the lex Aquilia had been extended, adapted and modernized in so many ways that a jurist from the time of its enactment would hardly have recognized the late classical (or Justinianic) delict of damnum culpa datum as specifically Aquilian, and any legal advice based merely on the wording of the lex would have been hopelessly inadequate.'
89. In fact, delicts are civil wrongs (torts). If the causative event is connected to the requirements unlawfulness and fault, the term delictual liability may well apply. If, however, the causative event is completely disconnected from both requirements, as it is in the case of strict liability, it may not.

duty form the core of the relationship of obligation, the concept of an obligational liability presupposes the existence of such a relationship between the parties.[90]

The concept of a *non-obligational, tortious liability* could be defined either positively or negatively: on the one hand, it could be negatively defined by saying that non-obligational, tortious liability is every single liability that does not result from the breach of the creditor's right, or from the breach of the debtor's duty to perform; on the other hand, it could be positively defined, by saying that non-obligational, tortious liability is every single liability that results either from the breach of an absolute, general right – such as an injury to the person or to property – or from the breach of a general duty.[91]

Where there is a duty to compensate – where the defendant is under the duty to compensate the plaintiff for the damages he sustained – the alternatives would be two, and no more than two: either the duty to compensate results from the breach of a special, specific duty to perform or it does not; this means that either the duty to compensate results from the breach of an obligation or it does not. If the duty to compensate results from the breach of an obligation, it would be fully appropriate to refer to *liability in contract* or, at least, to refer to *liability in obligation*. If it does not, it would be appropriate to refer to *liability in tort*. Where no contractual, no obligational liability could be found, there would be non-obligational, tortious liability.

The point is that the clear, all-comprehensive distinction between the two fundamental types of civil liability, obligational and non-obligational liability, immediately rules out intermediary liabilities.[92] It immediately rules out the so-called *third way* (*'Dritte Spur'*, *'terceira via'*) in the law of civil liability. Whether the all-comprehensive distinction between the two fundamental types of civil liability holds it depends on the merits of such a *third way*.

It is submitted that the so-called *third way* of civil liability is a good idea, steadily gaining ground among both scholars and judges.[93]

---

90. *See, for example*, E. Santos Júnior, Da responsabilidade civil de terceiro por lesão do direito de crédito (Coimbra: Livraria Almedina 2003) 211.
91. *See, for example*, E. Santos Júnior, Da responsabilidade civil de terceiro por lesão do direito de crédito, 211–212.
92. *See, for example*, M. Carneiro da Frada, Teoria da confiança e responsabilidade civil (Coimbra: Livraria Almedina 2004) 275.
93. *See, for example*, J. Baptista Machado, 'A cláusula do razoável', in: Obra dispersa, vol. I (Braga: Scientia Juridica 1991) 457–621, at 579–589 and 615–621; J.F. Sinde Monteiro, Responsabilidade por conselhos, recomendações ou informações (Coimbra: Livraria Almedina 1989) 507 ff; M. Carneiro da Frada, Contrato e deveres de protecção (Coimbra: Boletim da Faculdade de Direito 1994) 92 ff. and 259 ff.; M. Carneiro da Frada, Uma 'terceira via' no direito da responsabilidade civil. O problema da imputação a terceiros dos danos causados a terceiros por auditores de sociedades (Coimbra: Livraria Almedina 1997) 27 ff.; N.M. Pinto Oliveira, 'Deveres de protecção em relações obrigacionais', in: Scientia Juridica, 2003, 495–523; M. Carneiro da Frada, Teoria da confiança e responsabilidade civil, 757–766; L.M. Menezes Leitão, Direito das obrigações, vol. I – Introdução. Da consttuição das obrigações, 310 ff.; N.M. Pinto Oliveira, Direito das obrigações, vol. I – Conceito, estrutura e função das relações obrigacionais. Elementos das relações obrigacionais. Direitos de crédito e direitos reais (Coimbra: Livraria Almedina 2005) 48–55.

In the first place, liability resulting from *culpa in contrahendo* and from *culpa post factum finitum* does not fit either of the two categories.

On the one hand, they do not fit the concept of *obligational liability*.

The concept of an obligational liability refers to the breach of fundamental duties to perform. The concepts of pre-contractual and post-contractual liability refer to the breach of ancillary, reliance-based duties of conduct.

On the other hand, neither *culpa in contrahendo* nor *culpa post factum finitum* fit the concept of a non-obligational, tortious liability.

The concept of *non-obligational, tortious liability* refers to general duties – to duties among *strangers*, among persons *who do not know each other*. The concepts of *pre-contractual* and *post-contractual liability* refer to specific duties – to duties between persons who *do know each other*. In fact, *pre-contractual* and *post-contractual liability* require a special connection – a special relationship – between the parties (*Sonderverbindung*).

Culpa in contrahendo, as well as *culpa post factum finitum*, are 'concept[s] sui generis, floating freely between contract and tort'.[94]

Second, even within the classic causative events – even within sources of obligations – different relationships of obligation are to be treated differently.

In fact, relationships of obligations resulting from contracts are different from relationships of obligations resulting, for instance, from quasi-contracts, such as *negotiorum gestio*. It follows from such a difference as to duties – as to relationships of obligation – that principles and rules applying to contractual liability should not *automatically* apply to quasi-contractual liability, such as liability for the breach of obligations resulting from *negotiorum gestio*.[95]

In keeping with the conviction, there are intermediate liabilities; closed, rigid concepts of contractual and non-contractual, obligational and non-obligational liability should be abandoned. Contractual and non-contractual liability, obligational and non-obligational liability, should be referred to as types. Types are function-determined, value-determined, 'open-value concepts'.[96] In referring to contractual and non-contractual, tortious liability as types, open, flexible concepts should be preferred to closed, rigid concepts.

94. B.S. Markesinis/H. Unberath/A. Johnston, *The German Law of Contract. A Comparative Treatise*, 2nd edition (Oxford/Portland: Hart 2006) 92.

95. *See* Jorge Ferreira Sinde Monteiro, 'Rudimentos da responsabilidade civil', at 351, and L.M. Menezes Leitão, Direito das obrigações, vol. I – Introdução. Da constituição das obrigações, 288, 354–356.

96. On the concept of types, *see* e.g., K. Larenz/C.-W. Canaris, Methodenlehre der Rechtswissenschaft, 3rd edition (Springer: Berlin/Heidelberg 1995) 290 ff.; for the Portuguese translation, *see* K. Larenz, Metodologia da ciência do direito, 3rd edition (Lisboa: Fundação Calouste Gulbenkian 1997) 307 ff.; H.M. Pawlowski, Methodenlehre für Juristen, 3rd edition (Heidelberg: C.F. Müller 1999) 77–82; P. Pais de Vasconcelos, Contratos atípicos, (Coimbra: Livraria Almedina 1995); R. Pinto Duarte, Tipicidade e atipicidade nos contratos, (Coimbra: Livraria Almedina 2000); G. Sartor, 'Legal Reasoning: A Cognitive Approach to the Law', in E. Pattaro, *A Treatise of Legal Philosophy and General Jurisprudence* (Dordrecht: Springer, 2005), 158–159; F.J. Andrés Santos, 'Einleitung', in: F.J. Andrés Santos/Ch. Baldus/H. Dedek (eds), Vertragstypen in Europa. Historische Entwicklung und europäische Perspektiven (München: Sellier – European Law Publishers) 1–10.

Types aim at making *clear* and *understandable* the characteristic features of their object. They do have a core.[97] In spite of the fact they do have a core, 'part of their reference lies at the periphery'.[98] '[They] can be defined only by family resemblance.'[99] In determining whether there is a family resemblance, convergences and divergences as to the characteristic features of the object have to be weighed. Therefore, types 'make it possible to identify objects by recourse to weighing'.[100] It all comes then to determining the characteristic features of both contractual and non-contractual – of both obligational and non-obligational, tortious liability. It all comes then at determining which points of view are to be emphasized, and which are not.

In the first place, contractual and non-contractual liability typically relate to different values. Contractual liability typically relates to the value of (private) autonomy. The defendant is to be held liable, for he broke his promise. Non-contractual liability typically relates to the values of (public) heteronomy. The defendant is to be held liable, even though he promised nothing to no one.

Basic, fundamental interests relating to personality and property are to be protected by the State by means of general norms. Everyone's personality, as everyone's property, is to be protected by the law.

Second, contractual and non-contractual, tortious liability aim at different purposes. Whereas contractual liability is about changing the parties' economic situation by granting the creditor what he bargained for; non-contractual liability is all about keeping the parties' personality and property.

Contractual liability typically aims at the dynamic satisfaction of the parties' so-called *positive interests*; non-contractual, tortious liability typically aims at the static satisfaction of the parties' so-called *negative interests*.

Third, contractual and non-contractual liability typically aims at different purposes in different situations. Whereas contractual liability typically applies to contexts where the parties know each other; non-contractual, tortious liability applies in contexts where the parties do not know each other. Were it not for the damage, the plaintiff and defendant would never meet – they would be reciprocally anonymous, and reciprocally anonymous they would remain.[101]

Infringements of personality and property by persons who do not know each other (by strangers) clearly fall within the scope of non-contractual, tortious liability. Infringements of economic interests, protected by contract, by persons who do

---

97. In a sense, they are similar to Weber's ideal-types. '[They are] formed by the one-sided accentuation of one or more points of view and by the synthesis of a great-many diffuse discrete, more or less present and occasionally absent concrete individual phenomena, which are arranged accordingly to those one-sidedly emphasized viewpoints into a unified analytical construct (Gedankenbild)' – *see* Max Weber, *On the Methodology of the Social Sciences* (Illinois: The Free Press of Glencoe 1949) 90.
98. G. Sartor, 'Legal Reasoning. A Cognitive Approach to the Law', 159.
99. G. Sartor, 'Legal Reasoning. A Cognitive Approach to the Law', 159.
100. G. Sartor, 'Legal Reasoning. A Cognitive Approach to the Law', 159.
101. For further developments, *see* M. Carneiro da Frada, Contrato e deveres de protecção; M. Carneiro da Frada, Tutela da confiança e responsabilidade civil, 270–306; N.M. Pinto Oliveira, 'Tópicos sobre a distinção entre a responsabilidade contratual e a responsabilidade extracontratual', in: Estudos em comemoração dos vinte anos da Escola de Direito da Universidade do Minho (Coimbra: Coimbra Editora 2014) 513–526.

know each other (by the parties), clearly fall within the scope of contractual liability. *Culpa in contrahendo*, *culpa post factum finitum* and contracts with protective effects vis-à-vis third parties are harder cases, for they do not clearly fall within the scope of the established types.

I. Differences as to the Conditions of Contractual and Non-contractual Liability

15. There are five fundamental differences between the principles and rules applying to contractual and non-contractual, tortious liability.[102]

First, there is a difference as to compensation for *pure economic loss*. In contract, *pure economic loss* is to be compensated. In tort, it is not[103] – compensation for *pure economic loss* is but an exception, and in fact, it is an exception rather limited in scope.[104] Second, there is a difference as to the *burden of proof* of fault – Article 487(1) applies to non-contractual, tortious liability, and Article 799(1) applies to contractual liability. Third, there is a difference as to *liability for another's conduct* (i.e., to *vicarious liability*) – Article 500 applies to liability in tort, and Article 800(1) applies to liability in contract.

As to the difference between Article 487(1) and Article 799(1):

> When it comes at liability in tort, it is up to the plaintiff to demonstrate the defendant's fault.[105] It is up to the plaintiff to demonstrate that the defendant's conduct was either wilful or negligent. When it comes at liability in contract, it is up to the defendant – it is up to the debtor – to demonstrate that his conduct

---

102. For a comparative approach, *see, for example*, R. Zimmermann, *The Law of Obligations. Roman Foundations of the Civilian Tradition*, 902–906; Ch. von Bar, *The Common European Law of Torts, vol. I – The Core Areas of Tort Law, the Approximation in Europe and Its Accommodation in the System* (Oxford: Oxford University Press 1998) 459–512; H. Koziol, *Basic Questions of Tort Law from a Germanic Perspective*, 93–107.

103. *See* Portuguese Civil Code, Art. 483(1): 'Whoever, whether by wilful misconduct (dolus) or by negligence unlawfully infringes the rights of another person or any legal provision intended to safeguard the interests of others must compensate the injured party for damage arising from such violation.' It follows from the fact the formula 'the rights of another person' has been interpreted as referring to *absolute rights* – and to *absolute rights* only – that non-pecuniary damage is to be compensated only in exceptional cases.

104. *See* J.F. Sinde Monteiro, Responsabilidade por conselhos, recomendações ou informações (Coimbra: Livraria Almedina 1989) 187–199; M. Carneiro da Frada, Contrato e deveres de protecção, 176–177; N.M. Pinto Oliveira, 'Deveres de protecção em relações obrigacionais', 52 Scientia Juridica (2003) 495–523, at 519–521; N.M. Pinto Oliveira, Direito das obrigações, vol. I – Conceito, estrutura e função das relações obrigacionais. Elementos das relações obrigacionais. Direitos de crédito e direitos reais (Coimbra: Livraria Almedina 2005) 50–53; J.F. Sinde Monteiro, 'Responsabilidade delitual. Da ilicitude', in: Comemorações dos 35 anos do Código Civil e dos 25 anos da Reforma de 1977, vol. III – Direito das obrigações (Coimbra: Coimbra Editora 2007) 453–481, especially 464–465.

105. *See* Portuguese Civil Code, Art. 487(1).

was neither wilful nor negligent.[106] In the case of contractual liability, it follows from the presumption in Article 799 (1) that the burden of proof is reversed.

As to the difference between Article 500 and Article 800(1):

> There is a conceptual, structural difference between both Articles. Article 500 takes principal and his helper as different, separate persons. The principal is to be held liable in tort for the conduct of his helper. Article 800 (1) takes principal and his helper as one, and the same, person. In accordance with Article 800 (1), the principal (=the debtor) is to be held liable for the conduct of his helper, as if the helper's conduct was the principal's.[107]

The conceptual, structural difference between Articles 500 and 800(1) of the Portuguese Civil Code has three consequences:

The *first consequence* refers to the subjective requirements of liability.

Article 500(1) requires *subordination*. The principal is only to be held liable for his helpers' conduct in the case his *helpers* are *subordinates*. If there is no subordination, there will be no liability in tort. That is, the principal will not be held liable, for instance, for the conduct of an independent contractor.[108] Article 800(1) requires no *subordination* at all. The debtor is to be held liable for all acts and for all omissions of all persons concurring to performance.

In fact, Article 800(1) explicitly refers to *auxiliaries* or *helpers*. It follows from such a wording that the debtor for all acts, of all persons, helping him to carry out performance – all of them are auxiliaries, all of them helpers.

The *second consequence* refers to the objective requirements of liability.

Whereas Article 500(1) and (2) limits the principal's liability to cases where the helper is performing his task, and Article 800(1) does not.

The *third consequence* refers to the helper's liability for the damage.

Whereas Article 500(1) of the Civil Code requires the helper – the subordinate – to be himself liable for the damage, Article 800(1) does not.

In most, if not all, cases of contractual liability, it is not possible for the auxiliary to be held liable in contract vis-à-vis the creditor. There is a contract, and therefore, there is a relationship of obligation between the creditor and the debtor. There is no

---

106. *See* Portuguese Civil Code, Art. 799(1).

107. M. Carneiro da Frada, Contrato e deveres de protecção, 203–217; M. Carneiro da Frada, 'A responsabilidade objectiva por facto de outrem face à distinção entre responsabilidade obrigacional e aquliana', in: (1998) Direito e justiça 297–311; N.M. Pinto Oliveira, 'Cláusulas de exclusão e de limitação do dever de indemnizar em direito civil', in: Cláusulas acessórias ao contrato. Cláusulas de exclusão e de limitação do dever de indemnizar. Cláusulas penais, 3rd edition (Coimbra: Livraria Almedina 2008) 19–64, at 60–61; N.M. Pinto Oliveira, Princípios de direito dos contratos, 446–448.

108. *See* C.-W. Canaris, 'Schutzgesetze – Verkehrspflichten – Schutzpflichen', in: C.-W. Canaris/U. Diederichsen (eds), *Festschrift für Karl Larenz zum 80. Geburtstag* (Munich: C.H. Beck 1983) 27–110/in: *Gesammelte Schriften* (Berlin/Boston: de Gruyter 2012) 945–1024, especially at 1002–1005.

contract – and, therefore, there is no relationship of obligation at all – between the helper and the creditor. For there is no relationship of obligation, no contractual liability could arise.

The difference is rather significant, both theoretically and practically.

In the case of non-contractual, tortious liability, it makes full sense to hold both principal and subordinate jointly and solidarily liable for all damage.[109] In the case of contractual liability, it makes no sense at all – the debtor is to be held liable in the contract; the debtor's auxiliaries or helpers are not.

Fourth, there is a difference as to cases of the plurality of debtors. Article 512 states the general principle: Whenever there is a plurality of debtors, the obligation is deemed to be divided. Each debtor is bound to perform only part of the obligation.[110] In the case of non-contractual, tortious liability, Article 497 provides for an exception to the general principle. The duty to compensate qualifies as a solidary obligation. Each debtor – each tortfeasor – is bound to compensate in full. In the case of contractual liability, no article at all provides for an exception – therefore, the duty to compensate for all the damage the creditor sustained qualifies as a divided obligation.

Fifth, there is a difference in prescription. Whereas claims in tort are under a short limitation period of three years,[111] claims in the contract are normally under a long limitation period of twenty years.[112]

It has been argued that the short, three-year-limitation period should also apply to claims in the contract – at least in the case where performance is impossible, and the creditor is entitled to damages and to damages only.[113]

---

109. *See* Portuguese Civil Code, Art. 500(3).
110. For the distinction between solidary and divided obligations, *see*, for instance, Art. III – 4:102 of the (Draft) Common Frame of Reference: '(1) An obligation is solidary when each debtor is bound to perform the obligation in full and the creditor may require performance from any of them until full performance has been received. (2) An obligation is divided when each debtor is bound to perform only part of the obligation and the creditor may claim from each debtor only performance of that debtor's part.' – Art. 512 of the Portuguese Civil Code contains a definition of the concept of solidary obligations roughly equivalent to the definition enshrined in Art. 4:102 of the (Draft) Common Frame of Reference. There seems, however, to be a difference between the regimes of solidary obligations in the (Draft) Common Frame of Reference and in the Portuguese Civil Code. Article 4:102 of the (Draft) Common Frame of Reference allows the creditor to require performance from any of the debtors 'until full performance has been received'. Article 519 of the Portuguese Civil Code draws a line between claims which have been brought before a court of law and claims which have not. In the case the claim against one, and only one, of the debtors has been brought before a court of law ('interpelação judicial'), a limitation applies – the creditor may not claim performance from the others unless there is a relevant reason ('razão atendível') for such a proceeding, such as the insolvency, or the risk of insolvency, of the debtor from which performance has been required. In the case has not been brought before a court of law ('interpelação extrajudicial'), such a limitation does not apply, however.
111. *See* Portuguese Civil Code, Art. 498.
112. *See* Portuguese Civil Code, Art. 309.
113. Pedro de Albuquerque, 'A aplicação do prazo prescricional do n.º 1 do art. 498.º do Código Civil à responsabilidade civil contratual', in: 49 *Revista da Ordem dos Advogados* (1989) 793–837, especially at 800–804.

Even though there are some solid reasons in favour of such a shorter limitation period,[114] the thesis could not find acceptance in case law.

II. Differences as to the Effects of Contractual and Non-contractual Liability

16. In the case of liability in tort, Article 494 of the Civil Code applies, allowing the judge to reduce the amount of compensation: 'Where liability is based on mere fault, compensation may be fixed equitably at an amount lower than that corresponding to the damage caused, provided that the degree of fault of the wrongdoer, the financial situation of the wrongdoer and of the injured party, as well as the other circumstances of the case so justify.'[115] In the case of liability in contract, it has been argued that Article 494 should not apply.[116]

In the first place, contractual, obligational liability would be a form of performance. In spite of the fact it is not a specific performance, it should be construed as a performance by means of an equivalent. In a sense, contractual, obligational liability would be monetized performance. Second, contractual liability should conform to the creditor's *legitimate expectations.*

The requirement that contractual liability is certain, so as to conform to the creditor's *legitimate expectations*, would be stronger in the area of a contractual liability than in the area of non-contractual, tortious liability, and such a requirement would immediately rule out the application of Article 494.

It is submitted none of the two arguments is an obstacle against applying Article 494 to contractual liability, at least for consequential damage.

The Portuguese private law system clearly distinguishes the performance of the contract and damages for non-performance [for the breach of the contract]. Furthermore, it distinguishes the amount of damages corresponding to the value of the goods or to the value of the services the debtor failed to perform and consequential damages exceeding such a value.

In spite of this fact, Article 494 of the Civil Code should not apply to damages corresponding to the value of the goods or to the value of the services the debtor

---

114. *See*, thoroughly, R. Zimmermann, *Comparative Foundations of a European Law of Set-Off and Prescription* (Cambridge: Cambridge University Press 2004).

115. *See* A.G. Dias Pereira, 'Portuguese Tort Law: A Comparison with the Principles of European Tort Law', at 647. In M. Bussani/V.V. Palmer (eds), *Pure Economic Loss in Europe* (Cambridge: Cambridge University Press 2003) xxxv, the translation of Art. 494 of the Portuguese Civil Code reads as follows: 'If the liability is based upon negligence compensation may be equitably settled at a lesser amount so as to correspond to the damage caused, as long as the degree of culpability of the agent, his financial conditions and those of the injured party and other circumstances justify it.'

116. *See*, for instance, J.M. Antunes Varela, Das obrigações em geral, vol. I, 913; M.J. Almeida Costa, Direito das obrigações, 544; J. Ribeiro de Faria, Direito das obrigações, vol. II, 422–424; J. Calvão da Slva, Responsabilidade civil do produtor (Coimbra: Livraria Almedina 1990) 544.

failed to perform; it should apply at least to consequential damages exceeding such a value.[117] In contractual, as in tortious liability, 'full compensation [may be] an oppressive burden to the defendant'.[118]

III. Concurrence of Contractual and Non-contractual Claims – I

17. In general, cases of concurrence between principles, between rules, or between sets of principles and rules are to be resolved by applying one of three principles:

i. *Concurrence of claims may be cumulative.* In such a case, both principles, both rules, or both sets of principles and rules are to be applied side by side.
ii. *Concurrence of claims may be alternative or elective.* In such a situation, it is up to the plaintiff to decide which principle, which rule – which set of principles and rules is to be applied.
iii. Finally, the *concurrence of claims may be consumptive or mutually exclusive.* In such a situation, it is up to the judge to decide which principle, which rule, – which set of principles and rules is to be applied in accordance with the system's principles and values.[119] In the particular, specific case of concurrence between contractual and non-contractual, tortious liability, it should be asked which of the three principles is to apply.

The problem is apparent in the case of liability for medical malpractice – in a sense, liability for medical malpractice is always a liability between contract and tort.

In the first place, there is an important distinction between medical practice in *public hospitals* and medical practice in *private hospitals.* In public medicine, i.e., in the case of medical practice in public hospitals, the administrative courts are competent, and the law concerning *non-contractual, tortious liability* of the State applies

117. F. Pessoa Jorge, Ensaio sobre os pressupostos da responsabilidade civil, 365; A. Menezes Cordeiro, Da boa fé no direito civil (Coimbra: Livraria Almedina 1997, reprint) 638–639; L. Menezes Leitão, Direito das obrigações, vol. II – Transmissão e extinção das obrigações. Não cumprimento e garantias das obrigações, 7th edition (Coimbra: Livraria Almedina 2010) 260–261; J.C. Brandão Proença, A conduta do lesado como pressuposto e critério de imputação do dano extracontratual (Coimbra: Livraria Almedina 1997) 169–170, footnote 522; P. Mota Pinto, Interesse contratual negativo e interesse contratual positivo, vols. I and II (Coimbra: Coimbra Editora 2008) 840–841 (footnote 2361) and 938–940 (footnote 2360); N.M. Pinto Oliveira, Princípios de direito dos contratos, 723–735.

118. *See* Principles of European Tort Law, Art. 10:401, in: European Group on Tort Law, *Principles of European Tort Law. Text and Commentary* (Wien/New York: Springer 2005) 179–181.

119. *See* L. Enneccerus/H.-C. Nipperdey, Tratado de derecho civil. Parte general, vol. I/I (Barcelona: Bosch) 225–226 (§ 54a); K. Larenz/C.-W. Canaris, Methodenlehre der Rechtswissenschaft, 87–91; for the Portuguese translation, *see* K. Larenz, Metodologia da ciência do direito, 372–379; J. Baptista Machado, Âmbito de eficácia e âmbito de competência das leis (Coimbra: Livraria Almedina 1998, reprint) 214–217; M. Teixeira de Sousa, O concurso de títulos de aquisição da prestação (Coimbra: Livraria Almedina 1988) 101 ff.

(Law No. 67/2007, 31 December).[120] In private medicine, judicial courts are competent, and the Civil Code applies. In most cases, both the parties and the courts refer to the principles and rules on *contractual liability*. Second, within the sphere of private medicine, there is an important distinction between medical practice within and without the framework of a contractual relationship between doctor and patient.[121]

IV. Concurrence of Contractual and Non-contractual Claims – II

18. In some legal systems, the principle applying to concurrent claims in contract and in tort is rather clear. In France, for instance, it is clear that *concurrence between contract and tort is mutually exclusive*. Contractual liability excludes non-contractual, tortious liability.[122]

In Germany, it is clear that *concurrence between contract and tort is* not *mutually exclusive*. Contractual liability does not exclude non-contractual, tortious liability. It follows from such a preference for *cumulative concurrence* that the plaintiff may invoke provisions referring to contractual and provisions referring to non-contractual, tortious liability.[123]

In some legal systems, such as Portugal, the principle applying to such concurrent claims is not as clear as that.

---

120. The National Health Service is the largest health provider, thus administrative courts receive a substantial number of tort cases – *see, for example*, André Dias Pereira, 'Responsabilidade civil: O médico entre o público e o privado', 89 Boletim da Faculdade de Direito [da Universidade de Coimbra] (2013) 253–303.

121. *See* A.G. Dias Pereira, Direitos dos pacientes e responsabilidade médica (Coimbra: Centro de Direito Biomédico/Coimbra Editora 2015) at 624 ff.

122. On the French solution (principe du non-cumul), *see, for example*, P. Jourdain, 'La distinction des responsabilités délictuelle et contractuelle en droit positif français', in: Le droit français de la responsabilité civile confronté aux projets européens d'harmonisation. Recueil des travaux du Groupe de Recherche Européen sur la Responsabilité Civile et l'Assurance (GRERCA) (Paris: IRJS Editions 2012) 67–87; O. Moréteau, 'Grundfragen des Schadensersatz aus französischer Sicht', in: H. Koziol (ed.), Grundfragen des Schadensersatz aus rechtsvergleichender Sicht (Wien: Sramek 2014) 1–112, at 38–41.

123. For a comparative account, T. Weir, 'Complex Liabilities', in: *International Encyclopedia of Comparative Law* (Tübingen/Dordrecht/Boston/Lancaster: J.C.B. Mohr (Paul Siebeck)/Martinus Nijhoff 1983) 24–39; R. Zimmermann, *The Law of Obligations. Roman Foundations of the Civilian Tradition*, 904–906; Ch. von Bar, The Common European Law of Torts, vol. I – The Core Areas of Tort Law, the Approximation in Europe and its Accommodation in the System, 459–512; P. Schechtriem, 'The Borderland Between Tort and Contract – Opening a New Frontier', in: 21 Cornell International Law Journal (1988) 467–476; P. Ancel, 'Les conditions générales de la matière: rôles respectifs de la loi et du juge en matière de responsabilité civile, responsabilité délictuelle et responsabilité contractuelle', in: Le droit français de la responsabilité civile confronté aux projets européens d'harmonisation. Recueil des travaux du Groupe de Recherche Européen sur la Responsabilité Civile et l'Assurance (GRERCA) (Paris: IRJS Editions 2012) 735–749, especially at 748–749; and G. Dannemann, 'Point de vue extérieur', in: Le droit français de la responsabilité civile confronté aux projets européens d'harmonisation, 763–768, especially at 767–768.

In the first place, it has been argued that concurrence between contractual and non-contractual, tortious liability is *mutually exclusive*. Contractual liability was to be preferred to non-contractual, tortious liability.[124]

Second, it has been argued that concurrence is alternative (‘*sistema da opção*’). The plaintiff would be entitled to choose which set of principles and rules were to apply to his case. Furthermore, each set of principles and rules was to be taken as a whole. In the case, the plaintiff chose contractual liability; all principles and rules relating to contractual liability would apply. In the case he chose non-contractual, tortious liability, all principles and rules relating to non-contractual, tortious liability would apply, irrespective of whether they were more or less favourable to his interests.[125]

Third, it has been argued that concurrence is cumulative. The plaintiff would be entitled to combine principles and rules from both sets.[126]

In Germany, it has been suggested that at least two procedural schemes could apply, both of them reflecting the conception of concurrence as cumulative.

On the one hand, the plaintiff could be awarded two actions – an action in contract and an action in tort. Such a solution has been named as a *two-claims system* (in Portuguese: ‘*sistema da ação dupla*’). On the other hand, the plaintiff could be granted one action in both contract and tort. Such a system has been named as the *hybrid-claim system* (‘*sistema da ação híbrida*’).

In Portugal, it is unanimously accepted that the *two-claims system* is unacceptable or, at the very least, unjustified. In fact, nothing, either in principle or in practice, could justify that single damage caused by a single fact would require the plaintiff to bring two claims before the court.

For it is unanimously accepted that the *two-claims system* is unjustified to represent concurrence of claims in contract and tort as cumulative concurrence is equivalent to sustaining the *hybrid-claim system*.

In the judgments of 22 September 2011 and 2 June 2015, the Portuguese Supreme Court ruled in favour of the first solution. In the case of concurrence, liability in the contract was to be preferred to liability in tort.

In the judgments of 19 June 2001 and 22 February 2005, the Court ruled in favour of the second solution. The plaintiff would be entitled to choose the set of principles and rules most favourable to his interests. In the judgment of 25 February 2015, the Court ruled in favour of the third solution. The plaintiff would be entitled to combine parts of both sets – of both systems.

---

124. M.J. Almeida Costa, *Direito das obrigações*, 541–553; M.J. Almeida Costa, ‘O concurso da responsabilidade civil contratual e extracontratual’, in: *Ab uno ad omnes – 75 anos da Coimbra Editora*, (Coimbra: Coimbra Editora 1995) 555–565.
125. J.M. Antunes Varela, *Das obrigações em geral*, vol. I, 636–637; A. Pinto Monteiro, *Cláusulas limitativas e de exclusão da responsabilidade civil*, 425–433; A. Pinto Monteiro, *Cláusula penal e indemnização*, 713–714; P. Romano Martínez, *Cumprimento defeituoso – em especial na compra e venda e na empreitada* (Coimbra: Livraria Almedina 1994) 259–288.
126. A. Vaz Serra, ‘Responsabilidade contratual e responsabilidade extracontratual’, in: 85 *Boletim do Ministério da Justiça* (1959) 115–241, especially at 230–241; R. de Alarcão, *Direito das obrigações*, págs. 209–214; D. Moura Vicente, *Da responsabilidade pré-contratual em direito internacional privado* (Coimbra: Livraria Almedina 2001) 221–232; J.F. Sinde Monteiro, ‘Rudimentos da responsabilidade civil’, 352–353.

It is submitted that the first solution is untenable, although the Portuguese Supreme Court recently argued that the principles and rules referring to contractual liability were to be preferred for two reasons.

On the one hand, contractual liability would be the best solution from the perspective of the fundamental principles and values of private law. Contractual liability is closer to the principle of freedom of contract than a non-contractual, tortious liability, and freedom of contract ranks among the fundamental principles and values of any private law system.

On the other hand, contractual, obligational liability would be the best solution from the perspective of the victim. It would be, so the Portuguese Supreme Court says, the most favourable solution to the plaintiff.

It should be apparent that none of the two arguments holds.

In the first place, Portuguese tort law is much closer to German than to French tort law.[127] Second, it is not true that contractual liability is the best solution from the perspective of the fundamental principles and values of private law. It follows from the definition of contractual or obligational liability that principles and rules relating to contractual liability are to apply both to cases of breach of contractual obligations and to cases of non-contractual obligations. In the former, it could be argued that contractual liability is closer to freedom of contract. In the latter, it could not. Third and foremost, it is not at all true that contractual liability is always the best solution from the perspective of the plaintiff's legally protected rights and interests.

It is beyond doubt that the victim would be better off having the right to choose which of the two sets of principles and rules to apply to his case than not having such a right. It is also beyond doubt that the principles and rules referring to contract do not always leave the victim better off than the principles and rules relating to tort. In the case of a plurality of debtors, for instance, it is better to have a claim in tort than to have (only) a claim in contract. If contractual liability aims at awarding the victim additional, specific protection, such additional, specific protection should never leave the victim worse off. If contractual liability is a *majus*, it should never become a *minus*. It follows from such a principle that concurrence of claims in contract and in tort should always be taken as cumulative concurrence.[128]

V. General Clauses on Non-contractual: Tortious Liability

19. In keeping with the principles and rules in the Portuguese Civil Code, there are three fundamental, general clauses on non-contractual, tortious liability.[129]

In the first place, tortfeasors are to be held liable, under Article 483(1), if they infringe absolute rights (such as personality rights and property rights).

---

127. J.F. Sinde Monteiro, 'Anotação ao acórdão do Supremo Tribunal de Justiça de 12 de Novembro de 1996', in: 132 Revista de Legislação e de Jurisprudência (1999–2000) 90–96, at 96.
128. A. Dias Pereira, Direitos dos pacientes e Responsabilidade Médica, 753.
129. *See*, in English, A.G. Dias Pereira, 'Portuguese Tort Law: A Comparison with the Principles of European Tort Law', 628–632.

Second, they are to be held liable, under Article 483(1), if they infringe any statutory provision intended to safeguard the interests of others, and third, they are to be held liable, under Article 334, for any abuse of rights. Even though Article 334 of the Portuguese Civil Code nowhere refers to non-contractual, tortious liability for abuse of rights, it has been interpreted as a functional equivalent to § 826 of the German Civil Code.[130,131]

In keeping with the three general clauses in Articles 483 and 334 of the Portuguese Civil Code, the system of tort law depends on two principles.[132]

The *first principle* relates to the rights and interests to be protected by the law of torts. Article 483(1) of the Civil Code refers to an infringement on the rights of another person. In spite of the fact that it refers to rights of another person – without discriminating whether to absolute or to relative rights, or to both of them – it has been interpreted as referring to absolute rights and to absolute rights only. Therefore, Article 483(1) draws a line between interests that are protected by absolute, subjective rights and interests that are not.

The *second principle* relates to a fault, either in the form of wilful misconduct (*dolus*) or in the form of negligence. Article 483(1) and (2) draw a line between cases where the agent infringed another person's rights and interests being at fault – for he acted on his own wilful misconduct (*dolus*) or by his own negligence – and cases where he infringed another person's relevant rights and relevant interests being at no fault at all.

In the case of an infringement of another person's interests that are protected by absolute rights, liability depends on unlawfulness and fault – if there is a fault, liability is the rule; if there is no fault at all, liability is the exception. In keeping with Article 483(2), '[a]n obligation to pay compensation where there is no fault shall arise only in cases specified by law'.

In the event of an infringement of another person's interests that are not protected by absolute rights – that is to say, in the case of pure economic loss – liability is to be the exception, for it can only result from two things.

In the first place, the tortfeasor is to be held liable if he infringes statutory provisions intended to protect another person's interest (Article 483(1)). And second, he is to be held liable for pure economic loss if he incurs in abuse of rights (Article 334).

---

130. For the translation of § 826 of the German Civil Code, *see* B.S. Markesinis/H. Unberath, *The German Law of Torts. A Comparative Treatise*, 4th edition (Oxford/Portland: Hart Publishing 2002) 15: 'A person who wilfully causes damage to another in a manner contra bonos mores is bound to compensate the other for the damage.'

131. For the interpretation of Art. 334 of the Portuguese Civil Code as the third fundamental, general clause on non-contractual, tortious liability, *see* J.M. Antunes Varela, Das obrigações, 544–548; M.J. Almeida Costa, Direito das obrigações, 80–90 and 564; J. Ribeiro de Faria, Direito das obrigações, vol. II, 428–433; L. Menezes Leitão, Direito das obrigações, vol. I, 289–302; J.F. Sinde Monteiro, Responsabilidade por conselhos, recomendações ou informações, 535–582; J.F. Sinde Monteiro, 'Responsabilidade delitual. Da ilicitude', in: Comemorações dos 35 anos do Código Civil e dos 25 anos da Reforma de 1977, vol. III – Direito das obrigações (Coimbra: Coimbra Editora, 2007) 453–581; N.M. Pinto Oliveira, Princípios de direito dos contratos, 965–971.

132. *See*, for a similar account of German law, C.-W. Canaris, 'Grundstrukturen des deutschen Deliktsrechts', in: Versicherungsrecht 2005, 577–584/in: Claus-Wilhelm Canaris. Gesammelte Schriften. III – Privatrecht (Berlin: de Gruyter 2012) 1109–1126.

It should be stressed that while liability for the infringement of statutory provisions intended to protect another person's interests requires ordinary negligence – and no more than that – liability for abuse of rights requires more than that – it requires extraordinary, gross negligence.[133] In a sense, the exceptionally high degree of the tortfeasor's fault is to compensate for the exceptionally low degree of relevance of the interests he infringed.

§6. Protected Interests (Are All Interests Equally Protected; Are Subjective Rights More Protected Than Others?)

20. Perhaps in a still romantic way, the Portuguese CC concentrates the *General Principle* (Article 483) on the individual person who acts with fault and causes damage to another. Article 483(1) CC states, 'Whoever, whether by wilful misconduct (*dolus*) or by negligence unlawfully infringes the rights of another person or any legal provision intended to safeguard the interests of others, must compensate the injured party for damage arising from such violation.' Strict liability, liability for dangerous activities and liability for auxiliaries are seen as a deviance from the main rule. Article 483(2) confirms this idea by stating: 'an obligation to pay compensation when there is no fault shall arise only in cases specified by law'. Thus, fault liability is the principle, and strict liability is an exception. Neither an analogical application nor a general clause is accepted.

The *Principles of European Tort Law* start with a dynamic and plural source of tort liability, which indeed reflects the reality of our times. The drafters of the *Principles* reflect an urban society of risk rather than a rural society; an economy based on enterprises rather than on individual entrepreneurs might well be the explanation why the drafters of the *Principles* gave fault a place which is at the same level as an 'abnormally dangerous activity' or the liability for the 'auxiliary'.

The Portuguese CC structures the whole question on the basis of the General Principle of a faulty and wrongful behaviour of a person with the capacity to commit torts and from then on inserts exceptions, inversions of the burden of the proof, or particular regimes.

The *Principles* accept the concept of wrongfulness; they avoid the use of such 'name'.[134] That is understandable in an effort to conjugate different European traditions. For the CC, wrongfulness is also a basic concept in tort law. Article 483(1) enounces two types of wrongfulness: (1) violation of 'rights of another' (*erga omnes* rights); and (2) violation of legal provisions intended to protect the interests of others ('protective norms'). Moreover, the literature agrees that there is a third type of wrongful behaviour: intentional damage *contra bonos mores* (*Gute Sitten*) that is to be found in Article 334 – abuse of a right (*Rechtsmissbrauch*, *abuso do direito*).

133. *See* J.F. Sinde Monteiro, Obrigações. Aditamentos (Direito delitual) (Coimbra: 1994) 8; N.M. Pinto Oliveira, Princípios de direito dos contratos, 967–968.
134. *See* R. Zimmermann, in H. Koziol/B.C. Steininger (eds), *European Tort Law 2003* (2004).

As Koziol states, 'in essence, the European Group's *Principles* acknowledge wrongfulness as one decisive factor'.[135] In that respect, the *Principles* describe the scope of protection of interests (Article 2:102). The most extensive protection to *life, bodily or mental integrity, liberty and dignity* (Article 2:102(2)) is guaranteed by the *Principles*. So does the CC. In fact, Article 483(1) protects 'rights of another', which include *personality rights*. Articles 70–81 CC provide extensive protection of personality rights, including the General Personality Right (*Allgemeines Persönlichkeitsrecht*).[136]

Thus, the CC provides extensive protection to personality rights. The enumeration of protected rights in the *Principles* is only indicative; however, the catalogue of personality rights may be considered short, taking into account European case law.

Property rights' protection (including rights over intangible property) seems to be narrower than that of personality rights. That may well be the case also in court practice in Portugal. But technically, no distinction is made between the protection provided to personality rights and rights in rem since the law states that it is wrongful to violate (absolute) 'rights of another' (Article 483(1)).[137]

But the most important difference – at least in style – lies in paragraph (4) of Article 2:102. The *Principles* protect, to some extent, as a starting point, pure economic interests and contractual relationships (Article 2:102(4)).[138] This has been the subject of a hard discussion in Portugal. In fact, Article 483(1) establishes an obligation to compensate for damage caused whenever the 'rights of another' have been unlawfully violated. According to the intent of the author of the preparatory work on the Civil Code,[139] as well as the doctrine and prevailing jurisprudence, only the 'absolute rights' (*erga omnes*) are to be protected by tort law, and that is the traditional solution in Portuguese law. There was some influence from the German law and doctrine in the preliminary work of the current CC, although the formulation of

135. H. Koziol, 'The Concept of Wrongfulness under the Principles of European Tort Law', in: H. Koziol/B.C. Steininger (*supra* n. 24), 552 et seq.

136. Some authors (Oliveira Ascensão, Carvalho Fernandes) do not accept the concept of a general personality right. They state that Art. 70 provides a general clause, where one can include the fundamental rights provided by the extensive catalogue of our Constitution or by the European Convention on Human Rights or even the European Charter of Fundamental Rights (especially after the approval of the Constitutional Treaty).

137. *See* R. Zimmermann (*supra* n. 22), 12.

138. *See* the critics of R. Zimmermann (*supra* n. 22), 13–14. However, the intention of the drafters is not to provide such an extensive protection as Zimmermann states, as explains H. Koziol (*supra* n. 22), 243. The correct interpretation of the whole Art. 2:102 leads to a scarce protection of pure economic loss or contractual relationships under tort law.

139. A. Vaz Serra, Responsabilidade Civil (Requisitos), [1960] *Boletim do Ministério da Justiça* (BMJ), no. 92, 37 et seq. (122, no. 13) and Responsabilidade de Terceiros no Não-Cumprimento das Obrigações, [1959] BMJ, 85, 345 et seq.

Article 483(1) is considerably more open than the corresponding § 823 I of the BGB.[140] Thereinafter, the main doctrine and case law state that *relative rights* deserve no protection under tort law.[141]

Exceptionally, an action grounded in Article 483 and Article 334 (abuse of a right, intentional behaviour *contra bonos mores*) may be accepted in an intentional case of *inducement of breach of a contract*.[142] Another possibility may be the existence of *culpa in contrahendo*[143] or other legal instruments, such as 'contracts whose protective scope extends to certain third parties' (*Verträge mit Schutzwirkung zugunsten Dritter*).

---

140. *See* Sinde Monteiro, Manuel de Andrade und der Einfluss des BGB auf das Portugiesische Zivilgesetzbuch von 1966, in: E. Jayme/H.P. Mansel (eds), *Auf dem Wege zu einem gemeineuropäischen Privatrecht – 100 Jahre BGB und die lusophonen Länder* (1977), 41.
141. *See* Sinde Monteiro, Portugal, in: J. Spier (ed.), *The Limits of Expanding Liability, Eight Cases in a Fundamental Perspective* (1998). *See also* M Almeida, *A Responsabilidade Civil do Banqueiro Perante os Credores da Empresa Financiada* (2003) and M. Frada, O problema e os limites da responsabilidade dos auditores, [2002] *Direito e Justiça* 159–169.
142. *See* the recent work of S. Júnior, *Responsabilidade Civil de Terceiro por Lesão de Direito de Crédito* (2003). This dissertation deals with the question of liability of third parties that cause damage to a credit right of another. The traditional Portuguese doctrine advocates that a credit right only has *inter partes* effects, and thus – except in cases of abuse of right – a third party may not be held liable for violating it. On the contrary personality rights, real rights or intellectual property rights are absolute rights, with efficacy *erga omnes* and their violation might be argued against any wrongdoer. The author, however, after a comprehensive analysis of comparative law, defends that Portuguese law should follow the North-American (e.g., *tort of interference with contractual relations)*, French and Italian doctrine, which accepts, under some circumstances, that a third party might be held liable when breaching a credit right.
143. *See* E. Silva, *Da Responsabilidade Pré-Contratual por Violação dos Deveres de Informação* (2003).

Part I. Liability for One's Own Acts

Chapter 1. General Principles

§1. Unlawfulness and Fault

21. Unlawfulness is a condition of utmost importance in the case of non-contractual, tortious liability for one's own acts and omissions.

It is commonly held that non-contractual, tortious liability for one's own conduct depends on five cumulative requirements.[144]

In the first place, it depends on an act or an omission of the defendant, and second, it depends on the unlawfulness of such an act or omission.

In accordance with the prevailing view, unlawfulness may result: (i) from the infringement of subjective rights, (ii) from the infringement of objective law, in the form of an infringement of any statutory provision intended to protect another person's interests, and (iii) from abuse of rights.

Third, tortious liability depends on the fault of the defendant.

In keeping with the prevailing view, the defendant's fault may take either the form of wilful misconduct (*dolus*) or the form of negligence.

Fourth, tortious liability depends on the existence of damages and fifth, it depends on the existence of causation. It is submitted that there must be some type of causal connection between acts or omissions for which the defendant is to be held liable and the damage the plaintiff sustained.[145]

It should be apparent that such a scheme is far from perfect.[146]

---

144. *See, for example*, F.A. Pires de Lima/J.M. Antunes Varela (/ M.H. Mesquita), Código Civil anotado, vol. I, 471; J.M. Antunes Varela, Das obrigações em geral, vol. I, 525–563 and 562–597; M.J. Almeida Costa, Direito das obrigações, 557–606; R. Alarcão, Direito das obrigações, 238–286; J. Ribeiro de Faria, Direito das obrigações, vol. I, 413–539; J.F. Sinde Monteiro, 'Rudimentos da responsabilidade civil', 349–380; L. Menezes Leitão, Direito das obrigações, vol. I – Introdução. Da constituição das obrigações, 289.

145. van Dam argues that the provisions in §§ 823 and 826 of the German Civil Code contain five requirements for liability: (i) the violation of a codified normative rule (Tatbestandswidrigkeit), (ii) unlawfulness (Rechtswidrigkeit), intention or negligence (Verschulden), causation (Kausalität) and damage (Schaden) [*see* C. van Dam, *European Tort Law*, 2nd edition (Oxford: Oxford University Press 2013) 79]. – In page 136, however, the five requirements are reduced to three: Tatbestand, Rechtswidrigkeit and Verschulden.

146. For alternative schemes, *see* F. Pessoa Jorge, Ensaio sobre os pressupostos da responsabilidade civil, 52–57; A. Menezes Cordeiro, Direito das obrigações, vol. II, 278–282; M. Carneiro da Frada,

It has been pointed out that it deviates from Article 483(1) of the Portuguese Civil Code. In fact, Article 483(1) reads '[w]hoever […] unlawfully infringes the [subjective] rights of another person […] must compensate the injured party', thus distinguishing the requirement that the tortfeasor's act or omission infringes the subjective rights [of another person] from the requirement that the tortfeasor's act or omission is unlawful.

Furthermore, it has been pointed out that such a scheme fails to distinguish between causation establishing liability (*haftungsbegründende Kausalität*) and causation filling in liability (*haftungsausfüllende Kausalität*).[147]

Finally, it has been pointed out that such a scheme fails to represent the distinction between fault-based and no-fault, objective – thus strict – liability.

In the case of fault-based, subjective liability, the causative event is to be described by referring to an act or omission, to the requirement of unlawfulness, and to the requirement of fault. In the case of no-fault, objective, strict liability, it is far from clear whether the causative event is to be described by referring to an act, to an omission, or to unlawfulness.

In spite of this fact, it should be apparent that the scheme is far from perfect; it will be followed both by historical and pragmatic reasons.

It should be stressed that legal argumentation has a cultural and historical dimension. Legal argumentation depends on culture, and culture depends on history. It follows from the cultural and historical dimension of legal reasoning that academics and judges tend to prefer older constructions, based upon experience and tradition, to newer systems, based upon logic and reason.[148] Even if no argument could be derived from the historicity of legal argumentation, it should be stressed that it has a pragmatic dimension.

Portuguese lawyers are used to the old, traditional scheme – so used to the old scheme that they refer to the five requirements of non-contractual, tortious liability in most of the doctrinal writings and judicial decisions.

In following the old scheme, there are two things to be expected:

> In the first place, it is to be expected that the description of Portuguese tort law becomes more realistic and, second, it is to be expected that the discussion on the particular, specific features of Portuguese tort law concentrates on actual, effective, and substantive elements – paying full attention to matters of substance, and to matters of substance only.[149]

Direito civil. Responsabilidade civil. O método do caso, 72–83; N.M. Pinto Oliveira, Princípios de direito dos contratos, 615–622 (even though considering exclusively contractual, obligational liability).

147. *See, for example*, J.F. Sinde Monteiro, 'Rudimentos da responsabilidade civil', 383, and M. Carneiro da Frada, Direito civil. Responsabilidade civil. O método do caso, 80 and 100.

148. A. Menezes Cordeiro, Tratado de direito civil português, vol. II – Direito das obrigações, III. – Gestão de negócios. Enriquecimento sem causa. Responsabilidade civil, 433.

149. A. Menezes Cordeiro, Tratado de direito civil português, vol. II – Direito das obrigações, III. – Gestão de negócios. Enriquecimento sem causa. Responsabilidade civil, 433.

I. The Concept of One's Own Conduct

22. The concept of one's own conduct comprehends both positive and negative facts – positive facts, that is, acts, and negative facts, that is, omissions.

A. *One's Own Acts*

23. In the case of one's own acts, Article 483(1) applies. Liability for one's own acts depends on the fact that they are the expression of the human will.[150]

It follows from such a requirement that facts that are an expression of no human will at all, as well as facts that are the expression of the will of a third party, such as the facts a person is compelled to perform under the effects of an irresistible force or under the influence of hypnosis, are to be disregarded. There are no forms of human conduct at all – and, therefore, they cannot be assessed in terms of their unlawfulness.

B. *One's Own Omissions*

24. In the case of one's own omissions, Article 483(1) is supplemented by Article 486.

Liability for one's own omissions depends on the existence of a duty to act (= on the existence of a duty to take action). In keeping with Article 486, '[m]ere omissions shall give rise to an obligation to make reparation for the damage where, regardless of any other legal requirements, there was a duty, by law or by virtue of a legal act, to take the action which was not taken'.[151]

Among the specific legal provisions imposing a duty to act (to take action), Articles 491, 492 and 493 of the Portuguese Civil Code stand out.

Article 491 refers to the duty to supervise another person, either on account of that person's minority or on account of his mental or physical condition.[152] Article 492 refers to the duty to take action, conforming to due diligence, in the construction and maintenance of a building, so as to prevent the building from falling

150. *See* F.A. Pires de Lima/J.M. Antunes Varela (M. Henrique Mesquita), Código Civil anotado, vol. I, 471; J.M. Antunes Varela, Das obrigações em geral, vol. I, 527–529; M.J. Almeida Costa, Direito das obrigações, págs. 558–560; R. Alarcão, Direito das obrigações, 238–241; J. Ribeiro de Faria, Direito das obrigações, vol. I, 413–415; J.F. Sinde Monteiro, 'Rudimentos da responsabilidade civil', 360–361; L. Menezes Leitão, Direito das obrigações, vol. I – Introdução. Da constituição das obrigações, 289–290; A. Menezes Cordeiro, Tratado de direito civil português, vol. II – Direito das obrigações, III. – Gestão de negócios. Enriquecimento sem causa. Responsabilidade civil, 435–437.

151. On the interpretation of Art. 486 of the Portuguese Civil Code, *see* P. Nunes de Carvalho, Omissão e dever de agir em direito civil (Coimbra: Livraria Almedina 1999).

152. *See* Portuguese Civil Code, Art. 491: 'A person who is bound by law or by contract to exercise supervision over a person on account of minority, or of his mental or physical condition, is bound to make compensation for any damage which the latter unlawfully does to a third party, unless he fulfils his duty of supervision, or if the damage would have occurred notwithstanding the proper exercise of supervision.'

down.[153] Article 493(1) refers to the duty to supervise movable and immovable things, as well as to the duty to supervise animals,[154] and Article 493(2) refers to the duty to take action, conforming to due diligence, so as to prevent damage resulting from dangerous activities.[155]

*C. Liability for One's Own Omissions in the Case of Infringement of Duties to Prevent the Materialization of Damage in the Context of Social, Legally Relevant Contacts (*Verkerhrssicherungspflichten*)*

25. Even though Article 486 of the Portuguese Civil Code recognizes two, and only two, sources of the duty to act (=to take action), it is submitted that they are insufficient. Specific legal rules, such as the rules in Articles 491, 492 and 493, are to be supplemented by a general legal principle.

In Germany, the general principle applying to those cases has been derived from the doctrine of the so-called *Verkehrssicherungspflichten.*

The term *Verkehrssicherungspflichten* is difficult to translate into English.[156] In fact, it has already been declared 'untranslatable'.[157]

In spite of the fact that the term *duties of care* could be considered a candidate, using the English concept of *duties of care* to translate the German concept of *Verkehrssicherungspflichten* could, and indeed would, be misleading. It could suggest there is any kind of connection between the concept of the so-called *Verkehrssicherungspflichten*, relevant for the assessment of the conduct's *unlawfulness*, and the concept of the so-called *Sorgfaltspflichten*, relevant for the assessment of the defendant's *fault.*[158]

---

153. *See* Portuguese Civil Code, Art. 492: '(1) The owner of a building, or any other facility, which falls down due to a construction or maintenance defect, shall be held liable for all damage caused, unless he demonstrates either that his conduct conforms to the duty of diligence, or that damages would have occurred even if his conduct conformed to such a duty. (2) If the damage is caused by a maintenance defect, only the person under a statutory or contractual duty to maintain the building shall be held liable.'
154. *See* Portuguese Civil Code, Art. 493(1): 'Whoever detains movable or immovable things, and is bound to supervise them, as well as whoever is bound to supervise animals, shall be held liable for any damage caused by such things, or by such animals, unless he demonstrates that he has exercised due diligence, or that the damage would have occurred notwithstanding the proper exercise of diligence.'
155. *See* Portuguese Civil Code, Art. 493(2): 'Whoever causes damage to another person when performing a dangerous activity, is bound to make compensation for such a damage, unless he demonstrates he has taken all reasonable steps to prevent it.'
156. *See* B.S. Markesinis/H. Unberath/A. Johnston, *The German Law of Contract. A Comparative Treatise*, 86.
157. *See* F.H. Lawson/B.S. Markesinis, *Tortious Liability for Unintentional Harm in the Common Law and the Civil Law, vol. I – Text* (Cambridge: Cambridge University Press 1982) 78.
158. In a recent attempt to find an English equivalent to the German terms, Professor van Dam suggests societal safety duties to translate Verkehrssicherungspflichten and societal duties to translate Verkehrspflichten [C. van Dam, European Tort Law, 85].

In spite of the fact the translation is difficult and perhaps impossible, Professor Markesinis argues that the principle underlying all the doctrines of *Verkehrspflichten* could be summarized as follows: 'whoever by his activity or through his property establishes in everyday life a source of potential danger which is likely to affect the interests and rights of others, is obliged to ensure their protection against the risks thus created by him'.[159]

Professor Zimmermann suggests a similar definition,[160] stressing three points. In the first place, the so-called *Verkehrssicherungspflichten* are to be imposed both on whoever establishes and on whoever is in charge of a source of potential danger; second, they refer to sources of potential danger to the rights and interests enumerated in § 823(1) of the German Civil Code, that is to say, to the rights and interests relating to 'life, body, health, freedom, or any other right of another';[161] third, by consisting of duties to ensure the protection against certain dangers and risks, they require the obligee to take 'appropriate precautions to prevent the risk from materializing'.[162]

In Portugal, the terms *Verkehrspflichten* or *Verkehrssicherungspflichten* have been translated either under the name of 'deveres de prevenção do perigo'[163] or under the name of 'deveres (de segurança) no tráfego'.[164] The first term, 'deveres de prevenção do perigo', refers to the purpose of the duty. It can be translated as duties to prevent the materialization of a danger. The second term, 'deveres (de segurança) no tráfego', refers to the context of the duties to prevent the materialization of such a danger. It can be translated as duties in the context of social, legally relevant contacts.

Irrespective of the words, the doctrine of the so-called *Verkehrspflichten* or *Verkehrssicherungspflichten* is commonly accepted in Portugal.[165]

---

159. *See* B.S. Markesinis/H. Unberath, *The German Law of Torts. A Comparative Treatise*, 86.
160. *See* R. Zimmermann, *The Law of Obligations. Roman Foundations of the Civilian Tradition* 1046: 'anybody who either establishes, or is in charge of, a source of potential danger for the rights and interests (as enumerated in § 823 I BGB) of other people is obliged to take appropriate precautions to prevent the risk from materializing'.
161. This is, however, controversial – *see, for example*, C. van Dam, European Tort Law, 86.
162. *See* R. Zimmermann, *The Law of Obligations. Roman Foundations of the Civilian Tradition* 1046.
163. *See, for example*, J.M. Antunes Varela, '[Anotação ao] acórdão do Supremo Tribunal de Justiça de 26 de Março de 1980', in: Revista de Legislação e de Jurisprudência 114 (1981–1982) 35 ff.
164. *See, for example*, A. Menezes Cordeiro, Da boa fé no direito civil, 831–836; J.F. Sinde Monteiro, Responsabilidade por conselhos, recomendações ou informações, 300–307.
165. *See, for example*, J.M. Antunes Varela, '[Anotação ao] acórdão do Supremo Tribunal de Justiça de 26 de Março de 1980', 35 ff; F.A. Pires de Lima/J.M. Antunes Varela (/ M. Henrique Mesquita), *Código Civil anotado, vol. I*, 487–488; J.M. Antunes Varela, *Das obrigações em geral, vol. I*, 528–529; L. Menezes Leitão, *Direito das obrigações, vol. I – Introdução. Da constituição das obrigações*, 290–291; A. Menezes Cordeiro, *Tratado de direito civil português, vol. II – Direito das obrigações, III. – Gestão de negócios. Enriquecimento sem causa. Responsabilidade civil*, 571–589; A. Menezes Cordeiro, *Da boa fé no direito civil*, 831–836; J. Baptista Machado, 'A cláusula do razoável', 615–619; J.F. Sinde Monteiro, *Responsabilidade por conselhos, recomendações ou informações*, 300–307; M. Carneiro da Frada, *Contrato e deveres de protecção*, 163 ff., 202 (fn. 425) and 246 (fn. 508); M. Carneiro da Frada, *Uma 'terceira via' no direito da responsabilidade civil. O problema da imputação a terceiros dos danos causados a terceiros por auditores de sociedades*, 79–81; N.M. Pinto Oliveira, 'Sobre o conceito de ilicitude do artigo 483.º do Código Civil', in: *Estudos em homenagem a Francisco José Velozo* (Braga: Associação Jurídica

Article 486 of the Portuguese Civil Code reads that '[m]ere omissions shall give rise to an obligation to make reparation for the damage where […] there was a duty, by law or by virtue of a legal act, to take the action which was not taken'. In keeping with the doctrine of the so-called *Verkehrssicherungspflichten*, the reference to the duty, by law, to take action, which was not taken, is to be interpreted as comprehending both duties resulting from a general legal principle and duties resulting from specific legal, statutory provisions, such as Articles 491, 492 and 493 of the Civil Code.[166]

1. Comparing Article 486 of the Portuguese Civil Code with the (Draft) Common Frame of Reference and the Principles of European Tort Law[167]

26. Article 486 of the Portuguese Civil Code is rather different from the (Draft) Common Frame of Reference – at least in the following:

---

de Braga/Escola de Direito da Universidade do Minho 2002) 521 ff, especially at 542–544; M. Carneiro da Frada, *Teoria da confiança e responsabilidade civil*, 233–238, especially at 236–237 (fn. 236–237); J.F. Sinde Monteiro, 'Rudimentos da responsabilidade civil', 360–361; R. Ataíde, *Responsabilidade civil por violação de deveres no tráfego* (Coimbra: Livraria Almedina), especially at 253–279.

166. In a judgment of the Portuguese Supreme Court of 29 Nov. 2005, delivered by Justice Salvador da Costa, it is explicitly held that liability for omissions was independent from compliance with both legal, statutory provisions and administrative regulations. A was hit by a hockey disc while watching a hockey game in the stands from the field of sports club B. The disc hit the crossbar of the goal, changing direction towards the audience in the stands, hitting A in the face, causing her serious injuries. The audience only had protection nets in both ends of the hockey field, behind the goals, as required by the sports regulations in force at the time of the injury. A claimed to be compensated by the sports club B, host of the event, for the damage suffered. The Supreme Court ruled that the club had an interest in hosting the sporting event and that, therefore, it was required to take all appropriate security measures are taken. The fact that the sporting regulations were met was not sufficient to relieve the sports club from the obligation to ensure the safety of the spectators with stricter measures that those required by statutory provisions or by administrative regulations. If the defendant could reasonably foresee that the safety measures required by the law were insufficient, it was under the duty to go beyond the measures required by the law – In keeping, for instance, with the author of the preliminary work for the Civil Code, Professor Vaz Serra, statutes and (administrative) regulations would only relieve the defendant from the burden of safety in the case they were so exhausting that nothing more can be done to ensure the security of the event – For it is of common knowledge that the hockey disc configuration is propitious to ricochet upon impact, the Court held that the hockey club could reasonably foresee that the stands could be hit by the disc if not protected by nets, or other kind of barrier.

167. For a comparison between the (Draft) Common Frame of Reference and the Principles of European Tort Law, *see, for example*, C. van Dam, European Tort Law, 130–133; J. Spier, 'The Principles of European Tort Law of the European Group on Tort Law', in: European Group on Tort Law, *Principles of European Tort Law. Text and Commentary* (Wien/New York: Springer 2005) 12–18, especially at 17–18; G. Brüggemeier, 'Gemeinsamer Referenzrahmen (Entwurf), Buch VI: 'Außervertragliche Haftung für die Schädigung anderer' – eine kritische Stellungnahme', in: H.J. Ahrens/Ch. von Bar/G. Fischer/A. Spickhoff/J. Taupitz (eds), Medizin und Haftung. Festschrift für Erwin Deutsch zum 80. Geburtstag (Berlin/Heidelberg: Springer 2009), 749–768; M. Infantino, 'Making European Tort Law: The Game and Its Players', in: Cardozo Journal of International and Comparative Law 18 (2010) 45–87, especially at 60–78.

> Whilst Article 486 of the Portuguese Civil Code refers both to general principles and to specific rules, Articles 3:104 and 3:202 to 3:206 of the (Draft) Common Frame of Reference[168] refer exclusively to specific rules.[169]

It should be emphasized that the Portuguese legal system covers all the cases of liability referred to by Articles 3:104 and 3:202 to 3:206.[170]

Furthermore, it should be emphasized that the Portuguese legal system goes beyond (far beyond) Articles 3:104 and 3:202 to 3:206 of the (Draft) Common Frame of Reference, for Article 493(2) of the Portuguese Civil Code states a general principle, applying to all types of *dangerous activities*.

In contrast with the (Draft) Common Frame of Reference,[171] the provisions in the Principles of European Tort Law refer to four general clauses.[172]

In the first place, there is a duty to act positively to protect others from damage 'if law so provides'; second, there is a duty to act positively to protect others from damage if 'the actor creates or controls a dangerous situation'; third, there may be a duty to act positively to protect others from damage 'when the seriousness of the harm on the one side and the ease of avoiding the damage on the other side point towards such a duty' and, fourth and finally, there may be a duty to act positively to protect others from damage 'when there is a special relationship between parties'.

---

168. *See* Ch. von Bar/E. Clive (eds), Principles, Definitions and Model Rules of European Private Law. Draft Common Frame of Reference, 400–405.
169. Article 3:104 deals with *damage caused by children or supervised persons*. Arts 3:202, 3:203 and 3:206 deal with damage caused by *things* – Art. 3:202 refers to *immovable things* and Arts 3:203 and 3:206 refer to two types of *movable things*. In the case of Art. 3:203, to *animals* and, in the case of Art. 3:206, to *dangerous substances* – Arts 3:204 and 3:205 deal with damages caused by two types of *activities* – in the case of Art. 3:204, the relevant, dangerous activity consists of circulating *defective products* and, in the case of Art. 3:205, it consists of keeping and using *motor vehicles*.
170. In the first place, Art. 3:104 of the (Draft) Common Frame of Reference, on damages caused by children, corresponds to Art. 491 of the Portuguese Civil Code. Second, Art. 3:202 of the (Draft) Common Frame of Reference, on damages caused by immovable things, corresponds to Art. 492 of the Portuguese Civil Code. Third, Art. 3:203 of the (Draft) Common Frame of Reference, on damages caused by animals, corresponds to Arts 493(1) and 502 of the Portuguese Civil Code. Fourth, Art. 3:206 of the (Draft) Common Frame of Reference, on damages causes by dangerous substances, partly corresponds to Art. 493(2) of the Portuguese Civil Code. Fifth, Art.3:204 of the (Draft) Common Frame of Reference, on damages caused by defective products, corresponds to Decree-Law No. 393/89 of 6 Nov. 1989, as amended by Decree-Law No. 131/2001 of 24 Apr. 2001, and, sixth and finally, Art. 3:205 of the (Draft) Common Frame of Reference, on damages caused by motor vehicles, partly corresponds to Arts 503 to 508 of the Portuguese Civil Code.
171. For a comparison between Arts 3:104 and 3:202 to 3:206 of the (Draft) Common Frame of Reference and Art. 3:104 of the Principles of European Tort Law, *see* P. Widmer, 'La responsabilité pour choses et activités dangereuses dans les Projets européens', in: Le droit français de la responsabilité civile confronté aux projets européens d'harmonisation. Recueil des travaux du Groupe de Recherche Européen sur la Responsabilité Civile et l'Assurance (GRERCA) (Paris: IRJS Editions 2012) 251–277.
172. *See* European Group on Tort Law, *Principles of European Tort Law. Text and Commentary* (Wien/New York; Springer 2005) 1–10, at 5. Article 4:103 reads as follows: 'A duty to act positively to protect others from damage may exist if law so provides, or if the actor creates or controls a dangerous situation, or when there is a special relationship between parties or when the seriousness of the harm on the one side and the ease of avoiding the damage on the other side point towards such a duty.'

The comparison between the Principles of European Tort Law and Portuguese Tort Law is to be limited to the first three situations.

In case there is a special relationship between parties, duties to act positively to protect others from damage result from the concept of good faith.[173] It is submitted that liability for the infringement of specific duties resulting from good faith within the context of special relationships between the parties – for example, liability for *culpa in contrahendo*[174] – belongs neither to contractual nor to non-contractual, tortious liability. It qualifies as an intermediate liability between contract and tort – and, for it to qualify as an intermediate liability, it is to be ruled out from the area of tort law.

If the law provides for a duty to act positively to protect others, the provision in Article 4:103 of the Principles of European Tort Law is covered by the provision in Article 486 of the Portuguese Civil Code. If the defendant creates or controls a dangerous situation, the provision in Article 4:103 of the Principles of European Tort Law is covered by the development of the provision in Article 486 of the Portuguese Civil Code, conforming to the doctrine of the *Verkehrssicherungspflichten*. If, however, 'the seriousness of the harm on the one side and the ease of avoiding the damage on the other side point towards [the existence of] a duty [to act]', there could be a difference between both provisions.

In the commentary on Article 4:103 of the Principles of European Tort Law, Professor Widmer proposes the following example:

> This can be the case e.g. where a person realizes that another person is not aware of imminent danger and it would be sufficient to shout or to draw by other means the second person attention to the risk in order to warn her and prevent her from being injured.[175]

It is submitted that many cases relating to Article 4:103 of the Principles of European Tort Law fall within the scope of Article 220 of the Portuguese Criminal Code.

In the case of a serious threat to life, to the integrity or to the freedom of another person, public criminal law provides for a duty to act relevant to private tort law. It is, however, submitted that Article 4:103 of the Principles of European Tort Law goes beyond Article 220 of the Portuguese Criminal Code, for it applies to all cases of grave disproportion between the ease of avoiding damage and the (harmful) consequences of not avoiding it, by failing to prevent the materialization of an unlawful, unnecessary risk.

In spite of this fact, it is apparent that there is no equivalent to the third principle neither in Article 220 of the Criminal Code nor in Article 486 of the Civil Code, cases where 'the seriousness of the harm on the one side and the ease of avoiding the damage on the other side point towards [the existence of] a duty [to act]' could

---

173. *See* P. Widmer, '[Comment on] Article 4:103', in: European Group on Tort Law, Principles of European Tort Law. Text and Commentary, 86–90.
174. *See* P. Widmer, '[Comment on] Article 4:103', in: European Group on Tort Law, Principles of European Tort Law. Text and Commentary, 86–90, especially at 88.
175. P. Widmer, '[Comment on] Article 4:103', 88.

perhaps be construed as cases of abuse of rights.[176] It could be argued that there is a gap in the Portuguese private-legal system and that such a gap should be filled by referring to the abuse of rights. In cases of grave disproportion, omissions would contradict the ethical and moral values underlying Article 334 of the Portuguese Civil Code.

Even if it is assumed there is no gap at all, it should be recognized that the abuse of rights should apply both to abuses of the freedom to act and abuses of the freedom not to act. If the concept of abuse of rights is to be extended so as to apply to the abuse of the *freedom to act,* it could as well be extended so as to apply to the abuse of the *freedom not to act* (=to the abuse of the freedom to *refrain from taking action*).[177]

II. On the Requirement of Unlawfulness

27. Article 483(1) of the Portuguese Civil Code follows an intermediate approach[178] – a 'middle path'[179] – between French and English models.

French law defines torts by referring to a broad, all-encompassing general legal principle,[180] and English law defines torts by referring to narrow, specific legal rules[181] – in the words of Tony Weir, '[t]here is no general principle in English tort law to tell us when conduct is tortious […] and when it is not'.[182]

Contrary to both French law and English law, Portuguese tort law follows the model of §823 and 826 of the German Civil Code.[183]

176. *See see* P. Nunes de Carvalho, Omissão e dever de agir em direito civil, passim.
177. For a general discussion on the contribution of non-legislative codifications – such as the (Draft) Common Frame of Reference and the Principles of European Tort Law – to the development of private law, *see* N. Jansen, *The Making of Legal Authority. Non-Legislative Codifications in Historical and Comparative Perspective* (Oxford: Oxford University Press 2010), and N. Jansen, 'Dogmatising Non-legislative Codifications: Non-legislative Reference Texts in European Legal Discourse', in: R. Brownsword/H.-W. Micklitz/L. Niglia/S. Weatherill (eds), *The Foundations of European Private Law* (Oxford/Portland (Oregon): Hart Publishing 2011) 31–58.
178. *See*, for instance, C. van Dam, European Tort Law, 78 ff. – referring to German law.
179. *See*, for instance, W. van Gerven/J. Lever/P. Larrouche/C. von Bar/G. Viney, *Tort Law. Scope of Protection* (Oxford: Hart Publishing 1998), 55; D. Moura Vicente, Da responsabilidade pré-contratual em direito internacional privado (Coimbra: Livraria Almedina 2001), 188A.G. Dias Pereira, 'Portuguese Tort Law: A Comparison with the Principles of European Tort Law', 631–632. This recent trend is also followed by the Dutch, Swiss, Italian and Greek codifications. They take as a 'starting point a general provision founded on sufficiently flexible concepts to adjust to new situations, at the same time limiting or excluding certain heads of damage.'
180. For a short presentation of the French law of torts, *see, for example*, K. Zweigert/H. Kötz, Einführung in die Rechtsvergleichung, 3rd edition (Tübingen: Mohr Siebeck 1996) 619–625; R. Zimmermann, The Law of Obligations. Roman Foundations of the Civilian Tradition, 906; F. Ranieri, Europäisches Obligationenrecht, 1419–1421; C. van Dam, European Tort Law, 56 ff.
181. For a short presentation of the English law of torts, *see, for example*, K. Zweigert/H. Kötz, Einführung in die Rechtsvergleichung, 607–618; R. Zimmermann, The Law of Obligations. Roman Foundations of the Civilian Tradition, 908–914; F. Ranieri, Europäisches Obligationenrecht, 1428–1442; C. van Dam, European Tort Law, 108 ff.
182. T. Weir, *An Introduction to Tort Law* 2nd edition (Oxford: Oxford University Press 2006) 11.
183. For a short presentation of the German law of torts, *see, for example*, R. Hübner, *A History of Germanic Private Law* (Boston: Little, Brown and Company 1918) 576–579; K. Zweigert/H. Kötz,

It deviates from English law, for it contains general principles 'to tell us when conduct is tortious […] and when it is not'.[184] It deviates from French law for its general principles establish a hierarchy between interests, which are protected by subjective rights and interests, which are not.[185]

In fact, whereas 'French law does not provide an a priori limitation of the protected interests',[186] Portuguese law does so by requiring that the tortfeasor's act or omission infringes the rights of another person.

It has been argued that Article 483(1) of the Portuguese Civil Code deviates from the model in §823 and §826 of the German Civil Code.[187]

Article 483(1) would affirm a broad, comprehensive general clause,[188] and such comprehensive general clause would apply to all cases of infringement of another person's rights[189] and to many – if not most – cases of infringement of another person's legally protected interests.[190]

The concept of another person's rights would encompass both absolute rights and relative rights. Therefore, Article 483(1) of the Portuguese Civil Code would constitute the basic, fundamental provision of the complete system of civil liability, for

---

Einführung in die Rechtsvergleichung, 599–607; R. Zimmermann, *The Law of Obligations. Roman Foundations of the Civilian Tradition*, 905–906; F. Ranieri, Europäisches Obligationenrecht, 1421–1428; C. van Dam, European Tort Law, 78 ff.

184. It has been argued that such a general principle on non-contractual, tortious liability is somehow 'romantic', for it 'concentrates […] on the human person, who acts with fault and causes damage to another' [*see* A.G. Dias Pereira, 'Portuguese Tort Law: A Comparison with the Principles of European Tort Law', 629].

185. Article 1382 of the French Civil Code establishes no hierarchy at all among the interests protected by tort law. In keeping with Art. 1382, 'Any act whatever of man which causes damage to another obliges him by whose fault it occurred to make reparation' [on the non-hierarchical approach to the interests to be protected by French tort law, *see, for example*, H. Slim, 'Les intérêts protégés par la responsabilité civile en droit français', in: Le droit français de la responsabilité civile confronté aux projets européens d'harmonisation. Recueil des travaux du Groupe de Recherche Européen sur la Responsabilité Civile et l'Assurance (GRERCA) (Paris: IRJS Editions 2012) 113–133; G. Viney, 'Les intérêts protégés par le droit de la responsabilité civile. Synthèse', in: Le droit français de la responsabilité civile confronté aux projets européens d'harmonisation, 149–163; Luc Grynbaum, 'Point de vue extérieur', in: Le droit français de la responsabilité civile confronté aux projets européens d'harmonisation, 791–803; Stephan Lorenz, 'Point de vue extérieur', 805–811]. – Contrary to Art. 1382 of the French Civil Code, Art. 483 of the Portuguese Civil Code clearly distinguishes interests which are protected by subjective rights and interests which are not – and, by distinguishing interests which are and which are not protected, it clearly establishes a hierarchy among them. If the defendant's tort consists of infringing interests which are not protected by subjective rights, liability depends either on the infringement of legal provisions, intended to protect the interests of another person, or on abuse of rights.

186. C. van Dam, *European Tort Law*, 169.

187. *See, for example*, A.G. Dias Pereira, 'Portuguese Tort Law: A Comparison with the Principles of European Tort Law', 631–632.

188. *See*, for instance, A. Menezes Cordeiro, *Da boa fé no direito civil*, 636–639; P. Romano Martinez, *Cumprimento defeituoso – em especial, na compra e venda e na empreitada* (Coimbra: Livraria Almedina 1994) 273.

189. *See*, for instance, F. Pessoa Jorge, *Ensaio sobre os pressupostos da responsabilidade civil*, 298–299: In principle, would be enough for the plaintiff to affirm the existence of a subjective right, which has been infringed by the defendant, to hold the defendant liable for the damage he caused.

190. *See*, for instance, F. Pessoa Jorge, *Ensaio sobre os pressupostos da responsabilidade civil*, 302–307.

it could apply both to contractual, obligational liability and to non-contractual, non-obligational, tortious liability.[191] The concept of another person's interests would encompass, e.g., expectations.[192]

In affirming a broad, comprehensive general clause referring to subjective rights – to all subjective rights – Portuguese tort law would follow the tendency to avoid, at once, the problems of the French, the English, and the German models:

- To avoid the French model, for its general principles would be much too wide, '*virtually unlimited*', in scope.
- To avoid the problems of the English model, for its specific rules would be much too narrow in scope – for their approach to tort law would be a '*piecemeal approach*'.
- To avoid the problems of the German model, for the system resulting from § 823 and §826 of the German Civil Code would be '*overly compartmentalized*'.[193]

It all comes to determining the concept of '*rights of another person*'.

It is submitted that the concept of rights underlying Article 483(1) of the Portuguese Civil Code is to be interpreted so as to refer to absolute rights.

Even though 'Article 483 (1) does not expressly require an absolute right to be involved',[194] the prevailing view is that it applies exclusively to the infringement of absolute rights: 'only the violation of a so-called absolute right generates an obligation to compensate'.[195] Furthermore, it is submitted that the concept of absolute rights underlying Article 483(1) is to be interpreted so as to refer to personality rights and property rights.

Professors Bussani and Palmer accurately describe the situation:

> Portuguese courts and scholars recognize that in using the word 'unlawfully', Vaz Serra, the author of the 1966 code, intended to protect only 'absolute rights' and this 'legislative' intent is generally read into the provision. Accordingly, the Portuguese wrongdoer is liable, (1) when they violate an absolute right (purely financial loss is thus excluded); or (2) when the damage falls within the scope and aim of a protective statute: while the violation of a protective statute may give rise to compensation for pure economic loss, this is an exception to the general rule of no recovery. Portugal is therefore decidedly hostile to damages for this type of loss.[196]

---

191. *See*, for instance, P. Romano Martinez, Cumprimento defeituoso – em especial, na compra e venda e na empreitada 263.
192. *See*, for instance, F. Pessoa Jorge, Ensaio sobre os pressupostos da responsabilidade civil, 312–314.
193. *See, for example*, A.G. Dias Pereira, 'Portuguese Tort Law: A Comparison with the Principles of European Tort Law', 631–632.
194. *See, for example*, J.F. Sinde Monteiro, 'Case 2 – Portugal', in: M. Bussani/V.V. Palmer (eds), *Pure Economic Loss in Europe* (Cambridge: Cambridge University Press 2003) 202–204, at 203.
195. *See, for example*, J.F. Sinde Monteiro, 'Case 2 – Portugal', 202.
196. M. Bussani/V.V. Palmer, 'The Liability Regimes of Europe – Their Façades and Interiors', in: M. Bussani/V.V. Palmer (eds), *Pure Economic Loss in Europe* (Cambridge: Cambridge University Press 2003) 120 ff, at 155.

In a rather recent judgment, the Portuguese Supreme Court confirmed that, in principle, 'pure economic losses [...] are not recoverable in tort law'.[197]

Therefore, Article 483(1) of the Portuguese Civil Code can be interpreted neither 'as a French-like general clause'[198] – thus allowing recovery for all types of loss – nor as a modified 'French-like general clause' – thus allowing recovery for all types of loss resulting from the infringement of all types of (subjective) rights. The 'façade' of Article 483(1) could perhaps resemble Articles 1382 and 1383 of the French Civil Code. In that case, it would be, however, a '*somewhat misleading façade*', for the 'interior' – for the 'actual interior' – of Article 483(1) resembles § 823(1) of the German Civil Code.[199]

§ 823(1) of the German Civil Code reads: 'A person who wilfully or negligently injures the life, body, health, freedom, property, or other rights of another contrary to law is bound to compensate him for any damage arising therefrom.'[200]

It is apparent that 'the formulation in Article 483 (1) is considerably more open than the corresponding § 823 (1) of the [German Civil Code]',[201] for Article 483(1) contains no enumeration of the rights and interests to be protected.[202]

In spite of the fact that it is apparent that the formulation in Article 483(1) is '*considerably more open*', it is far from apparent whether the principles and rules arising from Article 483(1) of the Portuguese Civil Code are '*more open*', considerably or not, than the principles and rules arising from § 823 of the German Civil Code.

In what concerns personal, non-pecuniary loss, it is uncertain – it is doubtful, and rather doubtful indeed – whether the list in § 823(1) of the German Civil Code ever had a limitative, restrictive function.

In German legal doctrine, at the time the Civil Code was enacted, there was a dispute on whether personality interests were to be protected by subjective, personality rights. Savigny, for instance, argued that they were not.[203] The concept of a personality right 'as a proprietary right on one's own body' would be absurd.[204] Considering the dispute on the existence of subjective, personality rights, the list of

197. *See* the judgment of the Portuguese Supreme Court of 8 Sep. 2016 (M. Graça Trigo).
198. M. Bussani/V.V. Palmer, 'The Liability Regimes of Europe – Their Façades and Interiors', in: M. Bussani/V.V. Palmer (eds), *Pure Economic Loss in Europe* (Cambridge: Cambridge University Press 2003) 120 ff, at 155.
199. M. Bussani/V.V. Palmer, 'The Liability Regimes of Europe – Their Façades and Interiors', 155.
200. For the translation of § 826 of the German Civil Code, *see* B.S. Markesinis/H. Unberath, The German Law of Torts. A Comparative Treatise, 14.
201. *See* J.F. Sinde Monteiro, 'Case 2 – Portugal', 204; A.G. Dias Pereira, 'Portuguese Tort Law: A Comparison with the Principles of European Tort Law', 631.
202. Professors Bussani and Palmer refer to a 'numerus clausus list of protected rights' (M. Bussani/V.V. Palmer, 'The Liability Regimes of Europe – Their Façades and Interiors', 155). In spite of the fact § 823(1) of the German Civil Code contains a list of protected rights, it is far from clear whether it is a numerus clausus list. In fact, § 823 refers to 'another right' or to 'any other right' – *sonstiges Recht*. 'In using this concept, the legislator aimed to bring comparable rights within the ambit of the provision, such as rights regarding intellectual property (patents, trademarks, and copyrights), mortgages, names, portraits, and family law-related rights, such as the right to parental care' (C. van Dam, *European Tort Law*, 82).
203. F.C. von Savigny, System des heutigen römischen Rechts, vol. I (Berlin 1840) 334 ff. (§ 53).
204. *See* G. Brüggemeier, 'Protection of Personality Rights in the Law of Delict/Torts in Europe: Mapping Out Paradigms', in G. Brüggemeier/A. Colombi-Ciacchi/P. O'Callaghan, *Personality Rights*

personality interests in § 823(1) had a declarative function: in referring to life, body, health, and freedom, it aimed at making clear that personality interests are protected by tort law.[205]

Even if the list of personality interests in § 823(1) ever had any constitutive, limitative, and restrictive function, that function is long lost.

Under the influence of the German Basic Law (*Grundgesetz*) – especially under the influence of the principle of human dignity in Article 1(1) – the German courts came to admit the existence of the so-called general right to one's personality (*allgemeines Persönlichkeitsrecht*) and to count the general right to one's personality among the 'other rights of another' in § 823.[206]

In what concerns a pecuniary loss, it is certain that the list in § 823(1) of the German Civil Code had – and still has – a restrictive, limitative function.

In a positive sense, § 823(1) aims at making clear that pecuniary, economic losses arising either from the violation of property rights or from the violation of other rights similar to the property are to be compensated; in a negative sense, it aims at making clear that pecuniary, economic losses resulting neither from the violation of property rights nor from the violation of other rights similar to the property are not to be compensated. That is to say, it aims at making clear that pure economic loss is not to be compensated.

It is submitted that, in excluding compensation for pure economic loss, the concept of absolute, subjective rights in Article 483(1) of the Portuguese Civil Code performs a function fully equivalent to the enumeration of the rights and interests to be protected in § 823(1) of the German Civil Code.[207]

III. Liability for the Infringement of Subjective Rights

28. In the first place, Portuguese tort law contains a general clause on liability for the infringement of rights:

> [w]hoever, whether by wilful misconduct (dolus) or by negligence, unlawfully infringes the rights of another person [...] must compensate the injured party for damage arising from such violation.

IV. Liability for the Infringement of Absolute Rights

29. The concept of *rights of another person* in Article 483(1) of the Portuguese Civil Code is intended to comprehend *absolute rights*.

---

in European Tort Law (Cambridge: Cambridge University Press 2010) 5–37, at 19–20: 'A personality right understood as a property right in one's body does not make sense.'

205. *See* Ph. Heck, Grundriss des Schuldrechts (Tübingen: Mohr Siebeck 1929) 448–452; J.F. Sinde Monteiro, Responsabilidade por conselhos, recomendações ou informações, 183–184.

206. *See* B.S. Markesinis/H. Unberath, The German Law of Torts. A Comparative Treatise.

207. *See* J.F. Sinde Monteiro, Responsabilidade por conselhos, recomendações ou informações, 183–187; M. Carneiro da Frada, Contrato e deveres de protecção, 174 ff.; M. Carneiro da Frada, Teoria da confiança e responsabilidade civil, 238 ff.

In the first place, it comprehends *personality rights,* and second, it comprehends *property rights*. Third, it comprehends rights in rem, and fourth, it comprehends rights in personam to the use of things. The Portuguese Civil Code admits a third type of rights, somehow in-between rights in personam and rights in rem – the so-called *direitos pessoais de gozo* (in Portuguese) or *diritti personali di godimento* (in Italian) – and the concept of *rights of another person* comprehends such *tertium genus*.

Fifth, and finally, the concept of *rights of another person* in Article 483(1) of the Portuguese Civil Code clearly comprehends *possession*, controversial as it may be, whether *possession* is a subjective, absolute *right*.

V. Liability for the Infringement of Personality Rights

A. The General Clause in Article 70(1) of the Portuguese Civil Code

30. Article 70(1) of the Portuguese Civil Code adopts a general clause, thus providing for complete, extensive protection of *personality rights*:

> The law protects individuals against any unlawful offence or threat of offence to his physical or moral entity.[208]

It has been argued that Article 70(1) of the Civil Code corresponds to the so-called general right to one's personality – to the so-called *allgemeines Persönlichkeitsrecht*, as developed by German case law.[209]

In Germany, the general right to one's personality has been derived from two constitutional provisions – from Articles 1(1) and 2(1) of the Basic, Fundamental Law.[210] In Portugal, even though the text of the constitution did not establish the

208. *See*, for a comparative approach to the Portuguese law, Ch. von Bar, *The Common European Law of Torts, vol. I – The Core Areas of Tort Law, the Approximation in Europe and its Accommodation in the System* (Oxford: Oxford University Press 1998) 22 ff.

209. *See*, for instance, M. de Andrade, 'Esboço de um anteprojecto de Código das Pessoas e da Família na parte relativa ao começo e termo da personalidade jurídica, aos direitos de personalidade, ao domicílio', in: Boletim do Ministério da Justiça 102 (January 1961) 153–166; C.A. Mota Pinto/A. Pinto Monteiro/P. Mota Pinto, Teoria geral do direito civil, at 98 ff. and 207 ff.; O. de Carvalho, Teoria geral do direito civil. Sumários desenvolvidos para uso dos alunos do 2.º ano (1.ª turma) do curso jurídico de 1980/1981 (Coimbra: Centelha 1981) 179 ff.; D. Leite de Campos, 'Lições de direitos de personalidade', in: 67 Boletim da Faculdade de Direito [da Universidade de Coimbra] (1991) 129 ff.; R. Capelo de Sousa, O direito geral de personalidade (Coimbra: Coimbra Editora 1995); P. Mota Pinto, 'O direito ao livre desenvolvimento da personalidade', in: Portugal-Brasil ano 2000 – Tema Direito (Coimbra: Coimbra Editora 1999) 149 ff.; N.M. Pinto Oliveira, O direito geral de personalidade e a 'solução do dissentimento'. Ensaio sobre um caso de 'constitucionalização' do direito civil (Coimbra: Coimbra Editora 2002); P. Pais de Vasconcelos, Direito da personalidade (Coimbra: Livraria Almedina 2006).

210. The German Federal Constitutional Court carefully distinguishes the general right to one's freedom (*allgemeines Freiheitsrecht*) and the general right to one's personality (*allgemeines Persönlichkeitsrecht*). The general right to one's freedom protects the individual's liberty to do, or to refrain from doing, whatever they wish to do, or to refrain from doing. It emerges from the right to the free development of one's personality (Art. 2(1) of the German Fundamental Law

'*right to the free development of one's personality*' until 1997, the judgment of the Constitutional Court No. 6/84 of 18 January 1984 considered the general right to one's personality to be a consequence of the constitutional fundamental principle of *human dignity*.

In keeping with the judgment of 18 January 1984, the Portuguese Constitution, 'in its very first Article, declares that Portugal is a sovereign Republic founded on the dignity of the human person, thus accepting the principle that each and every right of the person – that is, to each and every aspect for which a general right to one's personality is necessarily revealed – must be given the highest degree of legal protection, and that highest degree of legal protection corresponds to what is enjoyed by fundamental rights'.[211]

With respect to German law, it is appropriate to speak of a certain *constitutionalization of private law*;[212] with respect to Portuguese law, it would be more appropriate to speak of a certain *civilization of constitutional law*.

It has been argued that the concept of a general right to one's personality is untenable on (purely) *theoretical grounds* – on the grounds that it would be impossible for a person to be, at once, both the subject and the object of the same subjective right[213] – and it has also been argued that the concept of a general right to one's personality is untenable on *practical grounds*.

In order to attain a certain degree of legal security, all absolute rights were to be derived from particular, specific provisions with a limited scope.

Since the general right to one's personality could never be derived from particular, specific provisions – since the scope of the general right could never be a determinate scope – it would seriously threaten legal security.

Instead of deriving a general right from the general clause in Article 70(1) of the Portuguese Civil Code, the judge should fill the gaps of the particular, specific provisions referring to personality rights in Articles 72 to 80. In doing so, in filling their gaps, the judge should consider the methods for the development of enacted statutory law in Article 10 – especially analogy.

That is to say that, instead of deriving a general right to one's personality from the general clause in Article 70(1), the judge should derive particular, specific rights from the particular, specific clauses in Articles 72 to 80.[214]

(*Grundgesetz*)). The general right to one's personality only protects the forms of conduct more important for forming and expressing one's individuality. It emerges from the coordination of two constitutional principles: the principle of human dignity (Art. 1(1)) and the right to the free development of one's personality (Art. 1(2)).

211. *See* the judgment of the Constitutional Court of 18 Jan. 1984 in: Boletim do Ministério da Justiça 340 (November 1984) 179.

212. *See* B.S. Markesinis/H. Unberath, *The German Law of Torts. A Comparative Treatise*, 28–32.

213. *See*, for instance, J. de Oliveira Ascensão, *Direito civil. Teoria geral, vol. I – Introdução. As pessoas. Os bens* (Coimbra: Coimbra Editora 2000) 87. It is submitted that such a critique would apply to all personality rights. In this respect, the general right to one's personality would be no different from any other personality right.

214. *See*, for instance, J. de Oliveira Ascensão, *Direito civil. Teoria geral, vol. I – Introdução. As pessoas. Os bens*, 87–88; A. Menezes Cordeiro, *Tratado de direito civil português, vol. I – Parte geral, III – Pessoas* (Coimbra: Livraria Almedina 2004) 80–82; L. Carvalho Fernandes, *Teoria geral do direito civil, vol. I – Introdução. Pressupostos da relação jurídica*, 4th edition (Lisboa: Universidade Católica Editora 2006) 225–227.

It is submitted that the practical results of both approaches would be equivalent. There should be no practical difference whatsoever between deriving personality from a general principle or from particular, specific rules, reasoning by analogy. Even if the practical results would be equivalent, there is a significant theoretical difference between both perspectives.

The concept of a general right to one's personality confirms the concept of the human person as unity; the concept of a plurality of personality rights confirms the concept of the human person as an assemblage of different fragments. If the person is to be taken as a whole – as something that cannot, and shall not, be divided – then the concept of a general right to one's personality is to be preferred to the plurality of personality rights.

In spite of accidental historical differences, it is submitted that the results of both Portuguese and German laws are essentially equivalent.

There is a striking similarity between both systems of constitutional law.

In Germany, the principle of human dignity results from Article 1(1) of the Fundamental Law; in Portugal, it results from Article 1 of the Constitution.

In Germany, the right to the free development of one's personality results from Article 2(1) of the Fundamental Law; in Portugal, the right to the development of one's personality results from Article 26(1) of the Constitution.

Furthermore, there is a striking similarity between both systems of tort law:

In Portugal, the tortfeasor is to be held liable for the infringement of the *general right to one's personality*, for it qualifies as an absolute, subjective right in the sense of Article 483(1) of the Civil Code. In Germany, the tortfeasor is to be held liable for the infringement of the general right to one's personality, for it qualifies as 'other right' in the sense of § 823(1).

B. The Particular, Specific Clauses in Articles 72 to 80 of the Portuguese Civil Code

31. The general clause in Article 70(1) of the Portuguese Civil Code is supplemented by the particular, specific clauses in Articles 72 to 80.

Articles 72 and 74 provide protection to the name and pseudonym.[215]

Articles 75 and 76 apply to confidential letters. Article 77 extends the scope of Articles 75 and 76 on letters to 'family or personal memoirs, or any other writings that have a confidential nature or which may concern the intimacy of private life'. Article 78 applies to non-confidential letters.[216]

---

215. *See*, for further developments, F.A. Pires de Lima/J.M. Antunes Varela (/ M.H. Mesquita), Código Civil anotado, vol. I, 105–107; C.A. da Mota Pinto/A. Pinto Monteiro/P. Mota Pinto, Teoria geral do direito civil, 214–215; A. Menezes Cordeiro, Tratado de direito civil português, vol. I – Parte geral, III – Pessoas, 155–152.

216. *See*, for further developments, F.A. Pires de Lima/J.M. Antunes Varela (/ M.H. Mesquita), Código Civil anotado, vol. I, 107–109; A. Menezes Cordeiro, Tratado de direito civil português, vol. I – Parte geral, III – Pessoas, 183–191.

As to *confidential letters*, Article 75(1) reads that their addressees 'shall keep its contents secret and shall not take advantage of any information acquired therefrom'.[217] It follows both from Articles 75(1) and 76(1) that confidential letters 'may only be published with the prior consent of their authors or that of the Court'. As to *non-confidential letters,* Article 78 reads that their addressees 'may only use them under such conditions that do not conflict with the expectations of their authors'.[218] It is submitted that Articles 75 to 78 are to apply also to modern messages, such as e-mails.

C. Closed Versus Open Personality Rights

32. In what concerns personality interests, there is a clear, fundamental distinction to be made between *closed rights* and *open rights.*

Whereas the content and limits of *closed rights*, such as the right to life and the right to bodily integrity, can be determined in advance with a high degree of precision, the content and limits of *open rights*, such as the general right to one's personality, cannot be determined in advance.

It follows that while *closed rights* are clearly defined and manifest,[219] *open rights* are not and cannot be clearly defined. They are thus *framework rights* (in German, *Rahmenrecht*; in Portuguese, *direitos-quadro*).

Whereas infringements of *closed, clearly defined rights* are easy to establish, infringements of *open, framework rights* are not.

In fact, it has always been stressed that the content and limits of *open, framework rights*, such as the right to the free development of one's personality, could not be determined in advance in a close, definitive way,[220] for they always depend on an assessment of the circumstances of the case.

Open, framework rights require the judge to balance competing interests.[221] That is to say that the content and limits of open, framework rights always depend on the 'interests of other in free development and in the exercise of rights, as well as [on] public interests'.[222] In deciding which interests are to prevail, the judge is to consider the circumstances of the case.[223]

---

217. For the translation of Art. 75(1) of the Portuguese Civil Code, *see* P. Pais de Vasconcelos/N. Ferreira, 'Case 12 – Portugal', in: G. Brüggemeier/A. Colombi-Ciacchi/P. O'Callaghan, Personality Rights in European Tort Law, 448.
218. For the translation of Art. 78 of the Portuguese Civil Code, *see* P. Pais de Vasconcelos/N. Ferreira, 'Case 12 – Portugal', in: G. Brüggemeier/A. Colombi-Ciacchi/P. O'Callaghan, Personality Rights in European Tort Law, 448.
219. *See* § 1293(3) of the 'Draft proposal submitted by the working group set up by the Federal Ministry of Justice for a new Austrian Law of Damages', referring to 'clearly defined and manifest personality rights', [in: H. Koziol, *Basic Questions of Tort Law from a Germanic Perspective*, 325–343 (328)].
220. *See* J.F. Sinde Monteiro, Responsabilidade por conselhos, recomendações ou informações, 228.
221. *See* O. de Carvalho, Teoria geral do direito civil, 38, and J.F. Sinde Monteiro, Responsabilidade por conselhos, recomendações ou informações, 228.
222. *See* § 1293(2) of the 'Draft proposal submitted by the working group set up by the Federal Ministry of Justice for a new Austrian Law of Damages', in: H. Koziol, *Basic Questions of Tort Law from a Germanic Perspective*, 327–328.
223. *See* J.F. Sinde Monteiro, Responsabilidade por conselhos, recomendações ou informações, 228.

It is submitted that the distinction between the two types of personality rights is of considerable importance, for instance, so as to resolve the problems relating to the relevance of the *exceptio veritatis* within the framework of liability for the infringement of credit and good name.

In fact, rights to credit and good name are open, framework rights.

Infringements to the rights to credit and good name are to be determined by balancing the interests of the person who makes relevant statements, and the interests of the person whose credit, honour and good name are at risk of being harmed. In a number of cases, the interests of the person who makes the relevant, harmful statements are protected by constitutional, fundamental rights, such as *freedom of expression* and *freedom of press*.

It follows from the constitutional relevance of the interests of both persons that 'the balance between the fundamental, constitutionally protected rights to honour, reputation and freedom of the press is to be reached according to the principles of proportionality, necessity and adequacy'.[224] In such a balance – conforming to the principles of necessity and proportionality – the starting point shall be that statements of true facts are not unlawful.[225]

D. Coordinating Articles 70 and 483 with Article 484 of the Portuguese Civil Code

33. Furthermore, the particular, specific clauses in Articles 72 to 80 are supplemented by Article 484 on the rights to credit and to good name:

> Whoever affirms or disseminates a fact which is able to harm the credit or good name of any person, private individual or legal person, is liable for the damage caused.[226]

It could be asked whether Article 484 of the Portuguese Civil Code is necessary.

224. *See* P. Pais de Vasconcelos/N. Ferreira, 'Case 1 – Portugal', in: G. Brüggemeier/A. Colombi-Ciacchi/P. O'Callaghan, *Personality Rights in European Tort Law*, 125.

225. *See*, for instance, J.F. Sinde Monteiro, Responsabilidade por conselhos, recomendações ou informações, 208–209 (footnote 106).

226. On the interpretation of Art. 484 of the Portuguese Civil Code, *see, for example*, F.A. Pires de Lima/J.M. Antunes Varela (/ M.H. Mesquita), *Código Civil anotado*, vol. I, 485–486; J.M. Antunes Varela, *Das obrigações em geral,* vol. I, 548–549; M.J. Almeida Costa, *Direito das obrigações,* 564–565; J. Ribeiro de Faria, *Direito das obrigações*, vol. I, 433–434; A. Menezes Cordeiro, *Tratado de direito civil português*, vol. I – *Parte geral*, III – *Pessoas*, 143–154; A. Menezes Cordeiro, *Tratado de direito civil português*, vol. II – *Direito das obrigações*, III. – *Gestão de negócios. Enriquecimento sem causa. Responsabilidade civil*, 551–561; L. Menezes Leitão, *Direito das obrigações*, vol. I – *Introdução. Da constituição das obrigações*, 303–305; J.F. Sinde Monteiro, 'Rudimentos da responsabilidade civil', 384–388; J.F. Sinde Monteiro, *Responsabilidade por conselhos, recomendações ou informações*, 208–209 (footnote 106); F.M. Albuquerque Matos, *Responsabilidade civil por ofensa ao crédito ou ao bom nome* (Coimbra: Livraria Almedina 2011).

In Germany, where there is no general clause on the protection of personality interests, it is easy to understand the reason why § 824 of the German Civil Code was adopted.[227]

In Portugal, where there is a general clause on the protection of personality interests, it is not easy to understand the reason why Article 484 of the Portuguese Civil Code was enacted. In fact, *credit* and *good name* seem to be *personality interests*. If they are *personality interests*, they are to be protected by *personality rights*.

It would follow from the very nature of *credit* and *good name* as *personality interests* that Article 70(1), in conjunction with Article 483(1) of the Portuguese Civil Code, should be sufficient to provide for their protection.

Therefore, it has been argued that Article 484 is not necessary and that it probably could be dismissed at no serious inconvenience at all.[228]

It is submitted that it all comes to defining *credit* and *good name*.

It has been suggested, with good reason, that there is a relationship of *speciality* between both concepts. *Good name* seems to refer to the general reputation of the person within the social circles where he or she lives and where he or she performs his or her professional duties.[229]

The concept of *credit* is a specification – and no more than a specification – of *good name*. *Credit* seems to refer to a special kind of reputation, which is business-related.[230] It seems to refer both to the ability and to the will of the person to perform his business-related duties. It can be defined as the *good name* of a *business person* who keeps promises.[231]

In what concerns general reputation – in what concerns *good name* – Article 484 of the Portuguese Civil Code may not be necessary. It could also be absent from the Portuguese Civil Code. The right to a *good name* fundamentally equates to the *right to honour* – and '[t]he right to honour has long been perceived as one of the specific personality rights which can be deduced from the general clause of Article 70'.[232] In what concerns specific, i.e., business-related reputation – in what concerns *credit* – however, Article 484 of the Portuguese Civil Code may well be necessary.

Although credit is a personality interest to be protected by personality rights, it is a personality interest whose infringement causes pecuniary loss.

227. In accordance with § 824(1), 'a person who maintains or publishes, contrary to the truth, a statement calculated to endanger the credit of another, or to injure his earnings or prospects in any other manner, must compensate the other for any damage arising therefrom, even if he does not know of its untruth, provided he ought to know', and, in accordance, with § 824(2), '[a] communication the untruth of which is unknown to the person making it does not thereby render him liable to make compensation, if he or the recipient of the communication has a justifiable interest in it'. For the translation of § 824 of the German Civil Code, *see* B.S. Markesinis/H. Unberath, The German Law of Torts. A Comparative Treatise, 14.
228. *See*, for instance, A. Menezes Cordeiro, *Tratado de direito civil português*, vol. I – *Parte geral*, III – *Pessoas*, 152, and L. Menezes Leitão, *Direito das obrigações*, vol. I – *Introdução. Da constituição das obrigações*, 304–305.
229. *See* F.M. Albuquerque Matos, *Responsabilidade civil por ofensa ao crédito ou ao bom nome*, 115.
230. *See* F.M. Albuquerque Matos, *Responsabilidade civil por ofensa ao crédito ou ao bom nome*, 116.
231. *See* F.M. Albuquerque Matos, *Responsabilidade civil por ofensa ao crédito ou ao bom nome*, 116.
232. *See* P. Pais de Vasconcelos/N. Ferreira, 'Case 1 – Portugal', in: G. Brüggemeier/A. Colombi-Ciacchi/P. O'Callaghan, *Personality Rights in European Tort Law*, 122–123.

In a sense, *credit* is a *personality interest* with a *double dimension*: on the one hand, it has a *non-pecuniary, personal dimension,* and, on the other hand, deviating from *normal* personality interests, it has a *pecuniary dimension.*[233]

In keeping with the *double dimension* of *credit*, Article 484 of the Portuguese Civil Code would perform at least two distinct functions.

In the first place, it would make clear that there may be an infringement of both the *credit* of *private individuals* and the credit of *private, purely legal entities*. In Portugal, it is far from clear whether *private, purely legal entities*, such as corporations, have *personality interests* to be protected by *personality rights*. Article 484 would make it clear that 'statement[s] calculated to endanger the credit of another, or to injure his earnings or prospects in any other manner' can do harm to corporations.[234]

Second, it would make it clear that there is a difference between statements oriented to facts and statements oriented to values. Infringements of credit resulting from *statements oriented to facts* – which are supposed to be value-neutral – should give rise to a duty to compensate. Infringements of credit resulting from *statements oriented to values* should not. In the case of *statements oriented to values*, freedom of expression should prevail.[235]

It is unclear whether Article 484 of the Portuguese Civil Code should apply to *all statements*, irrespective of whether they conform or do not conform to the truth or to false statements – *and to false statements only*.

Article 484 of the Portuguese Civil Code deliberately deviates from § 824 of the German Civil Code.[236] Article 484 applies to all statements 'which [are] able to harm the credit or good name of any person'. § 824 of the German Civil Code applies exclusively to statements 'contrary to the truth'.

In the absence of a statutory provision, similar to § 824 of the German Civil Code, limiting liability to statements *contrary to the truth*, there are two *mutually exclusive* models of decision competing in Portuguese courts.

The first model starts from the principle that all statements 'which [are] able to harm the credit or good name of any person' are unlawful.

Statements of true facts would give rise to an obligation to compensate the damage, unless they could only be justified on the grounds that they serve a *public interest* or, at least, a *legitimate, justifiable interest.*[237]

The second model starts from the principle that only false statements 'which [are] able to harm the credit or good name of any person' are unlawful.

233. *See* F.M. Albuquerque Matos, *Responsabilidade civil por ofensa ao crédito ou ao bom nome*, 116.
234. *See*, thoroughly, F.M. Albuquerque Matos, *Responsabilidade civil por ofensa ao crédito ou ao bom nome*, 363–383.
235. *See*, thoroughly, F.M. Albuquerque Matos, *Responsabilidade civil por ofensa ao crédito ou ao bom nome*, 263–316.
236. J.M. Antunes Varela, *Das obrigações em geral*, vol. I, 548–549 (footnote 2).
237. *See* F.M. Albuquerque Matos, *Responsabilidade civil por ofensa ao crédito ou ao bom nome*, 442–462.

In the event, most commonly, that the statement has been made or disseminated by a journalist, 'once the journalist proves that the affirmation published was true or that he/she had legitimate reasons to believe so, there is no place for the payment of damages (exceptio veritatis)'.[238]

Statements of true facts would not give rise to an obligation to compensate the damage arising therefrom unless they could infringe other personality interests or other personality rights of the person whose reputation is at stake (e.g., unless they could infringe his or her right to privacy).[239]

In a sense, the second model suggests that Article 484 of the Portuguese Civil Code is to be read as a functional equivalent to § 1323(1) of the 'Draft proposal […] for a new Austrian Law of Damages': 'The tortfeasor is liable for the distribution of true facts only if these were not generally known, there was no justified interest in their communication and the facts originate from the private sphere or if the distribution was manifestly designed to impair another person seriously.'[240]

E. Liability for the Infringement of Property Rights

1. Liability for the Infringement of Rights In Rem

34. It is apparent that the concept of rights of another person in Article 483(1) of the Portuguese Civil Code comprehends property rights.[241]

Article 1305 describes property by saying that the owner benefits from the rights to use, enjoy and dispose of things in a full and exclusive manner, within the limits of the law and observing the restrictions imposed on it.

Article 1302 seems to limit the concept of property rights. In accordance with Article 1302, property rights should be rights on corporeal, tangible things. Article 1303(2) seems, however, to expand the concept of property rights – in keeping with Article 1303(2), principles and rules on the property of corporeal, tangible things apply to copyright, industrial property, and intellectual property, even though they apply to them only 'on a subsidiary basis'. Therefore, principles and rules on the property of corporeal, tangible things apply to the property incorporeal, intangible things.

The ambiguity of Articles 1302 and 1303(2) explains the discussion on the concept of property. It has been argued that the concept of property is to be construed

238. *See* P. Pais de Vasconcelos/N. Ferreira, 'Case 1 – Portugal', in: G. Brüggemeier/A. Colombi-Ciacchi/P. O'Callaghan, *Personality Rights in European Tort Law*, 122–123.

239. *See*, for instance, J.F. Sinde Monteiro, *Responsabilidade por conselhos, recomendações ou informações*, 208–209 (footnote 106).

240. *See* H. Koziol, *Basic Questions of Tort Law from a Germanic Perspective*, 338.

241. For a presentation, in English, of the Portuguese system of rights in rem, *see* R. Pinto Duarte, 'Property Law', in: C. Ferreira de Almeida/A. Cristas/N. Piçarra (coord.), Portuguese Law. An Overview (Coimbra: Livraria Almedina 2007) 207–214, and S. Passinhas, 'Property Law – Portuguese Report', available at: http://www.eui.eu/Documents/DepartmentsCentres/Law/ResearchTeaching/ResearchThemes/EuropeanPrivateLaw/RealPropertyProject/Portugal.PDF.

so as to refer to corporeal, tangible things and it has been argued that it should be construed so as to refer to all things[242] – irrespective of whether they are corporeal or incorporeal, tangible or intangible.[243]

It is also apparent that the concept of *rights of another person* in Article 483(1) of the Portuguese Civil Code comprehends any other rights in rem.

Article 1306 of the Portuguese Civil Code states the principle according to which rights in rem are only recognized as such if they correspond to the types described by the law. In classifying the types of rights in rem described by the law, Portuguese legal doctrine habitually distinguishes three types of rights in rem – rights to use (*direitos pessoais de gozo*), rights to acquire (*direitos reais de aquisição*) and securities (*direitos reais de garantia*).

Book III, titles II to VI, of the Portuguese Civil Code, on the *law of property*, refers exclusively to *property* and to *rights to use*, different from property.

Articles 1439 ff. refer to usufruct (in Portuguese, *direito de usufruto*),[244] Articles 1484 ff., to the rights of use and residence (*direitos de uso e de habitação*),[245] Articles 1524 ff., to the rights to build, or to maintain a construction on land belonging to another person (*direito de superfície*) and Articles 1543 ff., to servitudes (in Portuguese, *servidões*).[246]

Book II, title II, chapter VI of the Portuguese Civil Code, on the *law of obligations*, deals with *securities*. The most important of them are mortgage (*hipoteca*) and pledge (*penhor*), '[…] the distinction between mortgage (hipoteca) and pledge (penhor) depend[ing] on the nature of the object of the security. When the object of security is an immovable, or a movable subject to registration, "hipoteca" is applicable; when the object of the security is a movable, a credit or another similar right, "penhor" is applicable'.[247]

There is no particular Book, no particular title, no particular chapter – and no particular section of the Portuguese Civil Code dealing with *rights to acquire*. They may result either from statute or from the contract – as in the case of Article 413 and Article 421 of the Portuguese Civil Code.

Article 483(1) applies to the infringements of property rights on both corporeal, tangible things and on incorporeal, intangible things.

---

242. On the case for a broad concept of *property*, comprehending rights on incorporeal, tangible things, *see* O. de Carvalho, *Direito das coisas* (Coimbra: Centelha 1977) 189–209.
243. For a summary of the discussion, *see* R. Pinto Duarte, *Curso de direitos reais* 3rd edition (Cascais: Principia 2013) 30–33.
244. Article 1439 defines usufruct as the right to enjoy a thing that belongs to another person fully, but temporarily, and without altering its form and substance [for the translation of Art. 1439 of the Portuguese Civil Code, *see* R. Pinto Duarte, 'Property Law', 210. S. Passinhas proposes a slightly different translation, replacing 'right to enjoy' with 'entitlement to use to property and to take its fruits' – *see* 'Property Law – Portuguese Report', at 1.3.].
245. *Direito de uso* consists 'of the faculty of using a thing belonging to another person within the limits of the needs of its holder and of its family' [*see* Portuguese Civil Code, Art. 1484(1)]. Whenever it applies to dwelling – i.e., whenever the object of the right of use is a home – the *right of use* transforms itself into the *right of residence* ['*direito de habitação*' – *See* Portuguese Civil Code, Art. 1484(2)].
246. Article 1543 defines servitudes as a charge imposed on a piece of land for the benefit of another piece of land belonging to a different owner.
247. R. Pinto Duarte, 'Property Law', 211.

It applies, e.g., to infringements of industrial property – such as property of trademarks[248] – and to infringements of intellectual property.[249]

Furthermore, Article 483(1) applies to the infringements of rights in rem, different from property, on corporeal, tangible things.

In what concerns the property and rights of use, different from property, there is no doubt that their infringements allow the owner to claim damages.

In what concerns rights to acquire and securities, there is, however, a doubt. It is far from clear whether rights to acquire and securities are really rights in rem.[250] In spite of the fact that it is far from clear whether they really are rights in rem, it is submitted that Portuguese courts would hold the tortfeasor liable for the infringement of both rights to acquire and securities.[251]

Finally, Article 483(1) of the Portuguese Civil Code applies to infringements of rights in rem, different from property, on incorporeal, intangible things – for instance, to the usufruct of copyright.[252]

F. Liability for the Infringement of Rights In Personam as to the Enjoyment and Use of Things

35. Articles 407 and 1682-A of the Portuguese Civil Code refer to *direitos pessoais de gozo*. The term is difficult to translate, for it refers to a hybrid. In fact, '*direitos pessoais de gozo*' are between property and contract. On the one hand, they are rights in personam (*direitos pessoais*). On the other hand, even though they are rights in personam, they are rights in personam as to the use of things (*direitos ... de gozo*).[253]

The concept of rights in personam as to the enjoyment and use of things is intended to be a broad, comprehensive concept. It aims at transforming into general category concepts and structures resulting, for example, from the principles and rules on specific contracts, as *locatio* and *commodatum*.[254]

The difference between *locatio* and *commodatum* lies in the fact that *locatio* depends on consideration, and *commodatum* does not. In both contracts, a party grants to another the use of a thing for a certain, determined period of time. In the

248. *See* Industrial Property Code (*Código da propriedade industrial*), Art. 347.
249. *See* Copyright Code (*Código dos Direitos de Autor e dos Direitos Conexos*), Art. 211.
250. For a suggestion that rights to acquire are not rights in rem, *see* M.H. Mesquita, *Obrigações reais e ónus reais* (Coimbra: Livraria Almedina 1990) 231 ff.
251. In public, administrative law, in the case of takings, compensation for the infringement of all rights different from property is provided for in Art. 32 of the Code of Takings (*Código das Expropriações*), approved by Decree-Law No. 168/99 of 18 Sep. 1999.
252. *See* Copyright Code, Art. 45.
253. *See*, for instance, J.F. Sinde Monteiro. 'Case 8 – Portugal', in: M. Bussani/V.V. Palmer (eds), *Pure Economic Loss in Europe* (Cambridge: Cambridge University Press 2003) 303–304 – suggesting that *direitos pessoais de gozo* are 'generally speaking, [...] 'personal right[s] to the enjoyment of something belonging to another'.
254. *See*, thoroughly, J.M. Andrade Mesquita, *Direitos pessoais de gozo* (Coimbra: Livraria Almedina 1999).

case of *locatio* (lease, tenancy), he or she does so in return for money.[255] In the case of *commodatum*, he or she does so in return for no money whatsoever – *Commodatum* is essentially free.

In spite of the fact that there is practical convergence between the effects of rights in personam as to the use of things and rights in rem, such as the rights of usufruct, use, and residence, there are also both theoretical and practical divergences. In the case of the lease – especially in the case of tenancy – there is a discussion on whether the tenant's right is in personam or in rem.[256] It has been suggested, on the basis of a good argument, that the tenant's right is neither in personam nor in rem, thus belonging to a *tertium genus*.[257] The conclusion applies to all rights in personam as to the use of things.[258]

In what concerns the lease – in what concerns, first and foremost, tenancy – the discussion on whether the tenant's right is in personam or in rem results from the fact that the tenant's position is strongly protected.

In the first place, the tenant may recur to the possessor's protection.

Second, even if the possessor's protection is insufficient, the tenant may recur to the law of torts to defend his or her right against third parties.

Article 1037(1) of the Portuguese Civil Code provided that the owner is under no duty to protect the tenant's right against third parties. It follows from Article 1037(1) that either the tenant's right is not to be protected against third parties or that it is to be protected by the tenant himself/herself. The first alternative is apparently untenable – thus, the second alternative is to be preferred.[259] Therefore, the tenant's right is an absolute right to be protected by Article 483(1) of the Portuguese Civil Code.[260]

In what concerns rights in personam as to the use of things different from the tenant's right, there are principles and rules similar to Article 1037(1). In the case of *commodatum*, for instance, Article 1133(1) applies. The arguments derived therefrom strongly suggest that all rights in personam as to the use of things are absolute

255. For a short presentation of the Portuguese system on lease, *see* S. Passinhas, 'Tenancy Law – Portugal', available at: http://www.eui.eu/Documents/DepartmentsCentres/Law/ResearchTeaching/ResearchThemes/EuropeanPrivateLaw/TenancyLawProject/TenancyLawPortugal.pdf.

256. *See*, for instance, J.F. Sinde Monteiro. 'Case 8 – Portugal', 303.

257. It should be stressed that such a qualification, as a *tertium genus*, depends on the immediate, 'physical' relationship, between tenant and thing. '[T]he particularities of the personal right to enjoyment compared with the credit rights only manifest themselves when there is 'immediacy' between the holder and the thing (sometimes there may be an initial, purely credit-related phase)' (*see* J.F. Sinde Monteiro. 'Case 8 – Portugal', 303).

258. *See*, for instance, M.H. Mesquita, *Obrigações reais e ónus reais*, 175–176; J.M. Andrade Mesquita, *Direitos pessoais de gozo*, 133–167; R. Pinto Duarte, *Curso de direitos reais*, 345–347; N.M. Pinto Oliveira, *Princípios de direito dos contratos*, 57–61.

259. *See*, for instance, M.H. Mesquita, *Obrigações reais e ónus reais*, 148–168; J.M. Andrade Mesquita, *Direitos pessoais de gozo*, 209–216.

260. *See*, thoroughly, J.M. Andrade Mesquita, *Direitos pessoais de gozo*, 171–249. It should be stressed that the particularities of the personal right to enjoyment compared with the contractual, obligational rights only manifest themselves when there is 'immediacy' between the holder and the thing.

rights – that all rights in personam as to the use of things are to be protected by Article 483(1) of the Portuguese Civil Code under the concepts of *rights of another person.*[261]

G. *Liability for the Infringement of Possession: Coordinating Article 483(1) with Article 1284 of the Portuguese Civil Code*

36. Finally, as to non-contractual, tortious liability for infringements of possession:

> In Portugal, as, for instance, in Germany and in Italy, possession depends on the 'actual power of control over the thing'.[262]

Article 1251 of the Portuguese Civil Code defines possession as a power revealed by the fact that someone acts in a way that corresponds to the exercise of property rights or to the exercise of any other rights in rem.[263]

It is controversial whether possession qualifies as a right in rem.

It has been argued that it is a right in rem.[264] It has been argued that it is no right at all.[265] In the case of corporeal, tangible things, possession would be closer to a physical relationship with the thing than to the concept of a legal, juridical relationship with another person.[266]

Controversial as it is whether possession qualifies as right in rem, Article 1284(1) of the Portuguese Civil Code aims at making clear – thus, consensual – that the possessor's interests are to be protected by tort law.

It follows from Article 1284(1) that, in the event of infringements to possession, the possessor who has been successful in his or her claim to maintenance or to the recovery of possession is entitled to claim damages for all losses he or she sustained, as a consequence of nuisance or trespass.[267]

It could be discussed whether Article 1284(1) is a deviation from the general clause in Article 483(1) or a specification – and no more than a specification – of the general clause in Article 483(1) of the Portuguese Civil Code. In spite of the fact that such a discussion is of theoretical significance, their results are, for all practical purpose, of no importance at all.

---

261. *See* J.F. Sinde Monteiro. 'Case 8 – Portugal', 303: 'In these circumstances (where there is "immediacy"), the personal right to enjoyment seems to merit aquilian protection under Article 483.'
262. *See* B.S. Markesinis/H. Unberath, *The German Law of Torts. A Comparative Treatise*, 51.
263. On the concept of possession, *see*, for instance, M. Rodrigues, *A posse. Estudo de direito civil português* (Coimbra: Coimbra Editora 1924), O. de Carvalho, 'Introdução à posse', in: *Revista de Legislação e de Jurisprudência* vol. 122 ff. (1989–1990 ff.), and A. Menezes Cordeiro, *A posse: perspectivas dogmáticas actuais* 3rd edition (Coimbra: Livraria Almedina 2000).
264. *See*, for instance, M. Rodrigues, *A posse. Estudo de direito civil português*, 33–40.
265. *See*, for instance, O. de Carvalho, 'Introdução à posse', passim.
266. *See*, for instance, B.S. Markesinis/H. Unberath, *The German Law of Torts. A Comparative Treatise*, 51: '[I]t is more [...] a physical relation to a thing than a right.'
267. *See*, for instance, F.A. Pires de Lima/J.M. Antunes Varela (/ M.H. Mesquita), *Código Civil anotado*, vol. III, 2nd edition (Coimbra: Coimbra Editora 1987) 59–60.

H. Liability for the Infringement of Contractual, Relative Rights?

37. In keeping with the author of the project of the Portuguese Civil Code,[268] the concept of *rights of another person* in Article 483(1) does not comprehend contractual, relative rights: 'in using the word "unlawfully", Vaz Serra, the author of the 1966 code, intended to protect only "absolute rights" and this "legislative" intent is generally read into the provision'.[269]

I. Liability for the Infringement of Objective Law

38. Second, Portuguese tort law contains a general clause on liability for the infringement of interests protected by the law:

> [w]hoever whether by wilful misconduct (dolus) or by negligence unlawfully infringes [...] any legal provision intended to safeguard the interests of others must compensate the injured party for damage arising from such violation.[270]

Whereas the first general clause in Article 483(1) of the Portuguese Civil Code corresponds to § 823(1) of the German Civil Code, the second general clause in Article 483(1) corresponds to § 823(2).

In the first general clause in Article 483(1) of the Portuguese Civil Code, as in § 823(1) of the German Civil Code, the element of unlawfulness is based upon the result.[271] In the second general clause in Article 483(1), as in § 823(2), that element is based upon the *behaviour* or the *conduct* of the defendant.[272] '[T]he element of unlawfulness [...] is here made to depend upon the notion of a violated protective norm (*Schutzgesetz*)'.[273]

In the first general clause in Article 483(1) of the Portuguese Civil Code, as in § 823(1) of the German Civil Code, the element of unlawfulness is defined by reference to the interests to be protected by the law – to the so-called *Rechtsgüter*[274] – and, in the second general clause in Article 483(1), as in § 823(2), it is defined by reference to particular, specific norms.

Koziol characterizes them as 'express behavioural rule[s] prohibiting the endangerment of rights and interests by specific proscribed behaviour'.[275]

---

268. *See* A. Vaz Serra, 'Responsabilidade de terceiros no não cumprimento de obrigações', in: *Boletim do Ministério da Justiça* 85 (April 195) 345–360.
269. M. Bussani/V.V. Palmer, 'The Liability Regimes of Europe – Their Façades and Interiors', 155.
270. For an analogous distinction between liability for the infringement of (subjective) rights and liability for the infringement of (objective) law, *see* J.D. Harke, *Besonderes Schuldrecht* (Berlin/ Heidelberg: Springer 2011) 435 and 461.
271. *See* H. Koziol, *Basic Questions of Tort Law from a Germanic Perspective*, 178.
272. *See* H. Koziol, *Basic Questions of Tort Law from a Germanic Perspective*, 178.
273. *See* B.S. Markesinis/H. Unberath, *The German Law of Torts. A Comparative Treatise*, 885.
274. *See* B.S. Markesinis/H. Unberath, *The German Law of Torts. A Comparative Treatise*, 885.
275. *See* H. Koziol, *Basic Questions of Tort Law from a Germanic Perspective*, 178.

Professor B.S. Markesinis argues that § 823(2) of the German Civil Code, '[i]n its ambit, […] is both wider and narrower than the first paragraph'.[276] It is wider since it covers pure economic loss, and it is narrower since it covers loss – both economic and non-economic – only in cases of interference with the particular, specific scope of a particular, specific statute. '[T]he illegality is defined by reference to the scope of the particular statute, which may be narrow, and not to the consequences of its violation'.[277]

The argument applies to the Portuguese system of tort law.[278]

In case there is no infringement of absolute, subjective rights whatsoever – that is to say, in the case of pure economic loss – the second general clause in Article 483(1) is necessary to establish liability.[279]

Professors Bussani and Palmer point out that, as a consequence of the limitation of Article 483(1) of the Portuguese Civil Code to absolute rights:

> Portuguese scholars and judges do not work out the notion of unlawfulness in an open-ended perspective. They usually handle the problem of recoverability by reference to those discrete provisions, scattered throughout the legal system, which are construed as safeguarding the particular right or interest in issue.[280]

Thus, if the plaintiff fails to prove there has been an infringement of legal, statutory provisions intended to safeguard the interests of others, he or she can only claim compensation in the case there is an abuse of rights:

> while the violation of a protective statute may give rise to compensation for pure economic loss, this is an exception to the general rule of no recovery.[281]

It follows from the close connection between German and Portuguese private-legal systems that the second general clause in Article 483(1) of the Portuguese Civil Code causes at least two problems – the first refers to the concept of a *legal, statutory provision* and the second to the concept of a legal, statutory provision *intended to safeguard the interests of others.*

---

276. *See* B.S. Markesinis/H. Unberath, *The German Law of Torts. A Comparative Treatise*, 885.
277. B.S. Markesinis/H. Unberath, *The German Law of Torts. A Comparative Treatise*, 885.
278. *See* J.M. Antunes Varela, *Das obrigações em geral,* vol. I, 536–542; M.J. de Almeida Costa, *Direito das obrigações,* 563; R. de Alarcão, *Direito das obrigações,* 242–244; J. Ribeiro de Faria, *Direito das obrigações*, vol. I, 418–425; J.F. Sinde Monteiro, *Responsabilidade por conselhos, recomendações ou informações,* 237–300; J.F. Sinde Monteiro, 'Rudimentos da responsabilidade civil', 365–366; A. Menezes Leitão, *Normas de protecção e danos patrimoniais primários* (Coimbra: Livraria Almedina 2008).
279. Professor van Dam emphasizes that '[t]he practical meaning of § 823 (2) lies particularly in the area of liability for pure economic loss, since § 823 (1) does not protect against this type of loss and § 825 requires the intentional behaviour of the tortfeasor' (C. van Dam, *European Tort Law*, 256). Even though there is a difference between Art. 334 of the Portuguese Civil Code and § 826 of the German Civil Code – for Art. 334 of the Portuguese Civil Code does not require an intentional behaviour of the tortfeasor – Professor van Dam's sentence could apply, *mutatis mutandis*, to Portugal.
280. M. Bussani/V.V. Palmer, 'The Liability Regimes of Europe – Their Façades and Interiors', 155.
281. M. Bussani/V.V. Palmer, 'The Liability Regimes of Europe – Their Façades and Interiors', 155.

J. The Concept of a Legal, Statutory Provision

39. The concept of a legal, statutory provision in Article 483(1) is to be defined in accordance with the concept in Article 1(2) of the Portuguese Civil Code.

In the first place, legal, statutory provisions relevant to Article 483(1) are required to be abstract and general (*'normas genéricas'*). Second, they are required to be grounded upon the authority of the State (*'emanadas dos órgãos estaduais competentes'*). Therefore, the scope of the term *'disposições legais'* in Article 483(1) is equivalent to the scope of the term *Schutzgesetz* in § 823(1).[282] In both cases, they are to be taken widely 'to refer to statutes (of private and public law, government decrees, local by-laws or ordinances (*Verordnungen*), food and drugs regulations, and police orders'.[283]

K. The Concept of a Legal, Statutory Provision Intended to Safeguard the Interests of Others

40. Whether a legal, statutory provision qualifies as a provision *intended to safeguard the interests of others* depends on three requirements. In the first place, the plaintiff's loss must correspond to the *infringement of a legal, statutory provision*; second, that *legal, statutory provision* must aim at protecting particular, private persons;[284] third, and finally, that *legal, statutory provision* must aim at protecting that particular, specific private person against that particular, specific loss. That is to say that *loss must fall within the scope of the provision which has been infringed.*[285] In Portugal, as well as in Germany, '[t]he fact that a statute meant to protect the public at large does not mean that it was not also intended to protect, within its protective ambit, a particular (legal or physical) person'.[286]

In determining whether the statute is meant to protect that particular person, the third requirement stands out, for it is the most important – *the loss must fall within the scope of the provision which has been infringed.* It is to be examined both subjectively and objectively. *Subjectively*, Article 483(1) implicitly requires that the *legal, statutory provision* aims at protecting the plaintiff. '[T]he victim must belong to the group of people who are to be protected by the [norm].'[287] The judge is to

282. *See*, for instance, J.F. Sinde Monteiro, *Responsabilidade por conselhos, recomendações ou informações*, 245–248.
283. *See* B.S. Markesinis/H. Unberath, *The German Law of Torts. A Comparative Treatise*, 885.
284. *See, for example*, C. van Dam, *European Tort Law*, 255 – referring to German law: 'If only the general or public interests are protected, the rule is not considered to be protective in the sense of § 823 (2).'
285. *See*, for instance, J.M. Antunes Varela, *Das obrigações em geral*, vol. I, 539; M.J. Almeida Costa, *Direito das obrigações*, 563; L.M. Menezes Leitão, *Direito das obrigações*, vol. I – *Introdução. Da constituição das obrigações*, 299.
286. *See* B.S. Markesinis/H. Unberath, *The German Law of Torts. A Comparative Treatise*, 887.
287. *See, for example*, C. van Dam, *European Tort Law*, 255.

ask whether 'the particular plaintiff is included in the protective ambit of the violated norm'.[288] *Objectively*, the third requirement implicit in Article 483(1) of the Portuguese Civil Code goes twofold.

On the one hand, Article 483(1) implicitly requires that the *legal, statutory provision* aims at protecting that particular plaintiff against that particular type of damage. 'It is not enough for the plaintiff to prove that it belongs to the class of persons that the violated statute wished to protect; he must also show that the mischief that has occurred was the one the statute wanted to avoid.'[289] On the other hand, Article 483(1) implicitly requires that the *legal, statutory provision* aims at protecting that particular plaintiff against that particular type of damaging conduct; in fact, 'certain [interests] are only protected against infringements by certain conduct'.[290] In the case there is an infringement of absolute, subjective rights, the first general clause is sufficient to establish liability and the second general clause is only necessary to establish the principles and rules applying to that liability – to establish, for instance, where the burden of proof is to fall.

L. *Coordinating Article 483 with Article 485 of the Portuguese Civil Code*

41. Article 485 of the Portuguese Civil Code refers to liability for mere advice, recommendation or information:

1. Mere advice, recommendation or information do not confer liability on whoever gives it, even though there may be negligence on their part.
2. The obligation to compensate exists, however, when the responsibility for damage has been assumed, when there is a legal duty to give advice, recommendation or information and this has been done with negligence or intent to harm, or when the behaviour of the agent constitutes a punishable act.

The existence of a particular, special provision on liability for advice, recommendation and information suggests that the regulation in Article 485 of the Portuguese Civil Code is complete, exclusive and special, for it deviates from the general principles and rules on pre-contractual, contractual and non-contractual, tortious liability.

In the case of liability for advice, recommendation and information, the general principles and rules on pre-contractual, contractual and non-contractual liability were to be replaced by the particular, specific principles and rules in Article 485.

The relationship between paragraph (1) and paragraph (2) of Article 485 would be a relationship of rule and exception. Article 485(1) would refer to the rule. In keeping with Article 485(1), the rule would be that there is no liability for advice, recommendation and information. Article 485(2) of the Portuguese Civil Code

288. *See* B.S. Markesinis/H. Unberath, *The German Law of Torts. A Comparative Treatise*, 887.
289. *See* B.S. Markesinis/H. Unberath, *The German Law of Torts. A Comparative Treatise*, 888.
290. *See*, *for example*, C. van Dam, *European Tort Law*, 255. In spite of the fact Professor van Dam writes ' rights', it is submitted he intends to refer to 'interests'. In the case 'rights' were involved, infringements would fall into the scope of the first general clause.

would refer to the exceptions. In keeping with Article 485(1), there would be three cases – and no more than three cases – of liability for advice, recommendation and information. In the first place, the author of the advice, recommendation or information would be under a duty to compensate in the event he or she assumed responsibility for the damage. Second, he or she would be under a duty to compensate in the event there was a legal duty to give that advice, that recommendation, or that information and he or she performed his or her duty either negligently or wilfully, with intent to harm. Third, he or she would be under a duty to compensate in the event his or her behaviour 'constitutes a [criminally] punishable act'.[291]

In his doctoral dissertation, Professor Sinde Monteiro convincingly argued for a new, alternative interpretation of Article 485 of the Portuguese Civil Code.[292]

On the one hand, Article 485(1) should not be interpreted so as to rule out liability arising from the general principles and rules on pre-contractual, contractual and non-contractual, tortious liability. On the other hand, Article 485(2) should not be interpreted as a complete, exhaustive list of cases of liability for advice, recommendation or information.

In Professor Sinde Monteiro's own words, 'a proper interpretation of this provision does not prejudice the application of the general principles of the law of obligations':[293]

> An earlier wording of this precept stated that the obligation to compensate existed when there was a legal duty to give advice 'or to proceed with diligence in giving advice'. A small alteration in the wording has changed the meaning completely. But, on pain of irremediable contradictions, it has to be admitted that this legal provision does not prejudice the application of the general principles of pre-contractual, contractual and aquilian responsibility, as clearly resulted from the project.[294]

In keeping with the wording of Article 485(1), there is a difference between 'advice, recommendation or information' and '*mere* advice, recommendation or information'.

Professor Sinde Monteiro sustains that advice, recommendation or information that normally confer liability – either in contract or in tort – cannot count as *mere* advice, recommendation or information for the purposes of Article 485.

The rule against liability, laid down in Article 485(1) of the Portuguese Civil Code, would apply to *mere* advice, recommendation or information. It would not apply to *qualified* advice, recommendation or information. If the behaviour of the author of advice, recommendation and information is relevant, for it meets the requirements of pre-contractual, contractual or non-contractual, tortious liability,

---

291. *See*, e. g., J.M. Antunes Varela, *Das obrigações em geral,* vol. I, 549–551; M.J. Almeida Costa, *Direito das obrigações,* 565–566; J. Ribeiro de Faria, *Direito das obrigações*, vol. I, 434–435.
292. *See* J.F. Sinde Monteiro, *Responsabilidade por conselhos, recomendações ou informações*, especially at 333–582 and 620–649; J.F. Sinde Monteiro, 'Rudimentos da responsabilidade civil', at 388–390.
293. J.F. Sinde Monteiro, 'Case 7 – Portugal', in: M. Bussani/V.V. Palmer (eds), *Pure Economic Loss in Europe* (Cambridge: Cambridge University Press 2003) 286–288, at 287.
294. J.F. Sinde Monteiro, 'Case 7 – Portugal', 288.

that advice, that recommendation, or that information is qualified by the legal system, or by the legal science, as having a particular property, that is enough to confer liability.[295]

The cases referred to in Article 485(2) would be examples – and no more than examples – of liability for advice, recommendation and information.

In spite of its text, Article 485(1) and (2) of the Portuguese Civil Code is to be interpreted as a 'declarative rule' or 'remissive rules',[296] allowing contractual and non-contractual, tortious claims resulting from general principles and rules.[297]

The new, 'remissive' interpretation of Article 485 of the Portuguese Civil Code is supported by comparative law: on the one hand, '§ 675 of the [German Civil Code] is frankly remissive in character' and, on the other hand, §1299 and §1300 of the Austrian Civil Code 'have to be examined against the background of the law on damage as a whole, of the law of contract and the theory of legal transactions'. 'It thus seems that the 'special provisions' of the European civil codes relative to responsibility for information are substantially less 'special' than a formal consideration leads one to believe'.[298]

VI. Unlawfulness of the Conduct or Unlawfulness of the Result (= Unlawfulness Established by the Result)?

42. In what concerns liability for the infringement of absolute, subjective rights, the criteria for assessing *unlawfulness* of the defendant's acts or omissions are under discussion.

The majority of authors prefer the so-called theory of unlawfulness of the result.[299] The minority prefers the so-called theory of unlawfulness of the conduct,[300] and in-between, there is an intermediate theory consistently gaining ground.[301,302]

---

295. *See* J.F. Sinde Monteiro, *Responsabilidade por conselhos, recomendações ou informações*, 620–649.
296. *See* J.F. Sinde Monteiro, *Responsabilidade por conselhos, recomendações ou informações* (Coimbra: Livraria Almedina 1990) 339–345.
297. *See* J.F. Sinde Monteiro, *Responsabilidade por conselhos, recomendações ou informações*, at 441–454.
298. J.F. Sinde Monteiro, 'Case 7 – Portugal', 288.
299. *See*, for instance, J.M. Antunes Varela, *Das obrigações em geral*, vol. I, 585–589.
300. *See*, for instance, J. Oliveira Ascensão, 'A teoria finalista da acção e o ilícito civil', in: *Revista da Faculdade de Direito da Universidade de Lisboa* (1986) 9–28; J. Ribeiro de Faria, 'Algumas notas sobre o finalismo no direito civil', in: 69/70 *Boletim da Faculdade de Direito* [da Universidade de Coimbra] (1993/1994).
301. *See*. for instance, J.F. Sinde Monteiro, *Responsabilidade por conselhos, recomendações ou informações*, 300–330; M. Carneiro da Frada, *Contrato e deveres de protecção*, 163–164; M. Carneiro da Frada, *Teoria da confiança e responsabilidade civil*, 235–236; N.M. Pinto Oliveira, 'Sobre o conceito de ilicitude do art. 483º do Código Civil', in: *Estudos em homenagem a Francisco José Velozo (Braga:* Associação Jurídica de Braga/Escola de Direito da Universidade do Minho 2002), 521–544; N.M. Pinto Oliveira, 'Responsabilidade civil em instituições privadas de saúde: problemas de ilicitude e de culpa', in: *Responsabilidade civil dos médicos* (Coimbra: Centro de Direito Biomédico da Faculdade de Direito da Universidade de Coimbra/Coimbra Editora 2005) 127–255.

In keeping with the theory of *unlawfulness established by the result*, there would be a rule and an exception. The rule would be that the infringements of absolute rights are *unlawful*. The result *infringement of absolute, subjective rights* would be enough to establish a *presumption* of *unlawfulness*. The exception would be that infringements of absolute rights are *lawful* in the event that a particular, specific defence applies – such as self-defence. The *presumption* resulting from the *infringement of absolute rights* would then be *rebutted*. 'The only thing that [could] remove the "unlawfulness" [would be] the presence of a legally recognized defence (*Rechtfertigungsgrund*).'[303]

In keeping with the theory of *unlawfulness established by the conduct*, the unlawfulness of infringements of absolute rights would depend on intention and negligence. '[U]nlawfulness should be determined by looking not at the result of the conduct but at the conduct itself (*Handlungsunrecht*).'[304] In the case that the infringement of the plaintiff's rights and interests is protected by Article 483(1), the first alternative is intentional, the defendant's conduct would always be unlawful. In the event the infringement of the plaintiff's rights and interests is unintentional, however, the defendant's conduct would be unlawful if – and only if – it failed to conform to the relevant standard of care. 'The mere violation of one of the [...] interests of Article 483 (1), 1st. alternative, if done unintentionally, does not necessarily satisfy the element of unlawfulness.'[305]

In keeping with the third, intermediate theory, there are two lines to be drawn.

In the first place, the law of torts is to draw a line between infringements of closed rights – such as rights to property and particular, specific personality rights – and infringements of open rights – such as the general right to one's personality.

In the case of infringements of open rights, the assessment of unlawfulness depends on a balance between competing and countervailing interests relevant to the case.

Second, in the case of infringements to closed rights, the law of torts is to draw a line between direct, immediate, and indirect, merely mediate infringements.

If there is a direct, immediate infringement of the plaintiff's absolute, subjective rights, the judge is to apply the theory of unlawfulness established by the result. 'If the defendant produces no justification, and a protective interest or right has been shown to have been violated, the element of unlawfulness is satisfied.'[306] If, however, there is an indirect, mediate infringement of absolute, subjective rights, the judge is to apply the theory of unlawfulness established by the conduct in a slightly modified form. Indirect, mediate infringements would only be unlawful in the event the defendant's conduct fails to conform to the duties to prevent the materialization

---

302. For a presentation of the three theories, *see*, for a brief historic reference, R. Zimmermann, *The Law of Obligations. Roman Foundations of the Civilian Tradition*, 976–978, and for longer, dogmatic developments, B.S. Markesinis/H. Unberath, *The German Law of Torts. A Comparative Treatise*, 79–83; H. Koziol, *Basic Questions of Tort Law from a Germanic Perspective*, 171–178; C. van Dam, *European Tort Law*, 231–233, especially at fn. 25.
303. B.S. Markesinis/H. Unberath, *The German Law of Torts. A Comparative Treatise*, 80.
304. B.S. Markesinis/H. Unberath, *The German Law of Torts. A Comparative Treatise*, 81.
305. B.S. Markesinis/H. Unberath, *The German Law of Torts. A Comparative Treatise*, 81 – referring to § 823 of the German Civil Code.
306. B.S. Markesinis/H. Unberath, *The German Law of Torts. A Comparative Treatise*, 80.

of danger in the context of social, legally relevant contacts (to the so-called *Verkehrspflichten* or *Verkehrssicherungspflichten).*

In what concerns liability for the infringement of statutory provisions intended to safeguard the interests of others, as well as in what concerns liability for abuse of rights, things are simpler. In both cases, unlawfulness refers to the conduct – to the defendant's acts or omissions that are contrary to the law, for they collide either with the specific provisions or with the general principles and values the community holds to be fundamental.

They may collide with particular, specific provisions. In that case, the defendant is to be held liable for the infringement of statutory provisions intended to safeguard the interests of others, as provided for in Article 483(1) of the Civil Code. They may collide with the general principles and values referred to by the concepts of good faith and good practice (*bonos mores*). In that case, the defendant is to be held liable for abuse of rights, as provided for in Article 334 in conjunction with Article 483(1) of the Civil Code.

In favour of the third, intermediate theory, there are at least three important arguments.

In the first place, it conforms to the distinction between the concepts of unlawfulness and fault. Second, it guarantees that the criterion of unlawfulness applying to the law of torts, within the framework of Article 483(1), is appropriate. Third, it guarantees that the criterion of unlawfulness applying to the law of torts, within the framework of Article 483(1), is consistent with the criterion of unlawfulness applying to the law of defences – especially in the case of self-defence (*see* Article 337 of the Portuguese Civil Code).[307]

VII. Selected Case Law on Unlawfulness for One's Own Acts and Omissions

43. In the judgment of the Portuguese Supreme Court of 8 October 2016, delivered by Justice Maria da Graça Trigo, the rule against liability for pure economic loss, as well as the exceptions to such a rule, were restated in rather clear and comprehensive terms.

A, The Milk Producers Cooperative, was prevented by B and by others (as owners of the bordering land) from circulating the trucks loaded with the concrete needed for the construction work. That happened in the context of a construction work aimed at the completion of the gathering of milk and transformation of land of its property into an industrial unit.

B and others claimed that the dirt path where the trucks intended to pass was their property and that a right of way in such land would only be given to a neighbour (C), who passed by on foot sporadically, with animals, an ox-cart and, at a later moment, a tractor.

In the process of construction of its industrial unit, A had proceeded to the raising of the land and to the widening of the path, initially until the entrance of his land

307. *See*, for instance, N.M. Pinto Oliveira, 'Sobre o conceito de ilicitude do art. 483º do Código Civil', 521–544.

and afterwards until C's land. When the construction was completed, B and others used a backhoe loader to dig the dirt soil with the sole purpose of preventing the circulation of the vehicles, which were to transport the concrete necessary for the completion of the construction work.

A brought proceedings against B and others demanding compensation for pecuniary damages (around EUR 30,000) which A suffered as a consequence of B's and others' action, namely the expenses incurred in the preparation of alternative accesses so as to continue the construction work, the costs of the forced interruption of the construction work and the expenses with the ulterior replacement of the path to its initial condition.

The Court of First Instance ruled in favour of these claims and consequently condemned the defendants to restore to the claimant the possession of the dirt path, to abstain from any action that would prevent or hinder access by the claimant to its land through the dirt path in question and pay compensation for damage. The Court of Appeal changed the findings of fact and revoked the first sentence on the grounds that the unlawfulness of the action requires the infringement of a third party's right, in the present case, the absolute right of possession of the path, the ownership of which was not established by A.

A appealed to the Supreme Court, claiming that the compensatory obligation may derive either from the unlawful infringement of an absolute right, or from the unlawful infringement of a statutory provision aimed at protecting third parties' interests, or from the agent's manifest abuse of a subjective right (*see* Article 334 of the Civil Code).

The Supreme Court considered that it could be concluded that B's and others' conduct amounted to a voluntary fact which caused damages to A. The main difficulty lay in answer to the question of whether such conduct could be qualified as unlawful. This qualification is intimately connected to the determination of the types of damages.

In the present case, the Court qualified the proven damage as *pure economic loss*, ruling that the specific circumstances justified them being compensated.

The compensation of pure economic loss could have been grounded either on the second type of unlawfulness established in Article 483(1) of the Portuguese Civil Code or on the third type of unlawfulness established in Article 334 of the Portuguese Civil Code.[308]

As to the second type of unlawfulness, relating to infringement of statutory provisions intended to protect third parties' interests, the Portuguese Supreme Court emphasized that Articles 2 and 3(1) of the Portuguese Road Traffic Code (*Código da Estrada*) are to apply only to public domain paths and to private domain paths open-to-public traffic.

Since the plaintiff failed to claim and prove that the halted path was either a public domain path or an open-to-public traffic private domain path, liability for the infringement of statutory provisions intended to protect third parties' interests was out of the question.

308. *See* the judgments of the Portuguese Supreme Court of 12 Sep. 2019 and of 26 Nov. 2020 both delivered by Justice Maria da Graça Trigo and the judgment of 15 Sep. 2022 delivered by Justice Manuel Capelo.

As to the third type of unlawfulness, relating to abuse of rights, the Portuguese Supreme Court qualified the conduct of the defendants as a *manifest and wilful infringement of the limits imposed by the principle of good practice.*

In keeping with a long-established doctrine, advanced, among others, by the drafters of the Portuguese Civil Code, Professor Antunes Varela, and developed by Professor Sinde Monteiro, Article 334 is an autonomous source of civil liability.

The absence of a subjective right *stricto sensu* would be of no relevance for the case, taking into account that the dominant position in the Portuguese doctrine and case law is a considerably wide interpretation of the expression of 'abuse of right', comprehending the abuses of legal positions, faculties or freedoms. The Court considered that the conduct of the defendants was so serious that one could question whether it was even included in the general freedom to act, as the defendants attempted to 'take the law into their own hands' while not having produced any evidence as to the requirements of direct action' (Article 336 of the Portuguese Civil Code, direct action). Therefore, 'a serious impairment of the minimum legal-ethical required in the social coexistence'[309] was at stake.

Having concluded that all requirements of non-contractual, tortious liability were met, the Portuguese Supreme Court sentenced the defendants to payment of compensation for the damage caused to the plaintiff, with a peculiar restriction: the expenses incurred by the plaintiff in putting the soil of the disputed path back to its original state.

These were not included in the compensatory amount due to the lack of an adequate causal connection between the defendant's conduct and the expenses.

§2. Concept of Fault (Which Behaviour Leads to Tort Liability?)

I. On the Requirement of Fault

44. In principle, liability depends on fault. That is to say, that subjective, fault-based liability is the rule and that objective, no-fault, strict liability is the exception.

The relationship between the rule and the exception is implicit in Article 483(1) and explicit in Article 483(2) of the Portuguese Civil Code. Whereas Article 483(1) aims at making clear that liability requires fault, either as wilful misconduct (*dolus*) or as negligence, Article 483(2) aims at making clear that the requirement of fault is necessary, unless exceptional cases specified by the law, that is, no-fault liability is exceptional and must be created by law:

> An obligation to pay compensation where there is no fault shall arise only in cases specified by law.

309. *See* M. Carneiro da Frada, *Teoria da confiança e responsabilidade civil* (Coimbra: Livraria Almedina 2003) at 164 ff.

In the case of liability for the infringement of absolute, subjective rights, as well as in the case of liability for the infringement of objective law – that is, in cases of liability under Article 483(1) – there is a clear distinction between unlawfulness and fault.

Unlawfulness is objective, for it refers either to the act or to the omission. The defendant's behaviour, as such, is to be blamed, for it is contrary to the law.[310]

In assessing unlawfulness, the judge is to determine whether there is either a violation of absolute, subjective rights or a violation of objective law in the form of statutory provisions intended to safeguard the interests of third parties.

Fault is subjective, for it refers to a person. The defendant's person is to be blamed, for he or she behaved as they did – that is, contrary to the law – even though they could behave, and should behave, differently – that is, according to the law.

In assessing fault, the judge is to determine whether there is either intention or negligence. Professor Markesinis rightly points out that fault indicates 'an attitude (the attitude of a person who intentionally or negligently causes damage to another)'.[311]

Article 483(1) of the Portuguese Civil Code clearly distinguishes the two elements.

In referring to '[w]hoever […] unlawfully infringes the rights of another person or any legal provision intended to safeguard the interests of others', Article 483(1) requires the defendant's behaviour to be unlawful. In referring to wilful misconduct (dolus) and negligence, Article 483(1) further requires the defendant to be at fault.

In the case of liability for abuse of rights, there is no clear distinction between the two elements. Liability for abuse of rights depends either on wilful or grossly negligent misconduct. The elements of unlawfulness and fault are thus intertwined.

In determining whether the exercise of a right 'manifestly exceeds the limits imposed by good faith, by good morals or by the social or economic purpose of the right', the judge is to consider subjective elements – for example, the defendant's intention.

II. Intention and Negligence

45. In Portugal – as in most legal systems – '[l]iability can exist for both intentional and negligent conduct. These are the two bases for fault liability, which is usually opposed to strict liability'.[312] Article 483(1) of the Portuguese Civil Code refers to both types of fault.

In the first place, it refers to intentional or wilful misconduct (*dolus*) and, second, it refers to negligence (mere fault). The concept of intentional, wilful misconduct (*dolus*) indicates cases where the agent predicts the harm as necessary, as probable

310. B.S. Markesinis/H. Unberath, *The German Law of Torts. A Comparative Treatise*, 79; unlawfulness 'indicates the violation of a legal norm in the absence of a legally recognised excuse'.
311. B.S. Markesinis/H. Unberath, *The German Law of Torts. A Comparative Treatise*, 79.
312. *See*, for instance, C. van Dam, *European Tort Law*, 225.

or merely possible and accepts it or intentionally fails to avoid it. The concept of negligence indicates cases where the agent fails to conform to the relevant standard of care.[313]

In what concerns the concept of wilful misconduct (*dolus*), it is commonly held that it comprehends *dolus directus*, *dolus necessarius* and *dolus eventualis*.

The definition of *dolus directus* in Portuguese tort law corresponds to the German definition of *Absicht*. The tortfeasor acts aiming at the harmful result.[314] The definition of *dolus necessarius* in Portuguese tort law corresponds to the German definition of *direkter Vorsatz*. The tortfeasor acts, knowing that the harmful result will occur and accepting it.[315]

The definition of *dolus eventualis* corresponds to the German definition of *bedingter Vorsatz*. The tortfeasor acts, knowing that the harmful result may occur and accepting it.[316,317]

The difference between *dolus necessarius* and *dolus eventualis* thus results from the intellectual element. In the case of *dolus necessarius*, the tortfeasor knows that the harmful result will occur. That is to say that he or she takes the harmful result as a certain consequence of their conduct. In the case of *dolus eventualis*, the tortfeasor only knows that the harmful result may occur. That is to say that he or she takes the harmful result as an uncertain, albeit possible, consequence of their conduct. The words intentional misconduct and wilful misconduct thus are slightly imprecise: 'A person acting with dolus eventualis does not actually intend to do harm but may hope that it does not occur.'[318]

---

313. On the concepts of wilful misconduct (dolus) and negligence, *see* A. Vaz Serra, 'Cu lpa do devedor ou do agente', in: *Boletim do Ministério da Justiça* 68 (1957), 13 ff.; M. Andrade, *Teoria geral das obrigações* 339–347; F.M. Pereira Coelho, *Obrigações. Obrigações. Sumários das lições ao curso de 1966/1967*, 146–155; J.M. Antunes Varela, *Das obrigações em geral* I 530–533, 542–544, 567–589; I. Galvão Telles, *Direito das obrigações* 345–363; M.J. de Almeida Costa, *Direito das obrigações* 578–579, 582–584; F. Pessoa Jorge, *Lições de direito das obrigações* 557–579; R. Alarcão, *Direito das obrigações* 241–267; A. Menezes Cordeiro, *Direito das obrigações* II 310–333; J. Ribeiro de Faria, *Direito das obrigações* I 415–428, 437–440, 451–469; L.M. Menezes Leitão, *Direito das obrigações*, *I – Introdução. Da constituição das obrigações*, 315–324; F. Pessoa Jorge, *Ensaio sobre os pressupostos da responsabilidade civil*, 75–102, 315–340, 355–367; J.F. Sinde Monteiro, 'Rudimentos da responsabilidade civil', at 349–390; A. Sá e Mello, 'Critérios de apreciação da culpa na responsabilidade civil', in: 49 *Revista da Ordem dos Advogados* (1989) 519–542.
314. Professor Markesinis gives the following example: 'I aim at a child standing behind a house window and I kill it' (*see* B.S. Markesinis/H. Unberath, *The German Law of Torts. A Comparative Treatise*, 84).
315. Professor Markesinis gives the following example: 'I set fire to a house in order to burn it *knowing* that a young child is inside and knowing (and accepting) that the inevitable result of my burning the house will be the death of the child' (*see* B.S. Markesinis/H. Unberath, *The German Law of Torts. A Comparative Treatise*, 84).
316. *See*, for instance, C. van Dam, *European Tort Law*, 227: 'the acting person is aware that occurrence of harm is possible and consents to the harm if it should occur'.
317. Professor Markesinis gives the following example: 'I hit a man on the head with the intention of injuring him; but I also realise that he *may* die as a result of the blow. Despite this knowledge, I persist with my action' (*see* B.S. Markesinis/H. Unberath, *The German Law of Torts. A Comparative Treatise*, 84).
318. *See*, for instance, C. van Dam, *European Tort Law*, 227.

In what concerns the concept of non-intentional, negligent misconduct, it is commonly held that it is to be elaborated on the basis of two distinctions. In the first place, there is a line to be drawn between advertent negligence and inadvertent negligence.[319] Second, there is a line to be drawn between particularly heavy, gross negligence (*culpa lata*), normal negligence (*culpa levis*) and particularly light negligence (*culpa levíssima*).

It shall be stressed that, in both advertent, conscious, and inadvertent, unconscious negligence, the acting person does not believe that the harmful event will take place.

If the agent does not believe that it is going to happen but predicts it as possible, there is adverting, conscious negligence. If the agent does not believe that it is going to happen and does not predict it as possible, there is inadvertent, unconscious negligence.[320]

Furthermore, it shall be stressed that the difference between *particularly heavy, gross negligence, normal, ordinary negligence* and *particularly light negligence* is one of degree.[321] In the case of particularly heavy, gross negligence (*culpa lata*), the tortfeasor fails to adopt minimal care. In the case of normal, ordinary negligence, the tortfeasor fails to adopt the care and diligence an average, reasonable person would adopt under comparable circumstances. In the case of particularly light negligence, the tortfeasor fails to adopt maximal care, that is only to be expected from exceptional persons.

The distinction between intentional and non-intentional, negligent misconduct tends to be of practical significance. In fact, Article 494 reads as follows:

> Where liability is based on mere fault, compensation may be fixed equitably at an amount lower than that corresponding to the damage caused, provided that the degree of fault of the wrongdoer, the financial situation of the wrongdoer and of the injured party, as well as the other circumstances of the case so justify.

It follows from the wording of Article 494 ('[w]here liability is based on mere fault') that liability for intentional, wilful misconduct and liability from non-intentional, negligent misconduct are to be subject to different regimes. In the case of liability for intentional, wilful misconduct, compensation must correspond to the damage caused – the judge has no discretionary power to fix compensation at a lower amount. In the event of liability for non-intentional, negligent misconduct, the

319. Professor Markesinis refers to concept of advertent negligence – or conscious negligence – by using the Latin word *luxuria* and to the concept of inadvertent, or unconscious negligence by using the Latin word *negligentia* (B.S. Markesinis/H. Unberath, *The German Law of Torts. A Comparative Treatise*, 84).

320. On the distinction between *dolus eventualis* and *advertent, conscious negligence, see* B.S. Markesinis/H. Unberath, *The German Law of Torts. A Comparative Treatise*, 84: 'Adverted negligence comes close to intention (dolus eventualis) in the sense that the actor (personally) foresaw the criminal consequences as likely to materialize. The difference, however, is that in the case of dolus the actor accepts the result whereas in the case of luxuria he does not. (Indeed, he goes ahead with his action in the belief that the criminal event will not materialise).'

321. B.S. Markesinis/H. Unberath, *The German Law of Torts. A Comparative Treatise*, 84.

judge has the discretionary power to fix the compensation, considering the factors referred to in the final part of that provision.

It is submitted that particularly heavy, gross negligence (*culpa lata*) is to be equated with intention (*dolus*) for the purposes of Article 494 of the Portuguese Civil Code.[322]

§3. Duty of Care

46. Article 487(2) of the Portuguese Civil Code determines the standard of care, according to which fault in the form of negligence is to be assessed:

> Fault shall be assessed, in the absence of any other legal criterion, by referring to the diligence expected from reasonable person [from a bonus paterfamilias], having regard to the circumstances of the case.

There is a formal difference between Article 487(2) of the Portuguese Civil Code and § 276(2) of the German Civil Code. Article 487(2) of the Portuguese Civil Code refers to the care and diligence expected from a *bonus paterfamilias*. § 276(2) of the German Civil Code refers to the care and diligence expected in daily affairs. That is to say that it refers to the care and diligence expected from a *reasonable person*:

> The person who fails to observe the ordinary care, which is required in everyday life, is guilty of negligence. This means doing what the reasonable man (or woman) would not have done or not doing what they would have done.[323]

There is, however, no substantial difference between the two provisions. The so-called *bonus paterfamilias*, referred to in Article 487(1) of the Portuguese Civil Code, is an average person (an average man or woman) of reasonable care and diligence.

Even if neither the German nor the Portuguese Civil Code state the factors relevant for assessing what the *bonus paterfamilias* would have done – or would not have done – it is submitted that the standard of care is to be established by 'balancing the expected risk, on one hand, and the precautions, on the other: "As the danger increases, so must the precautions increase."'[324] The expected risk is to be assessed by referring to the nature and value of the protected interest, the dangerousness of the activity, the probability that an accident will happen, and the seriousness of the damage resulting from such an accident. The appropriateness of the precautions required to prevent the risk from materializing is to be assessed by referring to the relationship of proximity or reliance between the persons involved, to

322. In Portugal, contrary, for instance, to Germany, the distinction between the various types of negligence is of some significance [on German law, *see*, for instance, B.S. Markesinis/H. Unberath, *The German Law of Torts. A Comparative Treatise*, 84].
323. B.S. Markesinis/H. Unberath, *The German Law of Torts. A Comparative Treatise*, 84.
324. H. Koziol, *Basic Questions of Tort Law from a Germanic Perspective*, 188.

the expertise of the person carrying on the dangerous activity, to the economic and social advantages of such an activity, and to the economic and social disadvantages – especially, to the costs – of the precautionary measures.[325]

The standard of care in Article 487(2) of the Portuguese Civil Code is objective for two reasons. In the first place, it is objective because it requires an abstract assessment. Second, it is objective because it requires an (abstract) assessment of the defendant's behaviour because it requires an (abstract) assessment of the defendant's conduct.

In accordance with a concrete, subjective assessment, the standard of care would be determined by referring to a particular, specific person – to the person of the defendant. That is to say that the standard of care would result from the normal, from the regular, from the usual care and diligence *of the person of the defendant.*

In accordance with an objective, abstract assessment, however, the standard of care would be determined by referring to no particular, specific person. The so-called *bonus paterfamilias* 'is nothing more than the anthropomorphic conception of justice'.[326]

That is to say that the standard of care would result from the normal, from the regular, from the usual care and diligence *of the person of a* bonus paterfamilias – *of the person of a reasonable defendant* – under the circumstances of the case.

In keeping with a concrete, subjective standard, the judge should compare the defendant's care and diligence under that particular, specific circumstance with the defendant's normal care and diligence under similar circumstances.

In the event the defendant acted less carefully – in the event the defendant acted less diligently – than he or she normally did, he or she would be at fault.

In keeping with an objective, abstract standard, the judge should compare the defendant's care and diligence, under that particular, specific circumstance, with a *bonus paterfamilias'* – with a reasonable person's care and diligence.

In the event the defendant acted less carefully, less diligently than a *bonus paterfamilias* – in the event the defendant acted less carefully, less diligently than a reasonable person – he or she would be at fault (he or she would be negligent).

Article 487(2) of the Portuguese Civil Code clearly requires an abstract, objective assessment of fault, for the standard of care is to be determined by referring to 'the diligence expected from reasonable person [from a *bonus paterfamilias*]'.

The reference to an abstract, objective assessment is, however, complemented by a reference to the 'circumstances of the case'.[327] In referring to the circumstances of the case, the judge is to consider socially typical functions. The circumstances of the case, referred to in Article 487(2) of the Portuguese Civil Code, comprehend the social, cultural, and professional environment in which the individual is placed.

325. *See*, for instance, H. Koziol, *Basic Questions of Tort Law from a Germanic Perspective*, 188, and C. van Dam, *European Tort Law*, 234.
326. B.S. Markesinis/H. Unberath, *The German Law of Torts. A Comparative Treatise*, 85.
327. *See, for example*, J.M. Antunes Varela, *Das obrigações em geral* I, 576.

Therefore, instead of a general reference to a single standard – to the *bonus paterfamilias* – Article 487(2) requires the judge to consider a set of specific references, a set of specific standards, applying to specific social groups – e.g., to specific professional groups.[328]

In Portugal – as, for instance, in Germany, France, and England – '[i]f the defendant belongs to a particular group or profession he will be judged against the standard expected to be attained by members of that profession'.[329]

If, for instance, the judge is to evaluate the conduct of a doctor, he or she is to compare the acts and omissions of such a doctor with the ones that we should expect of an average doctor in that particular, specific area of practice – and not simply to the conduct that we should expect from an average common man. A general medical practitioner will have to demonstrate the standard of care expected of general medical practitioners;[330] a specialized medical practitioner will have to demonstrate the standard of care expected of specialized medical practitioners in the same speciality. If, for instance, the judge is to evaluate the conduct of a lawyer, he or she is to compare the acts and omissions of such a lawyer with the ones we should expect from an average lawyer – and not simply to the conduct that we should expect from an average, common man.

The second reason why the standard of care in Article 487(2) is objective lies in the fact that it requires an assessment of the defendant's behaviour or conduct.

In fact, the standard of a *bonus paterfamilias* may apply either to an internal or to an external element. It may apply to an internal element, i.e., to the defendant's will. It may apply to an external element, i.e., to the defendant's behaviour or conduct. If the standards were to apply to the internal element – and to the internal element only – fault would be a defect in the tortfeasor's will. The wrongdoer would be at fault if – and only if – he or she failed to adopt the efforts expected from a *bonus paterfamilias*. If the standard were to apply to the external element, fault would be a defect in the tortfeasor's behaviour or conduct. The wrongdoer would be at fault if he or she failed to adopt the behaviour or conduct expected from a *bonus paterfamilias* – from a reasonable person.[331]

In practical terms, the difference between both concepts of fault is relevant in cases where the tortfeasor's abilities and knowledge are below the abilities and knowledge expected from a reasonable member of the tortfeasor's profession.

In accordance with the concept of *fault as a defect in the defendant's will* (in Portuguese: '*culpa como deficiência da vontade*'), the personal circumstances of the tortfeasor are relevant. The concept of *fault as a defect in the defendant's will* requires that the wrongdoer, *as he or she is – with the abilities he or she has –* applies their best efforts, so as to conform to the relevant standard.[332] If he or she

328. *See, for example*, J.M. Antunes Varela, *Das obrigações em geral* I, 576–577 (fn. 3).
329. B.S. Markesinis/H. Unberath, *The German Law of Torts. A Comparative Treatise*, 85.
330. *See*, for instance, B.S. Markesinis/H. Unberath, *The German Law of Torts. A Comparative Treatise*, 85 – with the following *caveat*: 'however, he will be negligent if he realizes (or ought to realise) that a specialised second opinion on the state of the health of his patient ought to have been obtained but was in fact never obtained'.
331. *See, for example*, J.M. Antunes Varela, *Das obrigações em geral* I, 577–581.
332. *See, for example*, J.M. Antunes Varela, *Das obrigações em geral* I, 578; N.M. Pinto Oliveira, *Princípios de direito dos contratos*, 438–439.

applies their best efforts, failing to perform the expected conduct, for they do not have either the abilities or the knowledge they were expected to have, they would be exempted from liability.

In accordance with the concept of *fault as a defect in the defendant's conduct* (in Portuguese: '*culpa como deficiência da conduta*'), the personal circumstances of the tortfeasor are irrelevant. The concept of *fault as a defect in the defendant's conduct* requires the wrongdoer either to acquire the abilities and knowledge he or she is expected to have or to refrain from exercising that particular, specific profession.[333] If he or she fails to perform the expected conduct, they would not be exempted from liability.

Whether they did or did not exert their best efforts would be immaterial:

> Shortcomings in knowledge or ability, tiredness, nervousness, excitement, or dejection [would be] no defences against liability.[334]

In keeping with the concept of fault as a defect in the defendant's will, the tortfeasor's personal ability and knowledge are always decisive. Someone equipped by nature with below than average abilities would thus be subject to no liability.

In keeping with the concept of fault as a defect in the defendant's conduct, the tortfeasor's personal ability and knowledge are never decisive. 'Someone equipped by nature with below average abilities [would] thus [be] subject to a type of strict liability.'[335]

The fact that he or she lacks average, normal abilities and knowledge should prevent them from participating in social interactions where they are likely to cause harm to others. If they did not refrain from participating in such particular, specific interactions, they should be held liable for their defective behaviour – for their defective conduct.

The foundation for such a strict liability would lie in 'the increased dangerousness emanating from a person not adequately equipped with ability'.[336]

In Germany, the concept of fault is normally defined as a defect in the defendant's conduct:

> The courts apply an objective standard (objektivierter or typisierter Fahrlässigkeitsmaßstab) which means that it is not the tortfeasor's personal knowledge and abilities that are decisive, but the typical knowledge and abilities of the professional group or the social or age group of the tortfeasor. The judge compares the conduct of a doctor with that of a typical doctor and the conduct of a driver with that of a typical driver. The person who does not meet this standard acts negligently, even if he personally cannot be blamed for his conduct.[337]

---

333. *See, for example*, J.M. Antunes Varela, *Das obrigações em geral* I, 578; N.M. Pinto Oliveira, *Princípios de direito dos contratos*, 438–439.
334. C. van Dam, *European Tort Law*, 232 – referring to German law.
335. *See* H. Koziol, *Basic Questions of Tort Law from a Germanic Perspective*, 204.
336. *See* H. Koziol, *Basic Questions of Tort Law from a Germanic Perspective*, 204.
337. C. van Dam, *European Tort Law*, 232.

In Austria, the concept of fault is normally defined as a defect in the defendant's will.

In justifying the preference for concrete, subjective standard in what concerns the tortfeasor's abilities and knowledge, it is argued that an abstract, objective standard would be incompatible with the requirements of human dignity. Liability for 'the increased dangerousness emanating from a person not adequately equipped with ability' leads – 'at least, insofar as the participation in general interactions necessary for an existence compatible with human dignity is concerned– to liability for existing, which will affect such a person particularly seriously given that he is already disadvantaged'.[338]

The rule according to which the tortfeasor's abilities and knowledge are to be assessed against the background of a concrete, subjective standard is, however, subject to exceptions. It applies neither to cases of liability for breach of contract,[339] nor to cases of fault-based, subjective liability of experts,[340] nor to cases of subjective, fault-based liability for the exercise of dangerous activities or for the use of dangerous things.[341]

In Portugal, the German approach has been followed – the concept of fault is defined as a defect in the defendant's conduct. In the first place, it is argued that it fits better the standard of care in Article 487(2) of the Portuguese Civil Code.

Second, it is argued that, in general terms, the results of the concept of fault as a defect in the defendant's conduct are to be accepted, for they are fair.

If the defendant causes damage, for he or she lacks either the abilities or the knowledge he or she is expected to have for being a part of a social or professional group, it is fair that he or she compensates the plaintiff for the damage they caused.[342]

Third, it is argued that, in particular, specific circumstances, where the results of the concept of fault as a defect in the defendant's conduct are not to be accepted – for they are unfair – the judge has the discretionary power to fix compensation at an amount lower than that of the damage caused. In fact, Article 494 of the Portuguese Civil Code explicitly requires the judge to consider 'the degree of fault of the wrongdoer'.[343]

Finally, it is commonly held that fault relates to the 'primary damage', that is, to the infringement – to the violation of the right or the protected interest.

Fault-based, subjective liability depends on the fact that the tortfeasor foresees that his acts or omissions infringe either absolute, subjective rights or objective law – it does not depend on the fact that the tortfeasor foresees that his acts or omissions cause damage.

That is to say that fault does not relate to consequential, 'secondary' damage.

---

338. H. Koziol, *Basic Questions of Tort Law from a Germanic Perspective*, 204.
339. *See* H. Koziol, *Basic Questions of Tort Law from a Germanic Perspective*, 205 ff.
340. *See* H. Koziol, *Basic Questions of Tort Law from a Germanic Perspective*, 207 ff.
341. *See* H. Koziol, *Basic Questions of Tort Law from a Germanic Perspective*, 207 ff.
342. *See, for example*, J.M. Antunes Varela, *Das obrigações em geral* I, 579; N.M. Pinto Oliveira, *Princípios de direito dos contratos*, 440.
343. *See, for example*, N.M. Pinto Oliveira, *Princípios de direito dos contratos*, 440–441.

It is submitted that the difference between both approaches to fault is limited by the criteria referring to the assessment of legal causation – especially by the requirement that the defendant's act or omission is abstractly appropriate to cause damage.[344]

I. On the Proof of Negligence

47. In keeping with Article 487(1), '[i]t shall be incumbent to the injured party to prove the fault of the person who caused the injury, unless there was a legal presumption of fault'.

It is submitted that Article 487(1) applies to liability for the infringement of absolute, subjective rights and, conversely, it is submitted that it does not apply to the following:

In the first place, it is apparent that it does not apply to the cases where there is a presumption of fault, such as to cases considered in Articles 491, 492 and 493.

Second, it is submitted that Article 487(1) does not apply to cases of infringement of legal, statutory provisions intended to safeguard the interests of third parties.

In Germany, there is a distinction between protective norms which prohibit a certain conduct and protective norms which prohibit a certain result.[345]

In the case of protective norms which prohibit a certain result, the plaintiff bears the onus of proving the defendant's fault; in the case of protective norms which prohibit certain conduct, by prescribing specific standards, he or she does not – 'fault will be presumed unless the defendant can positively disprove any fault on his part'. In spite of the fact that no particular, specific provision of the Civil Code refers to the problem, 'the case law has reversed the onus of proof and placed it squarely on the defendant'.[346]

It is submitted that, in Portugal, a corresponding presumption should apply.[347]

Third, it is submitted that Article 487(1) does not apply to cases of infringement of legal duties to prevent the materialization of danger in the context of social, legally relevant contacts (to cases of infringement of the so-called *Verkehrssicherungspflichten*).[348]

---

344. *See* H. Koziol, *Basic Questions of Tort Law from a Germanic Perspective*, 201: 'liability is restricted by objective criteria, in particular adequacy and the protective purpose of the rule on which liability is based'.

345. *See, for example*, C. van Dam, *European Tort Law*, 256.

346. *See* B.S. Markesinis/H. Unberath, *The German Law of Torts. A Comparative Treatise*, 886.

347. *See,* for instance, J.F. Sinde Monteiro, *Responsabilidade por conselhos, recomendações ou informações*, 263; N.M. Pinto Oliveira, 'Sobre o conceito de ilicitude do artigo 483.° do Código Civil', in: *Estudos em homenagem a Francisco José Velozo* (Braga: Associação Jurídica de Braga/Escola de Direito da Universidade do Minho 2002) 521–544, at 543–544 (footnote 61); M. Carneiro da Frada, *Teoria da confiança e responsabilidade civil*, J.F. Sinde Monteiro, 'Rudimentos da responsabilidade civil', 365; A. Menezes Leitão, *Normas de protecção e danos patrimoniais primários*, 650.

348. *See,* for instance, N.M. Pinto Oliveira, 'Sobre o conceito de ilicitude do artigo 483.° do Código Civil', 543–544 (footnote 61).

§4. CAPACITY (INFANTS, MINORS)

I. The Principle According to Which Non-imputable Persons Cannot Be Held Liable for Damages

48. Article 483(1) of the Portuguese Civil Code is to be read in conjunction with Articles 488 and 489. Articles 488 and 489 refer to imputability – to the so-called tortious capacity. It follows from the purpose and from the scope of both Article 488 and Article 489 that imputability refers to the ability – to the competence – to commit torts.

Article 488 requires that, for a person to be held liable, within the framework of subjective, fault-based liability, he or she must be capable of understanding and forming intent:

1. A person who for any reason was incapable of understanding or of forming intent when the injurious event occurred, shall not be liable for its consequences, unless he wilfully caused himself to be in that condition, and the condition was temporary.
2. Persons who are aged less than seven years or are subject to a psychiatric disorder shall be deemed not to bear any liability.

In the first place, Article 488(1) aims at defining imputability or tortious capacity.

In accordance with Article 488(1), imputability depends on two elements.

On the one hand, imputability depends on an intellectual element. The tortfeasor must be capable of understanding – he or she must be able to realize the content and the consequences of their acts and omissions.[349] On the other hand, it depends on a voluntary element. The tortfeasor must be capable of forming intent – he or she must be able to conform their acts or omissions according to that understanding.[350]

Second, Article 488(1) aims at establishing a general principle.

In general, there is no liability if the person is not imputable. Considering that imputability requires the person to be capable of understanding and forming intent, that is to say, that, in general, there is no liability if the person, at the moment of the relevant act or omission, was incapable of understanding or forming intent.[351]

Third, Article 488(2) aims at complementing the general principle with two particular, specific rules:

---

349. *See, for example*, M.M. Veloso [Gomes], 'Children as Tortfeasors under Portuguese Law', in: M. Martin-Casals (ed.), *Children in Tort Law*. Part I: *Children as Tortfeasors* (Wien/New York: Springer 2006) 311–343, at 312–313.

350. *See, for example*, M.M. Veloso [Gomes], 'Children as Tortfeasors under Portuguese Law', 313: 'Capacity to understand (art. 488, 1 CC) means capacity to realize the consequences of one's own acts and to evaluate them. In modern terminology, we could say that it means intellectual capacity and emotional intelligence.'

351. *See, for example*, in general terms, H. Koziol, *Basic Questions of Tort Law from a Germanic Perspective*, 200: 'Ultimately only such persons can be blamed for their conduct as are in possession of the necessary powers of discernment, i.e., who are in a position to recognise the wrongfulness of their conduct and to behave duly and properly.'

- first, Article 488(2) establishes a presumption of lack of imputability in minors younger than seven years old;[352]
- second, Article 488(2) establishes a presumption of lack of imputability in persons whose legal competence has been limited, on the grounds of a mental or psychological disorder.

It follows from Article 488(1) and (2) that Portuguese law does not set a specific age from which people may be held liable. Therefore, '[c]hildren can be [held] liable if they have the capacity to understand the consequences of their acts and the capacity to act according to that understanding'.[353] In spite of the fact that Article 488(2) does not set a specific age, the seven-year threshold is usually respected. In practical terms, the rebuttable presumption in Article 488(2) has never been rebutted.[354]

II. Deviations to the Principle According to Which Non-imputable Persons Cannot Be Held Liable for Damages

49. The principle affirmed in Article 488(1), according to which incompetent persons are not to be held liable for their behaviour, is limited by the exception enshrined in Article 489.

In keeping with Article 489(1), 'if the act causing the damage has been performed by a non-imputable person, the said person, on grounds of equity, may be sentenced to make total or partial compensation for the damage, to the extent that compensation cannot be obtained from a third party charged with the duty of supervision'.[355]

In the cases referred to in Article 483(1), liability is based upon fault. In the cases referred to in Article 498(1) – for there can be no fault of non-imputable persons – liability is based upon equity. In the cases referred to in Article 483(1), liability is based upon the concept of commutative, corrective justice. In the cases referred to in Article 489(1), liability is based upon the concept of distributive justice. Liability under Article 489(1) is 'strict liability […] for risks related to personal status or circumstances'.[356]

In the first place, Article 489(1) requires the plaintiff to consider whether compensation can be obtained from the persons charged with the duty of supervision.

352. For an assessment of the rule in Art. 488(2), *see* M.M. Veloso [Gomes], 'Children as Tortfeasors under Portuguese Law', 312: 'The age of seven was clearly chosen due to the German influence and the acceptance of the reasons of the German approach. It does not correspond to a marked age in terms of the Portuguese educational program, since children start primary school at the age of six years. Still, in terms of moral development and of knowledge of social rules, the age of seven is regarded as a starting point.'
353. *See* M.M. Veloso [Gomes], 'Children as Tortfeasors under Portuguese Law', 311.
354. M.M. Veloso [Gomes], 'Children as Tortfeasors under Portuguese Law', 311.
355. Article 489(1) of the Portuguese Civil Code roughly corresponds to the first part of § 829 of the German Civil Code.
356. M.M. Veloso [Gomes], 'Children as Tortfeasors under Portuguese Law', 317.

Article 491 of the Portuguese Civil Code reads that '[a] person who is bound by law or by contract to exercise supervision over a person on account of minority, or of his mental or physical condition, is bound to make compensation for any damage which the latter unlawfully does to a third party, unless he fulfils his duty of supervision, or if the damage would have occurred notwithstanding the proper exercise of supervision'.

It follows from Article 491 that compensation cannot be obtained from a third party if there is none bound, either by law or by contract, to exercise supervision, if the person bound to exercise supervision demonstrates that he or she properly exercised supervision if he or she demonstrates that damage would have occurred notwithstanding the proper exercise of supervision and if he or she is insolvent (if they have no means).

Second, if compensation cannot be obtained from a third party, the plaintiff is to consider whether compensation can be obtained from the non-imputable person.

Article 489(1) of the Portuguese Civil Code requires the act of the non-imputable person to be unlawful. Furthermore, Article 489(1) requires that the act of the non-imputable person is of such a nature that in the case it was the act of an imputable person, it would meet the requirement of fault. '[T]he [non imputable person] must have acted in such a way that, if he/she were imputable, he/she would be liable in tort'.[357]

Finally, Article 489(1) requires that equity justifies total or partial liability.[358]

Even if all requirements are met, the plaintiff's right to compensation is subject to three limits. First, the judge has the discretionary power to decide whether the non-imputable person is to be held liable.[359] Article 489(1) reads that the non-imputable person '*may be sentenced to make* ... compensation for the damage' (emphasis added).

Second, the judge has the discretionary power to determine whether the non-imputable person is to be held totally or partially liable.[360] Article 489(1) reads that the non-imputable person 'may be sentenced to make total or partial compensation'.

Third, in keeping with Article 489(2), compensation on the grounds of equity, as provided for in Article 498(1), is subject to a limit:

> Compensation shall be calculated so as not to deprive the non imputable person of the means which he needs for his own maintenance according to his status and condition in life and for the fulfilment of his statutory duties to furnish maintenance to others.[361]

It follows from Article 489(2) that the amount of compensation can interfere neither with the non-imputable person's right to maintenance nor with third parties' rights of maintenance, i.e., 'with the right of maintenance that third parties can

357. M.M. Veloso [Gomes], 'Children as Tortfeasors under Portuguese Law', 317.
358. M.M. Veloso [Gomes], 'Children as Tortfeasors under Portuguese Law', 316.
359. M.M. Veloso [Gomes], 'Children as Tortfeasors under Portuguese Law', 317–318.
360. M.M. Veloso [Gomes], 'Children as Tortfeasors under Portuguese Law', 317–318.
361. Article 489(2) of the Portuguese Civil Code roughly corresponds to the second part of § 829 of the German Civil Code.

claim from the non imputable person'. In what concerns the right of maintenance of the non-imputable person, it is submitted that the limit established in Article 489(2) 'goes beyond the traditional content of maintenance'. '[I]n contrast to the general rule (Article 2003 of the Portuguese Civil Code), "status" and "condition" are to be taken into consideration'.[362]

362. M.M. Veloso [Gomes], 'Children as Tortfeasors under Portuguese Law', 318.

Chapter 2. Specific Cases of Liability (Are All Tortfeasors Subject to the Same Rules?)

§1. Liability of Professionals

I. In General (Is There a Higher Standard of Care?)

50. Liability of legal practitioners, liability of medical practitioners, as well as the liability of builders and architects, are instances of professional liability.[363]

In general, the required standard of care is that of a *bonus paterfamilias* in the concrete situation. Therefore, the professional has a higher standard of care compared with an ordinary citizen.

II. Medical Practitioners

A. *Liability of Medical Practitioners*

51. There is an important distinction between medical practice in *public hospitals* and medical practice in *private hospitals*. In public medicine, i.e., in the case of medical practice in public hospitals, the administrative courts are competent, and the law concerning *non-contractual, tortious liability* of the State applies (Law No. 67/2007, 31 December).[364] In private medicine, judicial courts are competent, and the Civil Code applies. In most cases, both the parties and the courts refer to the principles and rules on *contractual liability*. The requirements for establishing liability are similar in both jurisdictions. There are only some differences concerning the burden of proof, the limitation for action and vicarious liability. In the case of public medicine, the doctor is only liable in redress and only if he acted with gross negligence;[365] however, in public medicine, the patient has the burden of proof since it is considered an extra-contractual relation. In a private law relationship, the burden of proving fault is (normally) on the side of the doctor.[366]

Within the sphere of private medicine, there is an important distinction between medical practice within and without the framework of a contractual relationship between doctor and patient.

---

363. For a comprehensive survey of particular principles and rules regarding particular, specific professions, *see* J.C. Brandão Proença. 'A responsabilidade civil extracontratual nos 50 anos de vigência do Código Civil: um olhar à luz do direito contemporâneo', in: E. Vaz Sequeira/F. Oliveira e Sá (eds), *Edição comemorativa do cinquentenário do Código Civil* (Lisboa: Universidade Católica Editora 2017) 313–388, at 323–324.
364. The National Health Service is the largest health provider, thus administrative courts receive a substantial number of tort cases – *see, for example*, André Dias Pereira, 'Responsabilidade civil: O médico entre o público e o privado', 89 Boletim da Faculdade de Direito [da Universidade de Coimbra] (2013) 253–303.
365. Article 8(1) Law No. 67/2007, 31 December.
366. Concerning the burden of proof, *see*: Jorge Ribeiro Faria, O ónus da prova na responsabilidade civil médica – reflexões em torno do direito alemão, [2004] *Revista da Faculdade de Direito da Universidade do Porto*, Vol. 1, 117–195.

Within the framework of a contractual relationship between doctor and patient, there is an important distinction between obligations of means and obligations of result. Even if there are specific medical procedures, such as medical analysis or medical tests, which may hypothetically be considered, on a case-by-case basis, as obligations of the result, it is submitted that the physician's obligations are, in general, obligations of means and not of result.[367]

The standard applied to evaluate medical liability is an objective one. Decisive is the competence of the reasonably careful and competent practitioner in his area of competence. The medical profession has a very relevant role in determining the standard of care. First, the decisions of the Medical Association's disciplinary board are normally taken into consideration. Second, medical expert-witnesses are heard by the judges, and their opinion is normally respected. Although the patient has, in general, the burden of proof of the failure to comply with the standards, in some cases, the courts accepted an inversion of the burden of proof.[368]

There are only some exceptional cases of strict liability (clinical trials,[369] organ donation,[370] exposure to radiations,[371] product liability and vicarious liability).

A *no-fault compensation system* is not provided, nor is it being discussed at a political level. Some academics agree with the so-called Scandinavian model.[372]

---

367. *See* A.G. Dias Pereira, Direitos dos pacientes e responsabilidade médica (Coimbra: Centro de Direito Biomédico/Coimbra Editora 2015) at 624 ff.
368. For example, Supreme Court of Justice 24 Apr. 2007 ([2007] CJ-STJ, I, 105–113): during an aesthetic surgery arose a serious adverse reaction to anaesthesia and the patient died. This decision of the Supreme Court is important since it opted clearly for the doctrine according to which the *inversion of the burden of proof* typical on contract law also applies in medical contract. The doctors were found liable since they could not prove that the death was attributable to an unexpected reaction of the patient's physiology to the anaesthetic drugs, rather than to a malperformance of the anaesthetic procedure. It had been proved that the anaesthetist had no previous contact with the patient and had not read her medical file thoroughly.
369. Law No. 21/2014 of 16 Apr. 2104 (Clinical Research Act) (with amendments), Art. 15°, 1. *See* for a similar norm in previous legislation – J.C. Loureiro/A. Dias Pereira, 'Portugal Country Report', in E. Deutsch/H.L Schreiber/A. Spickhoff/J. Taupitz, *Clinical Trials in Medicine – European Rules on Trial*, Springer, 2004, 259–293.
370. Law n° 12/93 of 22 Apr. 1993 (with amendments) (Harvesting and Transplanting Human Organs and Tissues) – Art. 9 (Right to assistance and compensation).
371. Article 178.° of Decree-Law No. 108/2018 applies for private entities and Law 67/2007 risk liability of public entities.
372. Rui Prista Cascão, A Responsabilidade Civil e a Segurança Sanitária, [2004] *Lex Medicinae – Revista Portuguesa de Direito da Saúde*, no. 1., 97–106. This article analyses the shifts in medical malpractice in recent years and criticizes the dominant approach to prevention of medical injury based on deterrence on the provider level. He presents a critique to the deterrence-based approach to the prevention of medical injury, and points out the advantages of a systems approach, where the cooperation of healthcare providers in the design of safety strategies achieves a more efficient and pro-active approach to prevent medical injury. Several successful examples of liability systems, such as the Scandinavian no-fault insurance schemes or French law after the 2002 reform, are presented to substantiate the advantages of prevention through risk management in a systems approach over preventive focus based on deterrence throughout provider specific liability in the context of a blame culture. The author concludes by providing some guidelines that are essential to render concrete that model of prevention: (1) Shift from provider specific liability towards institutional liability of hospitals; (2) Strict liability in case of injury caused by technological risks or hospital-acquired infections and (3) Alternative resolution of disputes and non-litigious, non-adversarial settlement of claims.

With regard to the first source of medical liability (technical errors), the standard of care can be derived from the actual state of medical care.[373]

With regard to the second source of medical liability, the violation of the rights of patients, Portugal ratified the *European Convention on Human Rights and Biomedicine*. This Convention consolidates some Patient's Rights that were already provided in the Criminal Code (e.g., Professional confidentiality, informed consent) or other legislation. Previously expressed wishes and the role of the family in the informed consent process should, however, be better clarified by national law.

Concerning informed consent, Portuguese criminal law, similar to Austrian criminal law, only aims to protect liberty; however, this solution is inconvenient and inadequate for civil law. Thus, also *physical integrity* (and *life)* are interests protected by tort law and both pecuniary and non-pecuniary damage shall be compensated in case of violation of informed consent.

The most important goal of informed consent is that the patient has an opportunity to be an informed participant in personal health care decisions. It is generally accepted that complete informed consent includes a discussion of the following elements: (a) the nature of the decision/procedure, (b) reasonable alternatives to the proposed intervention, (c) the relevant risks, benefits and uncertainties related to each alternative, (d) assessment of patient understanding, and (e) the acceptance of the intervention by the patient.

In order for the patient's consent to be valid, he must be considered competent to make the decision (minors and incompetent adults are subject to substitute consent) at hand, and his consent must be voluntary. The informed consent process should be seen as an invitation to participate in health care decisions. Comprehension on the part of the patient is equally as important as the information provided. The discussion should be conducted in layperson's terms, and the patient's understanding should be assessed along the way.

The right to be informed is not unlimited, as there is a *therapeutic exception;* that is, information may remain undisclosed if it would endanger the life or health of the patient. The patient has not only the right to be informed but also the *right not to be informed* as well (Article 10(2) Convention on Human Rights and Biomedicine). If the danger of not being informed, for the patient himself or others, outweighs the benefits, the information shall be provided.

If it is clear that the physician has an obligation to inform, there are doubts about how thorough the information shall be.[374]

The duty to inform includes risks, secondary effects, alternatives and many other subjects that are analysed in detail. Therapeutic privilege and the right not to know are also provided in the Criminal Code and in the Convention on Human Rights and Biomedicine, ratified by Portugal in 2001. Consent and refusal of treatment are

373. J. Sinde Monteiro/M.M. Veloso, 'Portugal', in M. Faure/H. Koziol, *Cases on Medical Malpractice in a Comparative Perspective*, Springer, 2001, 172–187.

374. PEL/Barendrecht/Jansen/Loos/Pinna/Cascão/van Gulijk, *Principles of European Law, Service Contracts*, 2007, Chapter 7, 837–838.

regulated in Portuguese criminal law and civil law: there is a right to refuse treatment even if that leads to death. The exceptions to informed consent include emergency and legal authorization (namely, compulsory internment of a person affected by a severe mental disorder).[375]

In Case Law, it is accepted that medical liability arises not only from technical errors but also from a failure to inform the patient properly or from failure to obtain his informed consent.[376] Two very important decisions were published in the last couple of years.

In the Judgment of the Supreme Court of Justice of 2 June 2015, the liability of the defendant for the *violation of informed consent* and for pecuniary damage and non-pecuniary damage was fully accepted, considering the right to self-determination of the patient in healthcare and the right to physical integrity.

On 22 March 2018, the Supremo Tribunal de Justiça (STJ) produced an important ruling in an increasingly complex and important field in the life of the Portuguese: medical liability for breach of adequate information. The Supreme Court of Justice upheld that the conviction applied the theory of the *lack of informed consent*. According to the STJ, it was clear from the file that she had not been informed that in her case there was a greater risk of perforation than normal, given that she had previously been operated on with a malignant tumour in the colon, which had prevented her from deciding not to take the risks of drilling. And this loss of opportunity to decide gave rise to the right to compensation. As the patient was retired, there were almost no pecuniary damages; the compensation was EUR 28,000.00 since the patient suffered pain for some months and had to carry a colostomy bag for several months, which disabled her from social activities. The Supreme Court made a strict interpretation of the doctrine since the standard patient criteria were not considered enough. The Court decided for the *concrete patient criteria*, that is, the doctor should have explained the concrete risks of the concrete patient: a woman of old age who had undergone previous surgeries had a much higher risk of perforation. Therefore, general information about that risk was considered not valid; therefore, the medical intervention was not justified by a valid informed consent, and the risks that materialized had to be compensated by the doctor. This was a leading case in this area and quite naturally created an important controversy in the medical profession.

III. Legal Practitioners

52. The concept of legal practitioners requires definition. It can be limited to advocates, attorneys of law and barristers (*advogados*),[377] but it can also be

375. *See* André G. Dias Pereira, O Consentimento Informado na Relação Médico-Paciente. Estudo de Direito Civil, Coimbra Editora, 2004.

376. André Dias Pereira, A Consagração do Direito ao Consentimento Informado na Jurisprudência Portuguesa Recente, *in* Estudos em Homenagem ao Prof. Doutor Guilherme, J. Loureiro, A.D. Pereira, C. Barbosa (eds), Vol. 3, *Segurança do Paciente e Consentimento Informado* (Almedina, 2016) 161–179.

377. On the liability of attorneys of law and barristers, *see*, for instance, J.C. Moitinho de Almeida, *Responsabilidade civil dos advogados* (Coimbra: Coimbra Editora 1985); O. Guedes da Costa, 'A

extended to solicitors (*solicitadores*) and to notaries (*notários*). In the following, the concept will be taken to comprehend all three categories. In Portugal, the difference between attorneys of law and solicitors is quite strict. First, while attorneys of law and barristers necessarily hold a law degree, solicitors do not, for they may simply hold a solicitor's degree. Second, while attorneys of law and barristers have rights of audience before courts of law, solicitors do not.

A. *Liability of Attorneys of Law, Barristers and Solicitors*

1. Liability for the Practice of Acts Reserved to Attorneys of Law, Barristers and Solicitors

53. In what concerns attorneys of law, barristers and solicitors, Law No. 10/2024 of 19 January 2024 determines acts that can only be practised either by attorneys of law and barristers registered at the Bar Council (Ordem dos Advogados) or by solicitors registered at the Solicitor's Council (Ordem dos Solicitadores e dos Agentes de Execução). If someone being neither an attorney of law nor a solicitor practices an act reserved to attorneys of law, barristers and solicitors may be held liable. On the one hand, he or she may be held liable towards his or her client. In that case, a presumption of fault applies.[378] On the other hand, he or she may be held liable towards the Bar Council and/or the Solicitor's Council.[379] It follows from Law No. 10/2024 that damages awarded either to the Bar Council or to the Solicitor's Council are to be applied in actions aimed at preventing third parties from practising acts reserved to attorneys of law, barristers and solicitors.

2. Civil Liability of Attorneys of Law and Barristers under the Regulation of the Bar Council

54. The Regulation of the Bar Council (*Estatuto da Ordem dos Advogados*), approved by Law No. 145/2015 of 9 September 2015,[380] refers to civil liability of attorneys of law and barristers in two provisions. In the first place, it refers to the civil liability of lawyers in Article 104. Second, it refers to the civil liability of intern lawyers in Article 196, paragraph (5), sub-paragraph (b).

Article 104, paragraph (1) provides that every practising lawyer is required to subscribe to compulsory insurance. The minimum amount of compulsory insurance shall be determined by the General Council of the Bar at a fixed amount, equal or

---

responsabilidade civil profissional do advogado', in: *Responsabilidade civil profissional* (Lisboa: Centro de Estudos Judiciários 2017), available at http://www.cej.mj.pt/cej/recursos/ebooks/civil/eb_ResponsabilidadeProfissional.pdf.

378. *See* Art. 15, para. (1), of Law No. 10/2024 of 19 Jan. 2024.
379. *See* Art. 15(2) of Law No. 10/2024 of 19 Jan. 2024.
380. Recently amendmed by Law No. 6/2024 of 19 Jan. 2024.

superior to EUR 250,000.[381] Article 104, paragraph (3) provides that every practising lawyer who subscribed to compulsory insurance is to benefit from a ceiling to his/her professional liability. The maximum amount of professional liability for slight negligence is limited to the minimum amount of compulsory insurance.

It should be emphasized that such a ceiling does not apply to cases of either wilful or grossly negligent misconduct. Furthermore, it should be emphasized that such a ceiling does not apply to cases where the practising lawyer declared that he did not want his or her professional liability to be subject to any limit [*see* Article 104, paragraph (4)].

3. Civil Liability of Solicitors under the Regulation of the Solicitor's Council

55. The Regulation of the Solicitor's Council (*Estatuto da Ordem dos Solicitadores e dos Agentes de Execução*), approved by Law No. 154/2015 of 14 September 2015,[382] refers to civil liability of solicitors in Article 123 and to civil liability of intern solicitors in Article 135.

Article 123 corresponds to Article 104 of the Regulation of the Bar Council and Article 135, paragraph (b) corresponds to Article 196, paragraph (5), sub-paragraph (b) of the Regulation of the Bar Council.

4. Case Law on Contractual Liability of Attorneys of Law, Barristers and Solicitors

56. With regard to liability in contracts of attorneys of law and barristers, the Supreme Court has established two fundamental principles. In the first place, contractual obligations of attorneys only involve a duty of best efforts.[383] Second, there shall be no liability of the lawyer, whenever he takes a decision that is to be included in the scope of his prudential, technical autonomy.[384] It follows that the lawyer will only be held liable if there is either intentional or grossly negligent misconduct.

In many, if not in most cases, the court condemns attorneys of law, barristers and solicitors for compensating plaintiffs for damages resulting from the loss of a chance.[385]

---

381. On the interpretation of Art. 104 of the Regulation of the Bar Council (Estatuto da Ordem dos Advogados), *see* the judgment of the Portuguese Supreme Court of 14 Dec. 2016, delivered by Justice António da Silva Gonçalves.
382. Amendmed by Law No. 7/2024 of 19 Jan. 2024.
383. *See*, for instance, the judgment of the Portuguese Supreme Court of 30 Apr. 2015, delivered by Justice Maria dos Prazeres Beleza, and the judgment of the Portuguese Supreme Court of 23 Mar. 2017, delivered by Justice Salazar Casanova.
384. *See* the judgment of the Portuguese Supreme Court of 23 Mar. 2017, delivered by Justice Salazar Casanova.
385. *See*, for instance, the judgment of the Portuguese Supreme Court of 30 Apr. 2015, delivered by Justice Maria dos Prazeres Beleza, as well as the judgments of 10 Feb. 2016 and 30 Mar. 2017, delivered by Justices Gabriel Catarino and Olindo Geraldes, respectively. More recently, the judgment No. 2/2022 of the Portuguese Supreme Court of 26 Jan. 2022, delivered by Justice Ana Paula Boularot.

57. With regard to liability in tort towards third parties, the Civil Procedure Code contains a provision holding legal practitioners liable for damages resulting from bad faith litigation.

Article 542 of the Civil Procedure Code defines bad faith litigation. 'He shall be deemed in bad faith who, either wilfully or with gross negligence, files a claim, or opposes a claim, being aware of the fact that either the claim or the opposition have no legal ground; invokes facts that have not occurred, or have not occurred in the way the party at question depicts them, or withholds facts that he or she knows have occurred, and are relevant to the decision; grossly infringes the duty to co-operate with the court; uses the legal process in a way that is manifestly to be blamed, with the purpose of achieving an unlawful purpose, of preventing the discovery of truth, of making it more difficult for the justice to follow its course, or to delay the enforcement of the decision.' In keeping with Article 544 of the Civil Procedure Code, the attorney of law, barrister, or solicitor may be held liable for bad faith litigation: Whenever the attorney of law, barrister or solicitor of the litigant has been directly and personally responsible for the acts showing his or her bad faith, the court shall communicate the fact to the Bar Council (Ordem dos Advogados) so as to apply the corresponding penalty and condemn the attorney to satisfy the other party on the part of the costs and damages resulting from such litigations.[386]

IV. Builders and Architects

58. There is an important difference between the liability of both architects and engineers and the liability of builders. Liability of architects and engineers results from defects in designing the project. Liability of builders results from defects in carrying out the project designed by architects and engineers. In spite of the fact that contractual liability tends to be more important than non-contractual, tortious liability, architects, engineers and builders may be held liable both in a contract and in tort.

A. Liability of Builders[387]

59. In the case of builders, there is no discussion as to the classification of the contract. Contracts to carry out a building project qualify as contracts to produce a work (*contratos de empreitada*) in the sense of Article 1207 of the Civil Code.

386. *See* the judgment of the Portuguese Supreme Court of 2 Jun. 2016, delivered by Justice António Joaquim Piçarra.

387. On the liability of builders, *see* P. Romano Martinez, *Cumprimento defeituoso. Em especial, na compra e venda e na empreitada* (Coimbra: Livraria Almedina 1994); P. Romano Martinez, *Direito das obrigações (parte especial). – Contratos – Compra e venda. Locação. Empreitada* 461 ff.; L. Menezes Leitão, *Direito das* obrigações, vol. III – *Contratos em especial* 11th edition (Coimbra: Livraria Almedina 2016); P. de Albuquerque/M. Assis Raimundo, *Direito das obrigações. Contratos em especial*, vol. II – *Contrato de empreitada*, 2nd edition (Coimbra: Livraria Almedina 2013); J. Cura Mariano, *Responsabilidade contratual do empreiteiro pelos defeitos das obra*, 6th edition (Coimbra: Livraria Almedina 2015); J. Sinde Monteiro, 'Responsabilidade civil do construtor', in: 16–19 *Revista de direito e economia* (1993) 723–730; A.C. Guedes, 'A responsabilidade do construtor no contrato de empreitada', in: *Contratos. Actualidade e evolução* (Porto: Universidade

Article 1208 of the Civil Code sets the standard according to which the contract to produce work is to be performed. It reads that '[t]he contractor must carry out the work in accordance with the terms agreed, and without defects that exclude or reduce either the value of the work or its suitability for normal use or the use set out in the contract'. In the case of builders, the standard in Article 1208 of the Civil Code is supplemented by Article 17 of Law No. 41/2015 of 3 June 2015 on the exercise of building activities, and Article 17 of Law No. 41/2015 reads that builders must carry out works under their responsibility conforming to the contract and complying with relevant laws and regulations.

In what concerns liability towards the owner of the work, general principles and rules apply.

The common scheme of remedies provided for in Articles 798 ff. of the Portuguese Civil Code is supplemented by a specific set of four remedies in Articles 1221 and 1222. Article 1221 recognizes the owner of the work the right to require the contractor to eliminate the work's defects and, in the case that elimination of the defects is impossible, the owner of the work has the right to require the contractor to build a new construction. Article 1222 recognizes that the owner of the work has the right to require the contractor to reduce the price and the right to terminate the contract. Article 1223 explains that neither of the rights provided for in Articles 1221 and 1222 rule out the general provisions on damages. It follows from the general provisions that contractual liability of builders depends on fault[388] and that fault is presumed.[389]

In what concerns liability towards third parties, there are four important things to be stressed. In the first place, the owner of the work is not liable for damages caused by the contractor to third parties. In fact, non-contractual, tortious liability for the behaviour of others depends on subordination,[390] and there is no subordination in the relationship between the owner of the work and the contractor.[391] Second, builders may be held liable for damages caused to third parties having a particular, specific connection with the owner of the work, for they have purchased the building from him. Third, builders may be held liable for damages caused to third parties having no connection whatsoever with the owner of the work. Fourth, and finally, it should be stressed that builders cannot be exempted from liability by arguing that either the architecture or the engineering project was defective. In that case, they

Católica 1997) 315–330; P. Romano Martinez, 'Compra e venda e empreitada', in: *Comemorações dos 35 anos do Código Civil e dos 25 anos da Reforma de 1977,* vol. III – *Direito das obrigações* (Coimbra: Coimbra Editora 2006) 235–263; J.L. Bonifácio Ramos, 'Responsabilidade civil dos intervenientes no processo de construção', in: *Estudos em Homenagem a Miguel Galvão Teles,* vol. II (Coimbra: Livraria Almedina 2012) 723–745, and H. Sousa Antunes, 'A responsabilidade civil dos intervenientes no processo de construção', in: 51 *Cadernos de direito privado* (2015) 3–25.

388. *See* Portuguese Civil Code, Art. 798.
389. *See* Portuguese Civil Code, Art. 799(1).
390. *See* Portuguese Civil Code, Art. 500(1).
391. *See* J. Sinde Monteiro, 'Responsabilidade civil do construtor', at 726.

must inform the owner of the work of the defect, and they will only be exempted from liability if the owner confirms that the work is to be carried out in conformity with the defective project.[392]

– As to liability for damages caused to third parties having a particular, specific connection with the owner of the work (i.e., as to liability towards acquiring third parties):

> Builders' liability towards acquiring third parties results from Article 1225 of the Civil Code: 'If the purpose of the contract is the construction, modification or repair of buildings or other real estate intended by its nature for long-term use and, within five years counting from delivery, or in the course of the agreed guarantee period, the work, due to a defect in […] the construction, modification or repair […] totally of partially falls down, or risks of falling down, or at least presents grave, serious defects, the contractor is responsible for the damage sustained by the owner of the work as well as by the damage sustained by any acquiring third party.' It is submitted that such liability results from the principle according to which acquiring third party is to be treated as the owner of the work himself.[393] Therefore, builders' liability towards acquiring third parties qualifies as contractual liability.[394]

– As to liability for damages caused to third parties having no connection with the owner of the work:

In the absence of particular, specific principles, Article 483(1) of the Civil Code applies:

> Whoever, whether by wilful misconduct (dolus) or by negligence unlawfully infringes the rights of another person or any legal provision intended to safeguard the interests of others must compensate the injured party for damage arising from such violation.

It should be emphasized that laws and regulations applicable to builders frequently qualify as legal provisions intended to safeguard the interests of others and that, even if there is no specific law or regulation, the doctrine of the *Verkehrssicherungspflichten* applies. If a builder, by his activity or through his property, 'establishes in everyday life a source of potential danger which is likely to affect the interests and rights of others', he is 'obliged to ensure their protection against the risks thus created by him'.[395]

Furthermore, in the case of urban projects (*operações urbanísticas*), Article 483 of the Civil Code is supplemented by Article 100-A of Decree-Law No. 555/99 of 16 December 1999, as amended by Decree-Law No. 136/2014 of 9 September 2014.

392. *See*, for instance, the judgment of the Portuguese Supreme Court of 29 May 2012, delivered by Justice Alves Velho.
393. *See*, for instance, the judgment of the Portuguese Supreme Court of 29 May 2012, delivered by Justice Alves Velho.
394. *See*, for instance, H. Sousa Antunes, 'A responsabilidade civil dos intervenientes no processo de construção', at 9.
395. *See* B.S. Markesinis/H. Unberath, *The German Law of Torts. A Comparative Treatise*, 86.

Decree-Law No. 555/99 of 16 December 1999 refers to the legal framework of the building (*regime jurídico da edificação e da construção*) and applies to all urban projects (*operações urbanísticas*). Article 2, paragraph (j), of Decree-Law No. 555/99 contains a broad definition of urban projects (*operações urbanísticas*) comprehending virtually all acts aimed at building using constructionsor using the soil, and Article 100-A (1) states a general principle – all legal persons that violate the duties inherent to their activity, arising either from a contract, from the law or from applicable regulations, are to be held liable for damages caused to third parties, as well as for the costs of restoring the situation which would exist if the urban order (*ordem urbanística*) had not been violated.

It should be emphasized that liability under Article 100(1) of Decree-Law No. 555/99 is fault-based, subjective liability. Article 100(1) explicitly refers to wilful misconduct and negligence. Such fault-based, subjective liability is to affect virtually all persons responsible for the urban project. They will be held joint and severally liable.[396]

Furthermore, it should be emphasized that builders may be subject to liability under Articles 492(1) and (2) and 493(1) of the Portuguese Civil Code.

Article 492(1) reads that '[t]he owner of a building, or any other facility, which falls down due to a construction or maintenance defect, shall be held liable for all damage caused […]'. The contractor may be held liable under Article 492(1), for instance, if a scaffold falls down.[397] Article 492(2) reads that '[i]f the damage is caused by a maintenance defect, only the person under a statutory or contractual duty to maintain the building shall be held liable', and the contractor may be the person under a duty to maintain the building. Article 493(1) reads that '[w]hoever detains movable or immovable things, and is bound to supervise them, as well as whoever is bound to supervise animals, shall be held liable for any damage caused by such things, or by such animals […]', and the contractor may detain immovable things, and be bound to supervise them. Article 493(2) reads that '[w]hoever causes damage to another person when performing a dangerous activity, is bound to make compensation for such a damage, unless he demonstrates he has taken all reasonable steps to prevent it', and the building activity may qualify as dangerous.

Compensation to the owner of the work, as well as to any acquiring third party, may comprehend both pecuniary loss and non-pecuniary loss. In the case of non-pecuniary loss, it may include damages arising from impediments to the use of the building.[398]

Article 11 of Law No. 41/2015 requires builders either to have an economical and financial capacity that guarantees the performance of the contract or to subscribe to third-party insurance that covers liability for the consequences of defective performance. Article 19 extends the rule to cases where builders are organized in joint ventures.

---

396. *See* Decree-Law No. 555/99 of 16 Dec. 1999, as amended by Decree-Law No. 136/2014 of 9 Sep. 2014, Art. 100–A(2), (3) and (4).
397. The example has been taken from J. Sinde Monteiro, 'Responsabilidade civil do construtor', at 727 (fn. 9).
398. *See*, for instance, the judgment of the Portuguese Supreme Court 14 Dec. 2016, delivered by Justice Tomé Gomes.

B. Liability of Architects and Engineers

60. In what concerns architects and engineers, there is a discussion as to the classification of the contract. It has been argued that the contract to design a project qualifies as a contract to produce a work. Article 1207 of the Civil Code defines contract to produce a work as 'the contract under which one of the parties undertakes the obligation to carry out a certain work for the other, for a determined price', and it has been argued that both corporeal and non-corporeal, intellectual works would fall within the scope of the legal definition.[399] It has been argued, however, that the contract to design a project never qualifies as a contract to produce a work, for *work* in the sense of Article 1207 could only be a corporeal, material work.[400] The Portuguese Supreme Court seems to favour the second approach.[401] Contracts of architects and engineers to design a project would be contracts for the provision of services, in the sense of Article 1154 of the Civil Code. In both cases, one of the parties – the architect or engineer – undertakes to provide the other party with a given result from his or her intellectual work. In spite of the fact that they are contracts for the provision of services, and contracts for the provision of services can take the form of mandate, deposit and contracts to produce a work, the Supreme Court holds that contracts of architects and engineers are not contracts to produce a work.

In what concerns contractual and non-contractual, tortious liability of both architects and engineers, general principles and rules are supplemented by Law No. 31/2009 of 3 July 1999, as amended by Law No. 25/2018 of 14 June 2018, and by Decree No. 555/99 of 16 December 1999, as amended by Decree-Law No. 10/2024 of 8 January 2024.

Law No. 31/2009 refers to the professional qualification required by all persons responsible for designing building projects.

Article 4(1) of Law No. 31/2009 requires building projects to be subscribed to either by architects or by engineers, and Article 4(2) requires them to associate with a project team (*equipa de projecto*). Article 19(1) of Law No. 31/2009 holds architects and engineers liable for all damages caused to third parties as a result of their own conduct. In accordance with the general principle in Article 483 of the Portuguese Civil Code, liability under Article 19(1) of Law No. 31/2009 depends on fault – architects and engineers are to be held liable for negligent infringements of their professional duties and for negligent infringements only. Article 19(1) of Law No. 31/2009 and Article 100-A (1) of Decree-Law No. 555/99 specify that relevant professional duties may arise from contract, from the law and from regulations, including technical regulations. Article 100(2), (3) and (4) of Decree-Law No. 555/99 makes it clear that all persons involved – architects, engineers, and builders – may

399. *See* A. Ferrer Correia/M.H. Mesquita, 'Anotação [ao acórdão do Supremo Tribunal de Justiça de 3 de Novembro de 1983]', in: 45 *Revista da Ordem dos Advogados* (1985) 129–158, followed by J. Brito Pereira, 'Do conceito de *obra* no contrato de empreitada', in: 54 *Revista da Ordem dos Advogados* (1994) 569–622.

400. *See* J.M. Antunes Varela, 'Parecer', in: 45 *Revista da Ordem dos Advogados* (1985) 159–197, followed by P. Romano Martinez, *Direito das obrigações (parte especial). – Contratos – Compra e venda. Locação. Empreitada*, 2nd edition (Coimbra: Livraria Almedina 2001) 386–393.

401. *See*, for instance, the judgment of 14 Dec. 2016, delivered by Justice Tomé Gomes.

be held joint and severally liable. Furthermore, Article 19(2) of Law No. 31/2009 holds architects and engineers liable for all damages caused to third parties as a result of their helpers' or auxiliaries' behaviour. Whereas architects' and engineers' liability for their own conduct depends on fault, liability for the conduct of their helpers and auxiliaries does not. Liability under Article 19(2) of Law No. 31/2009 is no-fault, strict liability.

Finally, Article 19(4) makes it clear that architects and engineers may be held liable for damages caused by acquiring third parties.[402] It has been argued that Article 19(4) of Law No. 31/2009 aims at extending the liability of builders for constructions intended for long-term use, as provided for in Article 1225 of the Civil Code, to architects and engineers. Article 1225 reads that 'if the purpose of the contract is the construction, modification or repair of buildings or other real estate intended by its nature for long-term use and, within five years counting from delivery, or in the course of the agreed guarantee period, the work, due to a defect in […] the construction, modification or repair […] totally of partially falls down, or risks of falling down, or at least presents grave, serious defects, the contractor is responsible for the damage sustained by the owner of the work as well as by the damage sustained by any acquiring third party'. Article 19(4) of Law No. 31/2009 would extend no-fault, strict liability for defects in the execution of the works to defects in the very conception and design; it would extend no-fault, strict liability of builders to architects and engineers, and it would extend no-fault, strict liability towards the owner of the work to any acquiring third party.[403] In spite of the fact that the argument is appealing, it is disputed whether the liability of architects and engineers under Law No. 31/2009 really corresponds to Article 1225 of the Civil Code. While the liability of builders may as well be a no-fault, strict liability, it is far from clear whether the liability of architects and engineers *for defective design* should be strict, i.e., independent from the infringement of professional standards.[404]

The Regulation of the Architects Council (*Estatuto da Ordem dos Arquitectos*)[405] explicitly provides for an obligation of the fully established architects to take out compulsory insurance for damages arising from the exercise of their profession.[406] The Regulation of the Engineers Council (*Estatuto da Ordem dos Engenheiros*)[407]

402. On the interpretation of Art. 19 of Law No. 31/2009 of 3 Jul. 1999, *see* J.L. Bonifácio Ramos, 'Responsabilidade civil dos intervenientes no processo de construção', in: *Estudos em Homenagem a Miguel Galvão Teles,* vol. II (Coimbra: Livraria Almedina 2012) 723–745, at 733, and H. Sousa Antunes, 'A responsabilidade civil dos intervenientes no processo de construção', in: 51 *Cadernos de direito privado* (2015) 3–25, at 20–21.

403. *See* J.L. Bonifácio Ramos, 'Responsabilidade civil dos intervenientes no processo de construção', at 733.

404. *See* H. Sousa Antunes, 'A responsabilidade civil dos intervenientes no processo de construção', at 21.

405. Approved by Decree-Law No. 176/98 of 3 Jul. 1998, and amended by Law No. 12/2024 of 19 Jan. 2024.

406. *See* the Regulation of the Architects Council (Estatuto da Ordem dos Arquitectos), Art. 51. If follows, however, from Art. 8(9) that the duty to take out compulsory insurance does not apply during internship, unless the practice of professional acts is allowed.

407. Approved by Decree-Law No. 119/92 of 30 Jun. 1992, and amended by Law No. 11/2024 of 19 Jan. 2024.

does not explicitly provide for such a duty. Article 24 of the Regulation, however, rules that trainee engineers are not required to take out insurance, and by ruling that trainee engineers are not, it suggests that fully established engineers are required to take out compulsory insurance for damages resulting from the exercise of their profession. That suggestion is confirmed, both in respect of architects and engineers, by Article 24 of Law No. 31/2009.

V. Others (Notaries, Tax Advisers, and Accountants, Banks)

A. *Liability of Notaries*

61. The Regulation of Notaries (*Estatuto do Notariado*), approved by Decree-Law No. 26/2004 of 4 February 2004, contains no substantive or procedural provisions on the liability of notaries. Article 23, paragraph (1), sub-paragraph (m) requires every notary to subscribe to compulsory insurance at a minimum amount of EUR 100,000. Article 27-D, paragraph (b) requires every intern notary to subscribe to compulsory insurance. Even if no fixed amount is defined, it should cover the risks inherent to the tasks assigned to him during the internship.

B. *Liability of Companies' Directors*[408]

62. In addition to the general provisions in the Civil Code, the Companies Act[409] establishes three particular, specific provisions on the liability of directors.

408. On the liability of companies' directors, *see* A. Menezes Cordeiro, *Da responsabilidade civil dos administradores das sociedades* comerciais (Lisboa: Lex 1996); J.M. Coutinho de Abreu, *Responsabilidade civil dos administradores de sociedades*, 2nd edition (Coimbra: Livraria Almedina 2010); M. Carneiro da Frada, 'A responsabilidade dos administradores na insolvência', in: 66 *Revista da Ordem dos Advogados* (2006) 653–702 = in: Manuel Carneiro da Frada, *Forjar o direito* (Coimbra: Livraria Almedina 2015) 413–457; P. Pais de Vasconcelos, 'Responsabilidade civil dos gestores das sociedades comerciais', in: 1 *Direito das sociedades em revista* (2009) 11–32; C. Serra, 'The Portuguese Classification of Insolvency of a Comparative Perspective', in: R. Parry (ed.), *Papers from the INSOL Europe Academic Forum/Milan Law School Joint Insolvency Conference, University of Milan Law School, Milan, Italy, 31 March-1 April 2011*, 2011, 3–16; R. Pinto Duarte, 'Responsabilidade dos administradores: coordenação dos regimes dos Código das Sociedades Comerciais e do Código da Insolvência e da Recuperação de Empresas', in: C. Serra (ed.), *III Congresso de direito da insolvência* (Coimbra: Livraria Almedina 2015) 151–173 = in: R. Pinto Duarte, *Escritos jurídicos vários 2000–2015* (Coimbra: Livraria Almedina 2015) 731–750; N.M. Pinto Oliveira, *Responsabilidade civil dos administradores. Entre direito civil, direito das sociedades e direito da* insolvência (Coimbra: Coimbra Editora 2015); A. Perestrelo de Oliveira, *Manual de governação das sociedades* (Coimbra: Livraria Almedina 2017); J.M. Coutinho de Abreu, 'Direito das sociedades e direito da insolvência: interacções', in: C. Serra (ed.), *IV Congresso de direito da* insolvência (Coimbra: Livraria Almedina 2017) 181–192; M. Carneiro da Frada, 'A responsabilidade dos administradores perante os credores entre o direito das sociedades e o direito da insolvência', in: C. Serra (ed.), *IV Congresso de direito da* insolvência (Coimbra: Livraria Almedina 2017) 193–202.

409. *Código das Sociedades Comerciais*, approved by Decree-Law No. 262/86 of 2 Nov. 1986, and amended, for the last (38th.) time, by Decree-law No. 89/2017 of 28 Jul. 2017.

In the first place, Article 72 of the Companies Act considers the 'internal' liability of directors towards the company.[410] Even though there is a discussion as to the nature of directors' duties towards the corporation, there is no discussion as to the nature of director's liability for the infringement of contractual and statutory duties – directors' liability towards the company is contractual liability. Therefore, Article 72 of the Companies Act is a specification, and no more than a specification, of the general provisions in Articles 798 and 799 of the Civil Code. In the second place, Articles 78 and 79 of the Companies Act consider the 'external' liability of directors towards third parties.

Article 79 has a broader, more comprehensive scope, applying to damages caused to any third party. It contains a reference, and no more than a reference, to the general provisions on civil liability – it gives any third party, such as any creditor, everything the general provisions on civil liability would give him.[411] Article 78 has a stricter scope, applying only to damages caused to creditors. It contains more than a reference to the general provisions – it gives creditors, and creditors only, more than the general provisions on civil liability would give them. In keeping with Article 78 of the Companies Act, directors are liable towards creditors for all damage resulting from the infringement of either contractual or statutory duties intended to safeguard the interests of creditors, if, as a consequence of such an infringement, the company becomes unable to pay its debts.[412]

In what concerns the liability of directors towards third parties, the Companies Act is to be read in conjunction with the Insolvency Act.[413] Article 186 of the Insolvency Act refers to the so-called classification of insolvency.[414] Insolvency may be

---

410. In keeping with the official translation of the Companies Act, available at the website of the Securities' Commission (*Comissão do Mercado de Valores Mobiliários*), Art. 72(1) reads 'managers or directors shall be responsible for damages caused by acts or omissions resulting from dereliction of their legal or contractual duties, unless the managers or directors can prove that they did not act intentionally or maliciously'. It is submitted that the word *maliciously* is misleading, for it suggests something that goes beyond mere negligence, and nothing more than negligence is required by Art. 72.

411. *See* Companies Act, Art. 79(1): 'managers or directors are also generally [liable] to the partners and third parties for damages resulting directly from the exercise of their duties' (translation available at: http://www.cmvm.pt/en/Legislacao/LegislacaoComplementar/EmitentesOfertasInformcaoValoresMobiliarios/Pages/Commercial-Company-Act.aspx?v=).

412. In keeping with the official translation of the Companies Act, available at the website of the Securities' Commission (*Comissão do Mercado de Valores Mobiliários*), Art. 78(1) reads: 'managers or directors shall be [liable] to the company's creditors if, because they wilfully ignore the provisions set forth by law or in the articles of association, designed to protect the company's assets, these become insufficient to pay for the company's debt' (translation available at: http://www.cmvm.pt/en/Legislacao/LegislacaoComplementar/EmitentesOfertasInformcaoValoresMobiliarios/Pages/Commercial-Company-Act.aspx?v=). It is submitted that the word *wilfully* is misleading, for it suggests that wilful misconduct (*dolus*) is required, and nothing more than mere negligence is required by Art. 78(1).

413. *Código da Insolvência e da Recuperação de Empresas*, approved by Decree-Law No. 53/2004 of 18 Mar. 2004, and amended for the last (17th.) time by Decree-Law No. 57/2022 of 25 Jul. 2022.

414. *See*, for a concise presentation in English of the relevant principles and rules, C. Serra, 'The Portuguese Classification of Insolvency from a Comparative Perspective', in: R. Parry (ed.), *The Reform of International Insolvency Rules at European and National Le vel* (Nottingham/Paris: INSOL Europe 2011) 3–16.

qualified as 'guilty' or 'not guilty' (accidental or random insolvency). '[T]he classification of insolvency as guilty implies that the court identifies a fault committed [by the debtor or, in the case of companies,] by the company's directors and a link between this fault and the company's insolvency or its aggravation.'[415] In spite of the fact the word 'guilty' may cause some confusion – for it may suggest that all types of fault are relevant, irrespective of the debtor's or directors' degree of fault – the fault committed must be either wilful or, at least, grossly negligent. In keeping with Article 186, Article 189(2)(a) of the Insolvency Act explicitly includes directors among the persons affected by the classification of insolvency, and Article 189(2)(e) and (4) reads that all persons affected are to be held joint and severally liable for all damage to creditors resulting from insolvency.

The provisions in both the Companies Act and the Insolvency Act apply, for instance, to cases where the director fails to file for insolvency. In fact, Articles 18 and 19 of the Insolvency Act require companies' directors to file for insolvency within thirty days counting from the moment they become aware of insolvency, and failure to comply with the duty to file for insolvency triggers directors' liability for damages to creditors resulting from the deepening of insolvency.[416]

C. *Liability of Companies' Auditors*[417]

63. In Portugal, assessment of facts relevant to the economic and financial situation of the company may be performed either by accountants (*contabilistas*) or by statutory auditors (*revisores oficiais de contas*).

---

415. *See* C. Serra, 'The Portuguese Classification of Insolvency from a Comparative Perspective', at 3.

416. *See*, for instance, N.M. Pinto Oliveira, 'Responsabilidade civil dos administradores pela violação do dever de apresentação à insolvência', in: 2 *Revista de direito comercial* (2018), at https://static1.squarespace.com/static/58596f8a29687fe710cf45cd/t/5ac6834b562fa7ae6133269f/1522959182313/2018-12.pdf.

417. On the liability of auditors, *see* M. Carneiro da Frada, *Uma 'terceira via' no direito da responsabilidade civil? O problema da imputação dos danos causados a terceiros por auditores de sociedades* (Coimbra: Livraria Almedina 1997); M. Carneiro da Frada, *Teoria da confiança e responsabilidade civil* (Coimbra: Livraria Almedina 2004) 180 ff., 392 (footnote 399), 686 (footnote 745), 644 (footnote 695) and 750 (footnote 829); L. Menezes Leitão, 'A responsabilidade civil dos auditores de uma sociedade cotada', in: 65 *Revista da Ordem dos Advogados* (2005), 663–675; M. Carneiro da Frada, *Direito civil. Responsabilidade civil. O método do caso* (Coimbra: Livraria Almedina 2006) 111–114; M. Azevedo de Almeida, 'A responsabilidade civil perante os investidores por realização defeituosa de relatórios de auditoria, recomendações de investimento e relatórios de notação de risco', 49 *Cadernos da Comissão do Mercado de Valores Mobiliários* (2010) 9–31; M. Azevedo de Almeida, *A responsabilidade civil por prospecto no direito dos valores mobiliários* (Coimbra: Faculdade de Direito da Universidade de Coimbra 2014); C. Ferreira de Almeida, 'Normas de imputação e normas de protecção no regime da responsabilidade civil pela informação nos mercados de valores mobiliários', in: 8 *Direito das sociedades em revista* (2016), 15–31; J. Melo Rodrigues/J. Ferreira, 'Responsabilidade pelo conteúdo do prospecto. O caso específico do revisor oficial de contas', in: 55 *Cadernos do Mercado de Valores Mobiliários* (2016), 167–183; M. Carneiro da Frada, 'Responsabilidade civil de terceiros na formação do contrato – um apontamento, nos 50 anos do Código Civil', in: A. Cardoso Guedes/N.M. Pinto Oliveira (eds), *Colóquio de direito civil de Santo Tirso. O Código Civil 50 anos depois: balanço e perspectivas* (Coimbra: Livraria Almedina 2017) 505–512.

Each profession is distinct – accountants and statutory auditors have different councils, the Council of Accountants (*Ordem dos Contabilistas Certificados*) and the Council of Statutory Auditors (*Ordem dos Revisores Oficiais de Contas*), and each council has a different regulation. The Regulation of the Council of Accountants has been approved by Law No. 139/2015 of 7 September 2015, and the Regulation of the Council of Statutory Auditors has been approved by Law No. 140/2015 also of 7 September 2015. As each council has a different regulation, accountants and statutory auditors are subject to different professional and deontological standards. It is submitted that statutory auditors are subject to higher professional standards, and the assessment of the facts most important to the economic and financial situation of the company is reserved for them.

Article 115 of the Regulation of the Council of Statutory Auditors explicitly refers to the civil liability of statutory auditors. Article 115(1) reads that '[i]n the exercise of public interest functions, statutory auditors shall be held liable to the company and to third parties for the damages they cause, either intentionally or negligently, under the conditions envisaged in the Companies Act and in identical legal provisions relating to any other companies or other entities'. It is submitted that the reference to the Companies Act is to be interpreted as a reference to Article 82 of the Companies Act. Paragraph (1) holds that statutory auditors shall be liable to the company and to its partners for damages resulting from wilful misconduct or from negligence and paragraph (2) holds that statutory auditors shall be liable to the company's creditors as set forth in Article 78. Article 115(2) reads that '[o]utside of the scope envisaged in the preceding paragraph, statutory auditors may limit their liability in accordance with civil law'.

It follows from the wording in Article 115(1) that liability of auditors in the exercise of public interest functions is to be equated with the liability of auditors. The definition of public interest functions results from Article 41 of the Regulation of the Council of Statutory Auditors. Public interest functions include the audit of accounts and related services provided to companies or other entities. Article 42 specifies that:

> [a]uditing activity encompasses the examinations and other services related to the accounts of companies or other entities, carried out in accordance with prevailing auditing standards, including:
> (a) The statutory audit of accounts performed in compliance with legal requirements and within the context of the oversight mechanisms of the entities or companies which are the object of an audit, in terms of which the appointment of a statutory auditor is required;
> (b) The audit of accounts carried out in compliance with legal, statutory or contractual provisions;
> (c) The services related to those referred to in the preceding sub-paragraphs, when they have a specific or limited objective or scope.

The most important case of liability of statutory auditors is a liability for the prospectus under Articles 149 to 154 of the Securities Code.[418]

Article 134(1) of the Securities Code reads that '[t]he carrying out of any public offer relating to securities should be preceded by the disclosure of a prospectus', and Article 135 requires the prospectus to contain 'complete, true, updated, clear, objective and lawful information, necessary to enable the addressees to make an informed assessment of the offer, the securities concerned thereby and the rights attached thereto, its specific characteristics and the assets and liabilities, economic and financial position of the issuer or the guarantor if any, and the prospects for the business and earnings of the issuer and the guarantor, if any'. Article 149 of the Securities Code contains the fundamental norm on liability for the prospectus:

1. The following [persons] are [to be held] liable for damages caused by the non-compliance with the contents of the prospectus in accordance with the provisions of Article 135, except in the case they prove to have acted without fault:
   a) The offeror;
   b) The members of the offeror's management body;
   c) The issuer;
   d) The members of the issuer's management body;
   e) The promoters, in the case of offer for subscription for the incorporation of a company;
   f) The members of the auditing body, accounting firms, chartered accountants and any other individuals that have certified or, in any other way, verified the accounting documents on which the prospectus is based;
   g) The financial intermediaries in charge of assisting with the offer;
   h) Any other entities that accept being appointed in the prospectus as responsible for any information, forecast or study included in the same.
2. Fault is judged according to the highest standards of professional diligence.
3. Liability is excluded if any of the individuals mentioned in sub-article 1 prove that the addressee knew or should have known about the shortcoming in the contents of the prospectus on the date of issue of the contractual declaration or when the respective cancellation was still possible.
4. Liability is excluded even if damages provided for in paragraph (1) result only from the summary of the prospectus, or any translation thereof, unless when read together with the other documents that make up the prospect, it contains misleading, inaccurate or inconsistent references or does not provide key information to allow investors to determine whether and when to invest in the securities in question.

418. *Código dos Valores Mobiliários*, approved by Decree-Law No. 486/99 of 21 Nov. 1999, and amended, for the last (28th) time, by Law No. 104/2017 of 30 Aug. 2017.

In keeping with Article 152, 'the compensation should place the injured party in the exact situation it would be in if, at the moment of acquisition or alienation of securities, the contents of the prospectus had been in accordance with the provisions of Article 135'.

The Regulation of the Council of Accountants (*Estatuto da Ordem dos Contabilistas Certificados*) requires accountants and accountant firms to take out compulsory insurance for damages arising from the exercise of their profession.[419] In the case of accountants, the minimum amount of compulsory insurance is EUR 50,000.[420] In the case of accounting firms, the minimum amount of compulsory insurance is EUR 150,000.[421] The Regulation of the Council of Statutory Auditors (*Estatuto da Ordem dos Revisores Oficiais de Contas*) also requires auditors and audit firms to take out compulsory insurance. In the case of auditors, the minimum amount of compulsory insurance is EUR 500,000 for each unlawful act[422] and, in the case of audit firms, that minimum amount is EUR 500,000 multiplied by the number of statutory auditors forming part of the firm.[423] In what concerns accountants, the provisions referring to compulsory insurance do not apply during an internship.[424] In what concerns statutory auditors, the provisions referring to compulsory insurance do apply during an internship, albeit in a modified form – the minimum amount of insurance must be proportionate to the type of acts the intern auditor is allowed to practice.[425]

D. Liability of Credit Rating Agencies[426]

64. Credit rating agencies are to comply with both European and Member States' rules.

At the European level, Regulation (EC) No. 1060/2009 of 16 September 2009, as amended by Regulation (EU) No. 513/2011 of 11 May 2011, and by Regulation (EU) No. 462/2013 of 21 May 2013, requires credit rating agencies to 'adopt, implement and enforce adequate measures to ensure that the credit ratings and the rating outlooks it issues are based on a thorough analysis of all the information that is

419. *See* Regulation of the Council of Accountants (Estatuto da Ordem dos Contabilistas Certificados), Art. 70(4), as to accountants, and Art. 121, at to accountant firms.
420. *See* Regulation of the Council of Accountants (Estatuto da Ordem dos Contabilistas Certificados), Art. 70(4).
421. *See* Regulation of the Council of Accountants (Estatuto da Ordem dos Contabilistas Certificados), Art. 121(2).
422. *See* Regulation of the Council of Statutory Auditors (Estatuto da Ordem dos Revisores Oficiais de Contas), Art. 87(1).
423. *See* Regulation of the Council of Statutory Auditors (Estatuto da Ordem dos Revisores Oficiais de Contas), Art. 87(2).
424. *See* Regulation of the Council of Accountants (Estatuto da Ordem dos Contabilistas Certificados), Art. 26(6).
425. *See* Regulation of the Council of Statutory Auditors (Estatuto da Ordem dos Revisores Oficiais de Contas), Art. 159(7).
426. On the liability of credit rating agencies under European and Portuguese law, *see* especially M. Carneiro da Frada, *A responsabilidade civil das agências de notação de risco* (rating) – *Ensaio de construção dogmático-crítica* (Coimbra: Livraria Almedina 2018).

available to it and that is relevant to its analysis according to the applicable rating methodologies'.[427] Furthermore, it requires credit rating agencies to 'adopt all necessary measures so that the information it uses in assigning credit ratings and rating outlooks is of sufficient quality and from reliable sources'[428] and to 'use rating methodologies that are rigorous, systematic, continuous and subject to validation based on historical experience, including back-testing'.[429]

Regulation (EU) No. 513/2011 of 11 May 2011 added Annex III to Regulation (EC) No. 1060/2009. In accordance with point 42 of Annex III,[430] '[t]he credit rating agency infringes Article 8(2) by not adopting, implementing or enforcing adequate measures to ensure that the credit ratings and rating outlooks it issues are based on a thorough analysis of all the information that is available to it and that is relevant to its analysis according to the applicable rating methodologies'. In keeping with point 43 of Annex III, '[t]he credit rating agency infringes Article 8(3) by not using rating methodologies that are rigorous, systematic, continuous and subject to validation based on historical experience, including back-testing'. If credit rating agencies commit the infringements listed in Annex III, Article 35a (1) of Regulation No 1060/2009[431] applies: 'Where a credit rating agency has committed, intentionally or with gross negligence, any of the infringements listed in Annex III having an impact on a credit rating, an investor or issuer may claim damages from that credit rating agency for damage caused to it due to that infringement.' Investors may claim damages 'where [they] establish[] that [they have] reasonably relied […] on a credit rating for a decision to invest into, hold onto or divest from a financial instrument covered by that credit rating'.[432]

It follows from Article 35a of Regulation (EC) No. 1060/2009, as amended in 2013, that liability under European law 'does not exclude further civil liability claims in accordance with national law'.[433] Article 485 of the Portuguese Civil Code states the principle according to which liability for information is exceptional. In spite of its text, Article 485 is to be interpreted as a 'declarative rule'[434] allowing contractual and non-contractual, tortious claims resulting from general principles and rules, such as from Article 483.[435]

It has been suggested that agencies' liability for careless, negligent ratings could result from the general principles of non-contractual, tortious liability. Article 8 of Regulation (EC) No. 1060/2009 of 16 September 2009, as amended by Regulation

427. *See* Regulation (EC) No 1060/2009 of the European Parliament and of the Council of 16 Sep. 2009 on credit rating agencies, Art. 8(2), as amended by Regulation (EU) No 462/2013 of the European Parliament and of the Council of 21 May 2013.
428. Regulation (EC) No 1060/2009, Art. 8(2) – as amended by Regulation (EU) No 462/2013.
429. Regulation (EC) No 1060/2009, Art. 8(3).
430. As amended by Annex II of Regulation (EU) No 462/2013.
431. Inserted by Art. 1 of Regulation (EU) No 462/2013.
432. Regulation (EC) No 1060/2009, as amended by Regulation (EU) No 462/2013, Art. 35a (3).
433. Regulation (EC) No 1060/2009, as amended by Regulation (EU) No 462/2013 of 21 May 2013, Art. 35a (3).
434. *See* J.F. Sinde Monteiro, *Responsabilidade por conselhos, recomendações ou informações* (Coimbra: Livraria Almedina 1990) 339–345.
435. *See* J.F. Sinde Monteiro, *Responsabilidade por conselhos, recomendações ou informações*, at 441–454.

(EU) No. 513/2011 of 11 May 2011 and by Regulation (EU) No. 462/2013 of 21 May 2013, could be interpreted as statutory provisions intended to safeguard the interests of investors.[436]

In keeping with Article 483 of the Portuguese Civil Code,[437] credit rating agencies would be held liable for any damage arising from such a violation. The reasoning could apply to Articles 7 to 12 of the Portuguese Securities Code. In accordance with Article 7, all information disclosed by rating agencies is to be clear, objective, true and up-to-date.[438]

If, however, non-contractual, tortious liability is inappropriate,[439] it has been suggested that agencies' liability for careless, negligent ratings could result either from *culpa in contrahendo* or from contractual or pre-contractual relations with protective effects vis-à-vis third parties or from liability for breach of trust.[440,441] In spite of the fact that the Portuguese Civil Code contains no principle or rule corresponding to § 313(3) of the German Civil Code, Portuguese scholars assume that German and Portuguese principles and rules on pre-contractual and contractual relations are equivalent.[442]

Under Portuguese law, as under German law, an obligation with duties to protect the rights and interests of the other party may come into existence in relation to persons who are not themselves intended to be parties to the contract. In this particular, specific case, liability would be justified by the fact that credit rating agencies, by laying claim to a particularly high degree of trust, substantially influence the conclusion of the contract.[443]

---

436. *See* M. Azevedo de Almeida, 'A responsabilidade civil perante os investidores por realização defeituosa de relatórios de auditoria, recomendações de investimento e relatórios de notação de risco' 2010 *Cadernos da Comissão do Mercado de Valores Mobiliários* 9–31, at 26–27.
437. Portuguese Civil Code, Art. 483(1): 'Whoever, whether by wilful misconduct (dolus) or by negligence unlawfully infringes the rights of another person or any legal provision intended to safeguard the interests of others must compensate the injured party for damage arising from such violation.'
438. *See* M. Azevedo de Almeida, 'A responsabilidade civil perante os investidores por realização defeituosa de relatórios de auditoria, recomendações de investimento e relatórios de notação de risco', at 15–16.
439. *See* M. Carneiro da Frada, 'Sociedades e notação do risco (*rating*) – a protecção dos investidores' in: *II Congresso Direito das Sociedades em Revista* (Coimbra: Livraria Almedina 2012) 341–346, at 343–344.
440. M. Carneiro da Frada, 'Sociedades e notação do risco (*rating*) – a protecção dos investidores', at 345.
441. The term 'liability from breach of trust' [suggested, for instance, by P. Widmer, '[The Concept of Unlawfulness:] Function and Relevance under Swiss Law', in: H. Koziol (ed.), *Unification of Tort Law: Wrongfulness* (The Hague: Kluwer Law International 1998) 115–127)] requires an explanation: in referring to liability for breach of trust we intend to refer to '*responsabilidade pela confiança*', '*responsabilità dall'affidamento*' or *Vertrauenshaftung* [for a comprehensive analysis of liability for breach of trust, *see* M. Carneiro da Frada, *Teoria da confiança e responsabilidade civil* (Coimbra: Livraria Almedina 2004)].
442. *See, for example*, A. Menezes Cordeiro, *Da modernização do direito civil, I. – Aspectos gerais* (Coimbra: Livraria Almedina 2004) 111–113; A. Menezes Cordeiro, *Tratado de direito civil português, II. – Direito das obrigações, I. – Introdução. Sistemas e direito europeu das obrigações. Dogmática geral* (Coimbra: Livraria Almedina 2009) 83–84; N.M. Pinto Oliveira, *Princípios de direito dos contratos* (Coimbra: Coimbra Editora 2011) 168–172.
443. *See* German Civil Code, § 311(3).

It follows that, under Portuguese law, [as well as under German law], general principles and general rules relating to liability for breach of trust would apply. Furthermore, it has been suggested that in some specific sectors, where there are particularly intense social and economic reasons to protect reliance, liability for breach of trust might go as far as to protect third parties, even if they cannot be determined in advance from the perspective of the agent.[444] It is submitted that such reasoning would apply to liability for credit ratings.

§2. Liability of Public Authorities (Conditions; Also Against Their Organs?: Is Compensation In Kind Possible?)

I. Liability of Public Authorities

65. The public authorities' liability is regulated by Law No. 67/2007 of 31 December, revoking the Decree-Law No. 48051 of 21 November 1967, which preceded the Portuguese democratic Constitution of 1976.

The Constitution's Article 22 states that:

> The State and remaining public authorities are civilly liable, jointly with his organs' holders, officials or agents, for actions or omissions practiced during the performance of a duty or because of it, if it results in the violation of the right, liberties, guaranties or causes harm to others.

In that light, the previous law was considered unconstitutional by many and by the Constitutional Court,[445] and after many attempts, Law No. 67/2007 was approved, only to be changed six months later by Law No. 31/2008 of 17 July. The latter altered its Article 7(2), following a decision by the Court of Justice of the European Communities.[446]

The Law is divided into five chapters: the first one dedicated to *general provisions*; the second to civil liability due to administrative function; the third to the one arising from the jurisdictional function; the fourth to the liability originating from the legislative and political power; and the fifth pertaining to compensation for the sacrifice.

It is applicable not only to public authorities, as stated, but also to legal persons governed by private law when they act with prerogatives of public powers or are regulated by principles of administrative law, as it is established in Article 1(2) and (5).

Following the general principles of tort law, Article 3 enshrines that (1) 'Those who are bound to repair the caused harm, according to this law, must recreate the

---

444. *See* M. Carneiro da Frada, *Teoria da confiança e responsabilidade civil*, at 743 (fn. 818).

445. For example, regarding its Art. 2.° n. °1, on the ruling n. ° 154/07, considering its interpretation as an administrative act had as void for complete lack of justification not being, in any case, grounds of wrongfulness apt to the consideration of public authorities as liable. *See*, http://www.tribunalconstitucional.pt/tc/acordaos/20070154.html.

446. *Decision Commission of the European Communities v. Portuguese Republic*, 10 Jan. 2008, Proc. C-70/06, which concluded that, concerning the transposition of the Directive 89/665/EEC.

situation as it would be if the harmful event hadn't occurred.' It proceeds to establish the priority of *natural reconstitution* over pecuniary compensation (2), 'The compensation is set in monetary value, unless it is unfeasible, prevents full reparation or it is excessively burdensome.' Finally, ergo Article 3(3), the reparable loss is global since it must encompass pecuniary and non-pecuniary harm, and also not only already consolidated detriments but also future losses.

As seen incidentally with Articles 505 and 570 of the Portuguese Civil Code, also Article 4 of this Law considers the concurrence of the injured party's fault to be relevant, giving the example of contributing to the aggravation of damage 'by choosing an erroneous legal procedure to eliminate a wrongful legal act'. If this is the case, the Court must decide, attending to each party fault's severity, if any, that a reduced or full compensation is due.

The limitation of action period is, in line with Article 5, the same as in Article 498 of the Civil Code, i.e., three years, being also applicable to all the general rules regarding suspension and interruption of this limitation of action period.

The *right to redress*, consecrated in Article 6, shares the three-year limitation of action period (*see* Article 5) and is, as of 2007, mandatory, notwithstanding any possible disciplinary action. For that effect, Article 6(2) '(...) the secretariat of the Court in which a legal person has been convicted will forward the judgment certificate, immediately after res judicata, to all the competent authorities to exert the right to redress'.

A. *Administrative Function*

66. In relation to liability due to the administrative function and powers, Article 7(1) establishes that 'The Portuguese State and all legal persons governed by public law (and some governed by private law, as seen above) are exclusively liable for all the damages caused by any actions or omissions arising from the negligent conduct of its organs' holders, officials or agents during the exercise of administrative powers and because of them.' In contrast, if the conduct of its organs' holders, officials or agents is exercised with misconduct or without the expected standard of diligence, Article 8(2) consecrates joint liability of the authorities and its representative, and the correspondent right to redress (3). If their actions are not associated with the pursuit of administrative powers, the organs' holders, officials or agents will be solely responsible, as it results from the conjugation of Article 8(1) and (2).

Article 7(3) enshrines the public authorities' liability for *faute du service*,[447] which means that the State or a public authority is liable even if any concrete action or author, by its representatives, can be identified but nonetheless is attributed to an abnormal functioning of service – defined by Article 7(4) as not meeting the expected standard of performance to not causing harm, considering the circumstances and the average results.

447. Regarded as an innovation, *see* M.J. Rangel de Mesquita, *O regime da responsabilidade civil extracontratual do Estado e demais Entidades Públicas e o Direito da União Europeia*, Almedina, 2009, p. 19.

The assessment of wrongfulness differs from the traditional civil law norm. Article 9 asserts that an action or omission is unlawful if the organs' holders, officials or agents disregard the provisions or constitutional, legal or regulatory principles, as well as technical regulations and standard duties of care (1); additionally, the wrongfulness can derive from *faute du service* (2).

Article 10 is dedicated to a fault, establishing a baseline reliant on each particular circumstance to measure the required diligence and aptitude (1). In (2), it anchors a presumption of negligence whenever an illicit act is committed, notwithstanding a proof of wilful misconduct. And (3) adds that 'besides all the other circumstances provided by law, negligence will also be presumed, *ex vi* civil liability's general principles, on any occasion where duties of care are violated'. The Civil Code regime is only applicable when there is a variety of liable parties, as determined by the referral of Article 10(4) to Article 497 of the Civil Code. The latter states that: (1) 'if several people are liable for the caused harm, theirs is a joint liability', and (2) 'the right to redress between the liable parties relies in each individual's fault and respective consequences of their actions, which are presumed equal'.

At last, Article 11(1) is dedicated to liability irrespective of fault, stating that 'The State and other legal persons governed by public law are liable for its activities, property or administrative services resulting damages, except if proven to had happen an event of force majeure or the concurrence of the injured parties' fault, case in which the Court can, attending all the circumstances, reduce or exclude any due compensation.'

When an action by a third party concurs to the existence or aggravation of damages, the State and other legal persons governed by public law are jointly liable with the third party, withal the right to redress – giving Article 11(2) an innovative character in contrast with the previous regime.[448]

B. Jurisdictional Function

67. In regard to the jurisdictional function, Article 12 of Law No. 67/2007 of 31 December 2007 refers to the regime of liability due to administrative powers (*supra*). However, that will not be the case whenever miscarriage of justice or magistrate's liability is involved. '(...) The Portuguese State is civilly liable for any damage arising from overtly unconstitutional or illegal court decisions, as well as from gross misjudgment in the assessment of facts', as enshrined in Article 13(1), being the claim substantiated on the repeal of the improper decision (2).

With respect to magistrates, Article 14 proclaims them to be directly civilly irresponsible, although there is a right to redress for the State if the magistrate operated with wilful misconduct (1), which is left to be decided ex officio by its disciplinary board (being the High Council of the Judicial Courts, of the Administrative and Fiscal Courts, or of the Public Prosecution Service), or by the Minister of Justice's incentive.

---

448. *See* M.J. Rangel de Mesquita, *O regime da responsabilidade civil extracontratual do Estado e demais Entidades Públicas e o Direito da União Europeia*, Almedina, 2009, p. 22.

In spite of the fact that there are no direct claims of particular, private persons against prosecutors and judges, there is a difference between cases of wilful misconduct and gross negligence and cases of slight negligence.

In the case where the State is held liable for evident mistakes of the judiciary, but there is neither wilful misconduct nor gross negligence on the part of the prosecutor or the judge, there is no recourse against either of them. The State is to bear the costs of compensating the plaintiffs. In the event that the State is held liable for evident mistakes of the judiciary, and there is either wilful misconduct or gross negligence on the part of the prosecutor or the judge, there is recourse against them. The State does not bear the costs of intentional or grossly negligent wrongdoing – thus, in this case, judges and prosecutors will be held liable for their acts and omissions.

C. Legislative and Political Function

68. According to Article 15(1), 'the State and both Autonomous Regions[449] are liable for abnormal damages to citizens' rights and interests legally protected caused by acts that violate the Constitution, international or EU law, or a legislative act of reinforced value'. The same goes for abnormal damages caused by normative omissions which impede the implementation of constitutional norms (3), inasmuch as the Constitutional Court previously recognizes unconstitutionality by omission (5). Exceptionally, Article 15(6) grants that if the aggrieved parties are numerous and there is a public interest in limiting the claimed compensation, the Court can set it equitably and without matching full compensation.

D. Compensation for Sacrifice

69. Law No. 67/2007's last chapter, which consists solely of Article 16, pertains to compensation for sacrifice, stating that 'The State and remaining legal persons governed by public law, must compensate all the individuals to whom, by reasons of public interest, burdens are enforced, or special and abnormal damages caused, being the compensation calculated in view of, namely, the extent of the caused harm.'

§3. Abuse of Rights (I.e., Injury Caused in the Exercise of Legal Rights; Abuse of Legal Procedure)

70. Portuguese tort law is to be interpreted as containing a general clause on liability for abuse of rights. It should apply to cases of wilful or grossly negligent causation of loss in a manner contrary to good morals.

Whereas the first general clause in Article 483 of the Portuguese Civil Code matches § 823(1) of the German Civil Code and the second general clause in Article

449. That is, Madeira and Azores.

483 matches § 823(2), there is no general clause in the Portuguese Civil Code that matches § 826 of the German Civil Code.

§ 826 of the German Civil Code reads that '[a] person who wilfully causes damage to another in a manner contra bonos mores is bound to compensate the other for the damage'.[450] Professor Markesinis informs that it 'was intended from the outset as an all-purpose residual provision, able to accommodate future expansion in the growth of the law of torts'.[451]

Subjectively, § 826 is the narrowest of the three general clauses, 'since it will be satisfied only if intention can be shown to exist'.[452] Objectively, it is the widest of the three general clauses, since it can be satisfied by any type of damage. 'Though subjectively narrow, § 826 is objectively wide – in fact, the most general, indeed amorphous provision of the Code.'[453]

Especially in the case of pure economic loss, the problems resulting from the absence of a general clause similar to § 826 of the German Civil Code have been solved by developing the principle in Article 334 of the Portuguese Civil Code on *abuse of rights*, as a general clause of tort law.[454]

Article 334 reads that '[t]he exercise of a right is illegitimate if such exercise manifestly exceeds the limits imposed by good faith, by good morals or by the social or economic purpose of the right'.

It has been argued that Article 334 could not fill the gaps in the Portuguese legal system for – at least – two reasons.

In the first place, the requirements mentioned in Article 334 could not be met in many, if not in most, cases of pure economic loss.

Article 334 clearly presupposes a (subjective) right and the exercise of a (subjective) right. In many, if not in most, cases of pure economic loss, damage results from the exercise of *freedoms*, *competences* and *faculties* that do not qualify as *rights*. In fact, pure economic loss normally results from an 'abuse' of the generic freedom to act or to refrain from acting.

Second, the effects mentioned would not include civil liability.

Considering the problems with Article 334, Professor Carneiro da Frada argued that judges should fill the gap by creating an unwritten norm.

The content of such an unwritten norm would correspond to the 'generic prohibition of injurious conduct contrary to good practice' (to good morals): whoever infringed the minimal ethical requirements for social coexistence should be held liable for damages resulting from such an infringement.[455]

---

450. For the translation of § 826 of the German Civil Code, *see* B.S. Markesinis/H. Unberath, *The German Law of Torts. A Comparative Treatise*, 15.
451. B.S. Markesinis/H. Unberath, *The German Law of Torts. A Comparative Treatise*, 888.
452. *See* B.S. Markesinis/H. Unberath, *The German Law of Torts. A Comparative Treatise*, 889 – adding that '[i]ntention is taken to include *dolus directus* and *dolus eventualis*'.
453. *See* B.S. Markesinis/H. Unberath, *The German Law of Torts. A Comparative Treatise*, 889.
454. *See* J.F. Sinde Monteiro, *Responsabilidade por conselhos, recomendações ou informações*, 545–582.
455. M. Carneiro da Frada, *Teoria da confiança e responsabilidade civil*, 164–174.

It is submitted that the discussion as to whether cases of pure economic loss are to be resolved by means of a written norm, namely by means of Article 334, or by means of an unwritten norm, namely by means of the 'generic prohibition of injurious conduct contrary to good practice'.

In favour of the former, it could be argued that liability for abuse of rights was accepted under the Civil Code of 1967; that the author of the preparatory work proposed that it should make its way into a particular, specific provision;[456] and that there is no sign at all that the legislator intended to deviate from the preliminary work, thus suppressing liability for abuse of rights.[457]

It is, therefore, submitted that recourse to an unwritten principle of law is unnecessary 'when we have a provision which can give direct support [to non-contractual, tortious liability for infringement of good morals]'.[458] Professors Bussani and Palmer sustain that 'the attempt to fashion a general clause of civil liability out of Article 334 (sanctioning the abuse of rights along the lines of § 826 BGB) has so far obtained only a little scholarly support'.[459]

The description does not fit, for the general clause of civil liability, fashioned out of Article 334, is widely recognized both by the academia and by the judiciary. In a recent and rather significant judgment, the Portuguese Supreme Court firmly held the thesis that either by recourse to the written norm in Article 334 or by recourse to an unwritten norm underlying the system, the plaintiff may be entitled to damages for pure economic loss.[460]

Objectively, the scope of Article 334 of the Portuguese Civil Code corresponds to the scope of § 826 of the German Civil Code. Subjectively, it does not – the scope of Article 334 goes beyond the scope of § 826. While § 826 requires intention, Article 334 of the Portuguese Civil Code does not.

Cases of intentional harmdoing always fall within the scope of Article 334. 'Whenever we are faced with an act that is contrary to boni mores if the agent has foreseen the possibility of damage and accepts it accordingly (dolus eventualis), it seems that abuse of law should be affirmed for the purposes of civil liability.'[461] Cases of non-intentional, merely negligent harmdoing may also occasionally fall within the scope of Article 334.

Professor Sinde Monteiro rightly emphasizes the fact that 'the letter of the law lets us go further, when this is justified, foregoing the proof of malicious damage: that is, serious or gross negligence would be enough'.[462]

Whenever we are faced with an act that is contrary to *boni mores*, even if the agent has not foreseen the possibility of damage, it seems that abuse of law should

456. *See* A. Vaz Serra, 'Abuso do direito (em matéria de responsabilidade civil)', in: *Boletim do Ministério da Justiça*, 85 (1955), 243 ff.
457. *See* J.F. Sinde Monteiro, 'Case 11 – Portugal', in: M. Bussani/V.V. Palmer (eds), *Pure Economic Loss in Europe* (Cambridge: Cambridge University Press 2003) 357–359.
458. *See* J.F. Sinde Monteiro, 'Case 11 – Portugal', 358.
459. *See* M. Bussani/V.V. Palmer, 'The Liability Regimes of Europe – Their Façades and Interiors', 155–156.
460. *See* the judgment of 8 Sep. 2016 (Maria da Graça Trigo). *See also* the judgments of Portuguese Supreme Court of 12 Sep. 2019 (Maria da Graça Trigo), of 26 Nov. 2020 (Maria da Graça Trigo) and of 15 Sep. 2022 (Manuel Capelo).
461. *See* J.F. Sinde Monteiro, 'Case 11 – Portugal', 359.
462. *See* J.F. Sinde Monteiro, 'Case 11 – Portugal', 359.

be affirmed, provided there is '"manifest abuse" of the limits imposed by the "good faith" or "boni mores" (or by the "economic or social goal" of the right)'.[463] It is thus submitted that there may be manifest abuse in cases of recklessness and even in cases of gross negligence.

§4. Injury to Reputation and Privacy (of Natural and Juristic Persons)

71. Article 79 deals at length with the *right to one's own image*:

1. The portrait of a person shall not be displayed or made public without his or her consent; after his or her death, consent is to be given by persons referred to in Article 71 (2).
2. Consent is not necessary when the display is justified, on the grounds that the person whose portrait is displayed is notorious, that he or she occupies a public office, that display is required by police or justice-related reasons, that it pursues scientific, didactic or cultural purposes, that the reproduction of the image is framed within a public place, or that it is framed within facts of public interest or which have taken place in public.
3. The image may not be displayed if [such a display] results in damage to the honour, reputation or decorum/basic decency of the person displayed.[464,465]

In spite of the fact there is no equivalent rule as to other dimensions of the person's identity, such as one's own voice, 'it is possible to use analogy in order to protect voice in the same way as the right to image is protected'.[466]

Article 80 considers the right to privacy in respect of the intimacy of private life ('reserva de intimidade da vida privada') by stating the general principles according to which 'everyone must respect the privacy of the intimacy of the private lives of others', and that 'the extent of this privacy is defined in accordance with the nature of the case and the condition of the persons'.[467]

---

463. *See* J.F. Sinde Monteiro, 'Case 11 – Portugal', 359.
464. For the translation of Art. 78 of the Portuguese Civil Code, *see* P. Pais de Vasconcelos/N. Ferreira, 'Case 3 – Portugal', in: G. Brüggemeier/A. Colombi-Ciacchi/P. O'Callaghan, *Personality Rights in European Tort Law*, 196–198.
465. *See*, for further developments, F.A. Pires de Lima/J.M. Antunes Varela (/ M.H. Mesquita), *Código Civil anotado*, vol. I, 109; C.A. da Mota Pinto/A. Pinto Monteiro/P. Mota Pinto, *Teoria geral do direito civil*, 213; A. Menezes Cordeiro, *Tratado de direito civil português*, vol. I – *Parte geral*, III – *Pessoas*, 193–204; D. Oliveira Festas, *Do conteúdo patrimonial do direito à imagem. Contributo para um estudo do seu aproveitamento consentido e* inter vivos (Coimbra: Coimbra Editora 2009).
466. *See* P. Pais de Vasconcelos/N. Ferreira, 'Case 14 – Portugal', in: G. Brüggemeier/A. Colombi-Ciacchi/P. O'Callaghan, *Personality Rights in European Tort Law*, 485–486. In elaborating their reasoning, the authors argue that it is reasonable – that it is sensible – not to allow 'someone's voice to be played, reproduced or commercialized without his or her consent'.
467. *See*, for further developments, F.A. Pires de Lima/J.M. Antunes Varela (/ M.H. Mesquita), *Código Civil anotado*, vol. I, 10; C.A. da Mota Pinto/A. Pinto Monteiro/P. Mota Pinto, *Teoria geral do direito civil*, 212–213; A. Menezes Cordeiro, *Tratado de direito civil português*, vol. I – Parte geral, III – Pessoas, 205–216; R. Amaral Cabral, 'O direito à intimidade da vida privada (Breve reflexão

§5. Interference by a Third Person with Contractual Relations

72. The question of whether interference with contractual relationships is lawful or unlawful was already discussed under the Civil Code of 1867. Professor Ferrer Correia argued that interferences with contractual relationships should be considered unlawful.[468] Professors Manuel de Andrade and Vaz Serra argued that it should not.[469] If Article 483(1) of the Civil Code of 1966 intended to decide the issue, it failed to do so.

The wording of Article 483 admittedly 'leaves some room for interpretation'.[470] Article 483 requires the infringement of 'subjective rights' – within 'subjective rights'; however, it does not distinguish between absolute and relative rights. It does not require the infringement of absolute rights. It 'does not expressly require an "absolute right" to be involved'.[471]

Professors I. Galvão Telles,[472] F. Pessoa Jorge,[473] A. Menezes Cordeiro[474] and E. Santos Júnior[475] argued in favour of a declarative – of a non-restrictive interpretation of the expression *rights of another person.*[476]

Professor E. Santos Júnior, for instance, suggested that Article 483(1) of the Portuguese Civil Code should apply to all cases of intentional interference with contractual relations: on the one hand, it should apply to the infringement of contractual, relative rights; on the other hand, however, it should apply only to the

---

acerca do artigo 80.º do Código Civil)', in: *Estudos em memória do Professor Doutor Paulo Cunha* (Lisboa: Faculdade de Direito da Universidade de Lisboa 1989) 373–406; P. Mota Pinto, 'O direito à reserva sobre a intimidade da vida privada', in: 69 *Boletim da Faculdade de Direito* [da Universidade de Coimbra] (1993) 479–586; P. Mota Pinto, 'A protecção da vida privada e a Constituição', in: 76 *Boletim da Faculdade de Direito* [da Universidade de Coimbra] (2000) 153–204; P. Mota Pinto, 'A limitação voluntária do direito à reserva sobre a intimidade da vida privada', in: *Estudos em homenagem a Cunha Rodrigues*, vol. II (Coimbra: Coimbra Editora 2001) 527–558.

468. A. Ferrer Correia, 'Da responsabilidade civil de terceiro que coopera com o devedor na violação de um pacto de preferência', 98 *Revista de Legislação e de Jurisprudência* (1966–1967), 355–360 and 369–374.
469. M. de Andrade (with R. de Alarcão), *Teoria geral das obrigações* 3rd edition (Coimbra: Livraria Almedina 1966) 48–53.
470. *See*, for instance, J.F. Sinde Monteiro, 'Case 2 – Portugal', 203.
471. *See*, for instance, J.F. Sinde Monteiro, 'Case 2 – Portugal', 203.
472. I. Galvão Telles, *Direito das obrigações*, 20.
473. F. Pessoa Jorge, *Lições de direito das obrigações* (Lisboa: AAFDUL 1966–1967) 599–603, and F. Pessoa Jorge, *Ensaio sobre os pressupostos da responsabilidade civil*, 138 (footnote 109).
474. A. Menezes Cordeiro, *Direito das obrigações*, vol. I, 262–265 and 274–282; A. Menezes Cordeiro, *Da boa fé no direito civil*, 647–648; A. Menezes Cordeiro, *Tratado de direito civil português*, vol. II – *Direito das obrigações*, I – *Introdução. Sistemas e direito europeu das obrigações. Dogmática geral,* 401–406; A. Menezes Cordeiro, *Tratado de direito civil português*, vol. II – *Direito das obrigações*, III. – *Gestão de negócios. Enriquecimento sem causa. Responsabilidade civil*, 445–448.
475. E. Santos Júnior, *Da responsabilidade civil de terceiro por lesão do direito de crédito* (Coimbra: Livraria Almedina 2003) especially at 437 ff.
476. *See also* P. Pais de Vasconcelos, 'O efeito externo da obrigação no contrato-promessa', in: 32 *Scientia Juridica* 3 ff.; R. Amaral Cabral, *A eficácia externa da obrigação e o n.º 2 do art. 406.º do Código Civil* (Braga: Livraria Cruz 1984); R. Amaral Cabral, 'A tutela delitual do direito de crédito', in: *Estudos em homenagem ao Professor Doutor Manuel Gomes da Silva* (Lisboa: Faculdade de Direito da Universidade de Lisboa 2001) 1025–1053.

intentional infringement of contractual, relative rights. Therefore, all cases of mere negligent interference should be disregarded.[477]

Professors Antunes Varela,[478] F.M. Pereira Coelho,[479] M.J. de Almeida Costa[480] and R. de Alarcão,[481] J. Ribeiro de Faria,[482] J. Sinde Monteiro[483] and L. Menezes Leitão[484] argued in favour of a restrictive interpretation of the expression *rights of another person.*[485] *Rights of another person*, in the sense of Article 483, should be *absolute rights* – and *absolute rights* only.

It has been argued that a distinction could be made between *attacks on a substratum of the credit* and *attacks on the credit itself.*[486]

Attacks on a substratum of the credit would comprehend *attacks* on objects that are instrumental to the performance of contractual obligations and *attacks* on the very subject of performance – i.e., on the very person of the debtor.

Among the *attacks* on the very object of performance would be, for example, the cases where the third party damaged an electricity cable, thus 'preventing performance of a contract to supply energy'; among the *attacks* on the very subject on the very person of the debtor would be, for example, the cases where the third party injures the debtor physically, 'thus preventing the debtor from performing an employment contract'.

Attacks on the credit itself would comprehend, for example – first and foremost – cases of collusion between the debtor and a third party.[487]

The arguments in favour of holding the third party liable would be weaker in the first and stronger in the second type of situation.[488]

In spite of the discussion, Portuguese doctrine, followed by the judiciary, prefers a restrictive reading of the concept of *rights of another person.*

---

477. E. Santos Júnior, *Da responsabilidade civil de terceiro por lesão do direito de crédito*, 594.
478. J.M. Antunes Varela, *Das obrigações em geral*, vol. I, 530–536.
479. F.M. Pereira Coelho, *Obrigações. Sumários das lições ao curso de 1966/1967*, 68–71.
480. M.J. de Almeida Costa, *Direito das obrigações*, 91–101, and M.J. de Almeida Costa, 'A eficácia externa das obrigações. Entendimento da doutrina clássica', in: 135 *Revista de Legislação e de Jurisprudência* (2006)130–136.
481. R. de Alarcão, *Direito das obrigações*, 82–89.
482. J. Ribeiro de Faria, *Direito das obrigações*, vol. I, 41–47.
483. J.F. Sinde Monteiro, *Responsabilidade por conselhos, recomendações ou informações*, 185–187, and J. Ferreira Sinde Monteiro, 'Rudimentos da responsabilidade civil', 361–365.
484. L.M. Menezes Leitão, *Direito das obrigações*, vol. I – *Introdução. Da constituição das obrigações*, 97–102.
485. *See also* J.C. Brandão Proença, *Direito das obrigações. Relatório sobre o programa, o conteúdo e os métodos de ensino da disciplina* (Porto: Universidade Católica 2007) 135–137; N.M. Pinto Oliveira, *Direito das obrigações*, vol. I, 251–276; N.M. Pinto Oliveira, *Princípios de direito dos contratos*, 965–1008; João Carlos Leal Amado, *Vinculação versus liberdade. O processo de constituição e extinção da relação laboral do praticante desportivo* (Coimbra: Coimbra Editora 2002) 347–357; Mafalda Miranda Barbosa, *Liberdade vs. Responsabilidade. A precaução como fundamento da imputação delitual?* (Coimbra: Livraria Almedina 2006) 86–102.
486. *See* J.F. Sinde Monteiro, 'Case 5 – Portugal', in: M. Bussani/V.V. Palmer (eds), *Pure Economic Loss in Europe* (Cambridge: Cambridge University Press 2003) 251–253 (252).
487. *See* J.F. Sinde Monteiro, 'Case 5 – Portugal', 252.
488. *See* J.F. Sinde Monteiro, 'Case 5 – Portugal', 252: 'In the second type of situation, there has been much discussion of the case where the third party, being aware of the existence of the credit right (usually a contract), colludes with the debtor in the non-fulfilment, principally when this leads to failure of the contract.'

'It is possible to say', as Professor Sinde Monteiro says, 'that the prevailing doctrine and case-law continue to oppose the external effect'.[489]

In both types of situations, third parties are not to be held liable for damages to the creditor resulting from the infringement of contractual, relative rights. '[I]n the case of inducing the failure of the contract, there is no unlawful act as such.'[490] The principle that third parties are not to be held liable for damages to the creditor is based upon the idea of a fundamental balance between the interests of the creditor and the interests of third parties – both the interests of the creditor and the interests of the third party deserve equal protection.[491] It applies to normal cases. It does not apply, however, to exceptional cases, such as cases of abuse of rights.

Article 334 of the Portuguese Civil Code on abuse of rights comprehends, for instance, cases of intentional conduct *contra bonos mores*.

In keeping with Article 334, 'the third party might be called upon to respond if the act were deemed very censurable and might be considered an abuse of right'.[492] It is submitted that cases of intentional interference with contractual, relative rights qualify as cases of abuse of rights:

> an action grounded in Article 483 and Article 334 […] may be accepted in an intentional case of inducement of breach of a contract.[493]

489. *See* J.F. Sinde Monteiro, 'Case 5 – Portugal', 252.
490. *See* J.F. Sinde Monteiro, 'Case 5 – Portugal', 252.
491. *See* J.F. Sinde Monteiro, *Responsabilidade por conselhos, recomendações ou informações*, 185–186 and, following Sinde Monteiro, L.M. Menezes Leitão, *Direito das obrigações*, vol. I – *Introdução. Da constituição das obrigações*, 100.
492. *See* J.F. Sinde Monteiro, 'Case 5 – Portugal', 252.
493. *See* A.G. Dias Pereira, 'Portuguese Tort Law: A Comparison with the Principles of European Tort Law', 631.

Part II. Liability for Acts of Others

Chapter 1. Vicarious Liability

§1. Liability for Another's Acts and Omissions

73. The concept of liability for another's acts and omissions comprehends two different types of liability: on the one hand, it comprehends fault-based liability for the infringement of a duty of supervision (Article 491); on the other hand, it comprehends no-fault, strict liability of the principal for acts and omissions of their agents, auxiliaries and employees.[494]

§2. Employee/Employer

74. No-fault, objective liability of the principal for acts and omission of their agents, auxiliaries and employees results from Article 500 of the Portuguese Civil Code:

1. A person who uses another to perform a task is liable, irrespective of fault, to make compensation for the damage that their agent, auxiliary or employee causes to third parties, provided that the latter also has the obligation to compensate.
2. Liability of the principal only exists if the act or omission was performed by the agent, auxiliary or employee, albeit intentionally or contrary to the instructions of the principal, in the exercise of the function assigned to him.
3. The principal who pays the compensation is entitled to claim full reimbursement from the agent, from the auxiliary, or from the employee, unless he also infringed a duty of care. In this case, the provisions of Article 497 (2) shall apply.[495]

---

494. For a comparative approach to liability for another's acts and omissions, *see* R. Zimmermann, *The Law of Obligations. Roman Foundations of the Civilian Tradition*, 1118 ff., B.S. Markesinis/H. Unberath, *The German Law of Torts. A Comparative Treatise*, 693–705; H. Koziol, *Basic Questions of Tort Law from a Germanic Perspective*, 210–225; C. van Dam, *European Tort Law*, 490–519; P. Gilliker, *Vicarious Liability in Tort. A Comparative Perspective* (Cambridge: Cambridge University Press 2010).

495. On the interpretation of Art. 500 of the Portuguese Civil Code, *see*, for instance, J.M. Antunes Varela, *Das obrigações em geral* I, 638–646; M.J. Almeida Costa, *Direito das obrigações*,

In the first place, Article 500(1) refers to the relationship between the principal and their agents, auxiliaries or employees.

It requires *subordination*. The principal is to be entitled to give orders and instructions to their agents, to their auxiliaries, and to their employees. It follows from Article 500 that there is no objective, strict tortious liability for acts and omissions of independent contractors.

Second, Article 500(1) requires the agent, auxiliary or employee to be liable to make compensation.

It is discussed whether the liability of the agent, auxiliary, or employee requires fault.

In accordance with the first theory, liability of the auxiliary must be fault-based, subjective liability. In keeping with a second theory, liability of the auxiliary or employee may be either subjective or objective – it may be either fault-based or no-fault, strict liability.

It is submitted that Article 500(1) makes no distinction. It requires the auxiliary or employee to be held liable – it does not require them to be held liable on any particular, specific grounds, such as a fault. Therefore, the principal is to be held liable, even if the auxiliary or employee is only subject to no-fault, strict liability.

It is also submitted, however, that in practical terms, the discussion is of no importance. Cases of vicarious liability to be decided by Portuguese courts typically are cases of vicarious liability for negligent misconduct of the auxiliaries or employees.

Third, Article 500(2) requires the act or omission to be performed by the agent, auxiliary or employee in the exercise of the function assigned to him.

The expression was borrowed from § 831 of the German Civil Code.

Professor Markesinis rightly points out that 'behind this not very informative expression lies one of the most litigated aspects of the whole law of vicarious liability'.[496] The judgment fully applies to Article 500(2) of the Portuguese Civil Code.

In Germany, as well as in Portugal, the requirements that the act or omission is performed by the agent, by the auxiliary or by the employee in the exercise of the function assigned to him is sometimes 'expressed in causal language'.[497]

614–620; J. Ribeiro de Faria, *Direito das obrigações* II, 406–420; P. Nunes de Carvalho, 'A responsabilidade do comitente', 48 *Revista da Ordem dos Advogados* (1988), 85–120; M. Carneiro da Frada, *Contrato e deveres de protecção*, 203–217; P.F. Múrias, 'A responsabilidade por actos de auxiliares e o entendimento dualista da responsabilidade civil', 37 *Revista da Faculdade de Direito da Universidade de Lisboa* (1996), 171–217; M. Carneiro da Frada, 'A responsabilidade objectiva por facto de outrem face à distinção entre responsabilidade obrigacional e aquiliana', in: *Direito e Justiça* 1998, at 297–311; M.G. Trigo, 'Responsabilidade civil do comitente (ou responsabilidade por facto de terceiro)', in: *Comemorações dos 35 anos do Código Civil e dos 25 anos da Reforma de 1977*, vol. III – *Direito das obrigações* (Coimbra 2007) 153–169; M.G. Trigo, *Responsabilidade civil delitual por facto de terceiro* (Coimbra: Coimbra Editora 2009); B.G. Lobo Xavier, 'Nota sobre a responsabilidade do trabalhador pelos actos dos trabalhadores', 51 *Revista de direito e estudos sociais* (2011), 9–41; C. Madaleno, *A responsabilidade obrigacional objetiva por fato de outrem*, doctoral dissertation, Faculdade de Direito da Universidade de Lisboa, 2014, 873 ff. (available at http://repositorio.ul.pt/bitstream/10451/22242/1/ulsd071777_td_Claudia_Madaleno.pdf).

496. B.S. Markesinis/H. Unberath, *The German Law of Torts. A Comparative Treatise*, 696.

497. B.S. Markesinis/H. Unberath, *The German Law of Torts. A Comparative Treatise*, 696.

In Germany, it is argued that there must be 'an internal, direct connection between the function assigned to the servant and the activity that has caused the harm'.[498]

The principal will be liable for his auxiliary or employee's acts and omissions if the fact that he assigned him a task to perform is to be considered a *cause* and, conversely, the principal will not be liable if the fact that he assigned him a task is not to be considered a *cause* of the damaging event. The fact that their employment provided them with the occasion or opportunity to perform these events is not sufficient.

In Portugal, the causal requirement of an internal, direct connection is elaborated by referring to the so-called *positive formulation* of the adequacy requirement. The fact that the principal assigned the agent, the auxiliary or the employee a task to perform is to be considered a *cause* of the damaging event if, and only if, such a task, for its very nature, normally increases the risk of that type of damaging result.[499]

The principal and his agent, auxiliary, or employee are jointly and severally liable.[500]

In external relations – i.e., in the relationship between both principal and auxiliary and the victim – they are both bound to compensate in full.[501] In internal relations – i.e., in the relationship between principal and auxiliary – Article 500(3) applies.

If there is no fault of the principal, he is entitled to claim full reimbursement from the agent, from the auxiliary, or from the employee. If, however, there is the fault of the principal, for he infringed a duty of care – for instance, in inspecting his auxiliary or employee – Article 500(3) explicitly refers to Article 497(2). In that case, liability is apportioned, taking into account the degree of fault of each tortfeasor and his contribution to damage.

§3. Independent Contractors

75. As we have seen, Article 500 does not apply only to employees but also to other persons who are under certain forms of *subordination.*

If the independent contractor is not under the requisites of Article 500, (s)he is responsible, and it will be very hard to demand strict liability from the 'principal' in case of damage to third parties.

498. B.S. Markesinis/H. Unberath, *The German Law of Torts. A Comparative Treatise*, 696.
499. *See*, for instance, J.M. Antunes Varela, *Das obrigações em geral* I, 642–643.
500. *See* Art. 497(1), which applies to no-fault, objective liability pursuant to Art. 499 of the Portuguese Civil Code.
501. *See* Arts 512 and 519 of the Portuguese Civil Code, on solitary obligations.

§4. Liability of Legal Entities for Acts of Their Organs (and for Acts of Persons Entrusted with the Power to Act Without Being an Organ)

76. According to Article 165, legal entities are liable for the acts of their organs. In the case of tort law, the rules of Article 500 apply. In the case of contractual liability, Article 800 is applicable.

As to the difference between Article 500 and Article 800(1):

> There is a conceptual, structural difference between both Articles. Article 500 takes principal and his helper as different, separate persons. The principal is to be held liable in tort for the conduct of his helper. Article 800 (1) takes principal and his helper as one, and the same, person. In accordance with Article 800 (1), the principal (=the debtor) is to be held liable for the conduct of his helper, as if the helper's conduct was the principal's.

The conceptual, structural difference between Articles 500 and 800(1) of the Portuguese Civil Code has three consequences:

The *first consequence* refers to the subjective requirements of liability.

Article 500(1) requires *subordination.* Article 800(1) requires no *subordination* at all. The debtor is to be held liable for all acts and for all omissions of all persons concurring to performance. In fact, Article 800(1) explicitly refers to *auxiliaries* or *helpers.* It follows from such a wording that the debtor for all acts, of all persons, helping him to carry out performance – all of them are auxiliaries, all of them helpers.

The *second consequence* refers to the objective requirements of liability.

Whereas Article 500(1) and (2) limits the principal's liability to cases where the helper is performing his task, and Article 800(1) does not.

The third consequence refers to the helper's liability for the damage.

Whereas Article 500(1) of the Civil Code requires the helper – the subordinate – to be himself liable for the damage, Article 800(1) does not.

In most, if not all, cases of contractual liability, it is not possible for the auxiliary to be held liable in contract vis-à-vis the creditor. There is a contract, and therefore, there is a relationship of obligation between the creditor and the debtor. There is no contract between the helper and the creditor.

The difference is rather significant, both theoretically and practically.

In the case of non-contractual, tortious liability, it makes full sense to hold both principal and subordinate jointly and solidarily liable for all damage (Article 500(3)). In the case of contractual liability, it makes no sense at all – the debtor is to be held liable in the contract; the debtor's auxiliaries or helpers are not.

Chapter 2. Liability of Parents, Teachers & Instructors (For Children, Minors, Students)

77. Fault-based, subjective liability for the infringement of a duty of supervision results from Article 491 of the Portuguese Civil Code:

> A person who is bound by law or by contract to exercise supervision over a person on account of minority, or of his mental or physical condition, is bound to make compensation for any damage which the latter unlawfully does to a third party, unless he fulfils his duty of supervision, or if the damage would have occurred notwithstanding the proper exercise of supervision.[502]

Article 491 applies both to parental liability for the torts of their children[503] and to non-parental liability of persons bound, by contract or by law, to exercise supervision.

It depends on the existence of a duty to exercise supervision; it requires that the duty to exercise supervision results either from the supervised person's minority or from his mental or physical condition;[504] finally, it requires that the infringement of the duty to exercise supervision is the cause of the damages a third party sustained.

The person who is bound by law or by contract to exercise supervision may escape liability if he or she proves either that he or she properly exercised supervision or that damage would have occurred notwithstanding the proper exercise of supervision.

In the case of Article 491, fault-based, subjective liability is aggravated, for there is a reversal of the burden of proof. It qualifies as a supervisory liability based on presumed negligence.[505] In the case of Article 500, fault-based, subjective liability is replaced by no-fault, objective, strict liability. The principal is held liable, irrespective of fault.

502. On the interpretation of Art. 491 of the Portuguese Civil Code, *see*, for instance, H. Sousa Antunes, *Responsabilidade civil dos obrigados à vigilância de pessoa naturalmente incapaz* (Lisboa: Universidade Católica 2000).
503. *See*, for instance, P. Gilliker, *Vicarious Liability in Tort. A Comparative Perspective*, 196 ff.
504. It is not necessary, however, that the supervised person lacks the so-called capacity to commit torts. In the case the supervised person is imputable, both the supervisor and the supervised person will be held jointly and severally liable [*see* Art. 497 of the Portuguese Civil Code]; in the case the supervised person is not imputable, however, only the supervisor will be held liable. If, for some reason, only the non-imputable person comes to be held liable, on the grounds of Art. 489 of the Portuguese Civil Code, he or she is entitled to claim full reimbursement from the supervisor.
505. C. van Dam, *European Tort Law*, 492.

Chapter 3. Liability for Things and Animals

78. In Portuguese law, the same norm regulates liability for dangerous activities and dangerous things.

Liability for dangerous activities and liability for dangerous things can be either fault-based or no-fault. The concepts of fault-based and no-fault, strict liability require re-examination.

In the first place, there are cases of pure fault-based liability, where the plaintiff is to demonstrate the defendant's negligence. Second, there are cases of impure fault-based liability. That is what happens when there is a presumption of fault – the ordinary standard of care applies, for the defendant is admitted to demonstrate that he behaved as a reasonable person would behave. Third, liability may be exactly in-between. That is what happens when there is more than a presumption of fault. The ordinary standard of care does not apply, for the defendant is only admitted to prove that he did behave as a more than a reasonable person would behave – for the defendant is to prove that he behaved with exceptional care, taking all precautions to prevent damage. Fourth, there are cases of impure, no-fault, strict liability. That is what happens when there is a presumption that damage resulted from that particular, specific risk foreseen by the law – the defendant is only admitted to demonstrate there was force majeure. Fifth, there are cases of pure no-fault, strict liability, where the defendant is not even admitted to prove force majeure.

It is submitted that the third type of liability is closer to no-fault than to fault-based liability. Whenever the defendant conforms to the ordinary standard of care, he is not at fault.[506] It is thus submitted that cases where *the defendant is only exempted from liability if he demonstrates that he behaved with exceptional, more than reasonable care, taking all precautions to prevent damage*, are cases of *no-fault, objective, strict liability*. Whether there is negligence is (maybe) open to discussion. It all depends on how negligence is defined – however, if there is negligence, there is negligence without fault.[507]

§1. On a General Clause of Aggravated Liability for Dangerous Activities

79. Article 493(2) of the Portuguese Civil Code reads as follows:

> Whoever causes damage to another person when performing a dangerous activity, is bound to make compensation for such a damage, unless he demonstrates he has taken all reasonable steps to prevent it.

The concept of dangerous activity apparently requires an aggravated risk of damage.

In order to determine whether there is an aggravated risk of damage, the judge is to consider both the nature of the activity and the nature of the equipment and

506. *See*, for instance, J. Calvão da Silva, *Responsabilidade civil do produtor*, 400–414.
507. *See* A. Ehnrenzweig, 'Negligence without Fault', 54 *California Law Review* (1966), at 1422–1477.

instruments the activity normally involves. Therefore, whether an activity is dangerous or not is something that can only be established considering all circumstances of the case.[508]

It is commonly held that the particularly high standard of care established in Article 487(2) does not affect the nature of liability for dangerous activities as a fault-based liability.

In requiring the defendant to demonstrate that he has taken all reasonable steps to prevent damage, Article 493(2) would confirm the standard of care established in Article 487(2) – the *bonus paterfamilias'* standard of care. The defendant is to take increased care, so as to prevent an increased danger from materializing in damage.

The difference between the general principles and rules on liability for one's own acts and omissions and the particular, specific rules on liability for dangerous activities would be limited to the burden of proof. In accordance with the general principles and rules on liability for one's own acts and omissions, the burden of proof rests on the plaintiff. It is up to the plaintiff to prove the defendant was negligent.[509] In keeping with the particular, specific rules on liability for (one's own) dangerous activities, the burden of proof rests on the defendant. It is up to the defendant to prove that he was not negligent – that he has taken all reasonable steps to prevent damage. Liability for dangerous activities would be a liability for presumed fault, for presumed negligence – and nothing else.

In the event the defendant wishes to rebut the presumption of fault that was created against him, he would have to prove that the standard of care required from any person – from any *bonus paterfamilias* – in his situation was met, so as to prevent damage.

In spite of the fact that it is commonly held that the particular standard of care established in Article 487(2) does not affect the nature of liability for dangerous activities, it is submitted that there is a difference between Article 487(2) and Article 493(2).

Whereas Article 487(2) would require the defendant to demonstrate he has taken the steps a reasonable person would have taken, Article 493(2) requires the defendant to demonstrate he has taken *all steps* to prevent damage. In requiring the defendant to demonstrate that he has taken *all steps to prevent damage,* Article 493(2) clearly goes beyond the ordinary standard of care established in Article 487(2).[510]

It is thus submitted that Article 493(2) of the Portuguese Civil Code is to be interpreted as a general clause of no-fault, strict liability for dangerous activities.[511]

---

508. *See*, for instance, F.A. Pires de Lima/J.M. Antunes Varela (/ M. Henrique Mesquita), *Código Civil anotado*, vol. I, 495.
509. *See* Art. 487(1) of the Portuguese Civil Code.
510. *See*, for instance, L. Menezes Leitão, *Direito das obrigações*, I. – *Introdução. Da constituição das obrigações*, 330; J.C. Brandão Proença, *Direito das obrigações. Relatório sobre o programa, o conteúdo e os métodos de ensino da disciplina*, 188; N.M. Pinto Oliveira, 'Responsabilidade objectiva', in: *Cadernos de direito privado,* special issue – *II Seminário dos Cadernos de Direito Privado* (2012) 107–121.
511. *See* N.M. Pinto Oliveira, 'Point de vue extérieur', in: P. Jourdain (ed.), *Le droit français de la responsabilité civile confronté aux projets européens d'harmonisation* (Paris: IJRS Editions 2012) 841–862; N.M. Pinto Oliveira, 'Responsabilidade objectiva', 107–121.

§2. On General Clauses of Aggravated Liability for Dangerous Things

80. The general principle on liability for dangerous activities in Article 493(2) of the Portuguese Civil Code is supplemented by a set of particular, specific rules on liability for animals, liability for movable things, as well as liability for immovable things.

As to liability for animals, two provisions apply. Article 493(1) of the Portuguese Civil Code applies to whoever is bound to supervise animals. 'Whoever detains movable or immovable things, and is bound to supervise them, *as well as whoever is bound to supervise animals*, shall be held liable for any damage caused by such things, or by such animals, unless he demonstrates that he has exercised due diligence, or that the damage would have occurred notwithstanding the proper exercise of diligence.' Article 503 of the Portuguese Civil Code applies to whoever uses animals in their own interest: 'Whoever uses any animals in their own interest shall be liable for any damage they cause, provided that such damage results from the special danger associated with their use.'

It follows from the wording in Article 493(1) that liability depends on the infringement of a duty to supervise – 'Whoever is bound to supervise animals shall only be held liable for damage resulting from the infringement of his duty to supervise.' It also follows from the wording in Article 493(1) that there are two presumptions – 'Whoever is bound to supervise animals is presumed to have infringed his duty, and damage to third parties is presumed to have resulted from the fact that the defendant infringed his duty.'

The presumptions in Article 493(1) are, however, rebuttable. The defendant is allowed to prove either that he did not infringe his duty to supervise or that there is no causal connection between the infringement of his duty to supervise and the damage third parties sustained. On the one hand, he is allowed to prove that he did not infringe his duty to supervise by demonstrating that he has exercised due diligence. On the other hand, he is allowed to prove that there is no connection between the infringement of his duty to supervise and the damage third parties sustained by demonstrating that 'the damage would have occurred notwithstanding the proper exercise of diligence'.

Whereas Article 493(1) still refers to fault-based, subjective liability – albeit to liability for presumed fault – Article 503 refers to no-fault, objective, strict liability.

In keeping with the general structure of the Portuguese Civil Code on no-fault, objective, strict liability, Article 503 refers to three requirements:

In the first place, it requires the defendant to have established or to be in charge of the particular, specific situation of danger referred to by the provision that consecrates strict liability. In the case of Article 503, it requires the defendant to have established or be in charge of such a particular, specific situation of danger by using animals.

Second, it requires the defendant to have an interest in that particular, specific situation of danger.

Third, it requires damage to result from the particular, specific situation of danger the defendant has established or is in charge of.

In the case of Article 503, the defendant is only to be held liable for damage resulting 'from the special danger associated with [the] use [of animals]'.

It is submitted that Article 505 of the Portuguese Civil Code is to apply, indirectly, by way of analogy, to cases of liability for animals, as enshrined in Article 503.

The defendant shall be allowed to escape liability by demonstrating either that damage is imputable to the plaintiff or to a third party or that damage results from force majeure unrelated to the special danger associated with the use of animals.[512]

In what concerns movable things, aggravated liability, based upon the presumption of fault in Article 493(1), applies: 'Whoever detains movable or immovable things, and is bound to supervise them, [...] shall be held liable for any damage caused by such things, [...] unless he demonstrates that he has exercised due diligence, or that the damage would have occurred notwithstanding the proper exercise of diligence.'

In what concerns immovable things, aggravated liability results from two provisions.

On the one hand, it results from Article 492:

1. The owner of a building, or any other facility, which falls down due to a construction or maintenance defect, shall be held liable for all damage caused, unless he demonstrates either that his conduct conforms to the duty of diligence, or that damages would have occurred even if his conduct conformed to such a duty.
2. If the damage is caused by a maintenance defect, only the person under a statutory or contractual duty to maintain the building shall be held liable.

On the other hand, it results from Article 493(1): 'Whoever detains [...] immovable things, and is bound to supervise them, [...] shall be held liable for any damage caused by such things, [...] unless he demonstrates that he has exercised due diligence, or that the damage would have occurred notwithstanding the proper exercise of diligence.'

In the case of buildings falling down, the owner is to be held liable for construction defects, maintenance defects, as well as supervision defects – i.e., for infringements of his duty to supervise. In spite of the fact that liability for maintenance defects and supervision defects may be transferred to third parties, according to Articles 492(2) and 493(1), normally, the owner will be liable for all types of defects. In the case of another's immovable things, as well as in the case of another's accidents caused by buildings, the owner is only to be held liable for the supervision of defects – in keeping with the fact that Article 492(1) and (2) is limited in scope, only Article 493(1) applies.

It has been suggested that Article 493(1) should apply, for instance, to accidents caused by animals on highways.[513] Article 12 of Law No. 24/2007 of 18 July has,

512. *See* J.C. Brandão Proença. *A conduta do lesado como pressuposto e critério de imputação do dano extracontratual* (Coimbra: Livraria Almedina 1998) 230–247 and 795–826.

513. *See*, for instance, J.F. Sinde Monteiro, 'Acidente na auto-estrada, provocado pelo atravessamento de um animal (anotação ao acórdão do Supremo Tribunal de Justiça de 12 de Novembro de 1996)', 131 *Revista de Legislação e de Jurisprudência* (1998–1999), 41–50, 106–113, 378–380; as well as

however, established the rule that the concessionary of a highway is to demonstrate that it complied with their duties of safety. Therefore, after Law No. 24/2007, whether Article 493(1) applies or does not apply to highways tends to be immaterial.

---

in 132 *Revista de Legislação e de Jurisprudência*(1999–2000), 28–32, 60–64, 90–96; J.F. Sinde Monteiro, 'Acidentes de viação – natureza e regime da responsabilidade da concessionária (anotação ao acórdão do Supremo Tribunal de Justiça de 17 de Fevereiro de 2000 e à sentença do Juiz do 3º Juízo de Competência Especializada do Tribunal da Comarca de Santo Tirso de 2 de Maio de 1996', 133 *Revista de Legislação e de Jurisprudência* (2000–2001), 17–32, 59–66.

Part III. Forms of Strict Liability

Chapter 1. Road and Traffic Accidents

§1. Road and Traffic Accidents [under Article 503 of the Portuguese Civil Code]

I. Requirements Regarding the Defendant: (Who Is to Compensate the Damage?)

81. Liability for traffic accidents[514] may be either fault-based, subjective liability or no-fault, strict liability. If there is a fault, either proved or presumed, of the driver, the general principle in Article 483(1) applies. In the case the driver is an agent, auxiliary or employee, Article 483(1) is to be read in conjunction with Article 500. Therefore, both the principal and his agent, auxiliary or employee will be held jointly and severally liable. If there is no fault of the driver, the particular, specific rule in Article 503(1) applies. In keeping with Article 503:

> Whoever is in possession of a road vehicle and uses it in his own interest, albeit by means of an agent, auxiliary or employee, shall be held liable for damage inherent to the vehicle's own danger, even if such a vehicle is not circulating.

514. On liability for traffic accidents, *see*, for instance, J.M. Antunes Varela, *Das obrigações em geral*, vol. I, 654–714; M.J. Almeida Costa, *Direito das obrigações*, 627–652; J. Ribeiro de Faria, *Direito das* obrigações, vol. II (Coimbra: Livraria Almedina 2001, reprint) 30–107; A. Menezes Cordeiro, *Tratado de direito civil português*, vol. II – *Direito das obrigações*, III. – *Gestão de negócios. Enriquecimento sem causa. Responsabilidade civil,* 663–680; L.M. Menezes Leitão, *Direito das obrigações*, vol. I – *Introdução. Da constituição das obrigações*, 369–381; Jorge Ferreira Sinde Monteiro, 'Responsabilidade civil – I. Introdução', in: 4 *Revista de direito e economia* (1978), 312–405; J.F. Sinde Monteiro, 'Responsabilidade por culpa, responsabilidade objectiva, seguro de acidentes (propostas de alteração ao Código Civil e ao Decreto-Lei n.º 408/79, de 25 de Setembro; considerações em torno de um seguro social de acidentes de trabalho e de trânsito)', in: 5 *Revista de direito e economia* (1979) 123 ff.; J. Sousa Ribeiro, 'O ónus da prova da culpa na responsabilidade civil por acidentes de viação', in: *Boletim da Faculdade de Direito* [da Universidade de Coimbra] – *Estudos em homenagem ao Professor Doutor José Joaquim Teixeira Ribeiro*, vol. II – *Iuridica),* 1980, 413–542; J.F. Sinde Monteiro, 'Acidentes de viação – Assento n.º 1/80', 57 *Boletim da Faculdade de Direito* [da Universidade de Coimbra] (1981), 231–243; R. Guichard, 'Acerca da responsabilidade civil objectiva por danos causados por veículos de circulação terrestre', in: *Revista de ciências empreariais e jurídicas* (2006); M. Graça Trigo, 'Das presunções de culpa no regime da responsabilidade civil por acidentes de viação', in: *Cadernos de direito privado* No. 32 (2010) 22–44; M. Graça Trigo, *Responsabilidade civil. Temas especiais*, 23–40.

There are a few fundamental differences between fault-based, subjective liability and no-fault, objective liability for traffic accidents.

In the case of fault-based, subjective liability, the duty to compensate is to be imposed on the driver. If the driver acts in his own interest, the picture looks simpler. Article 483(1) of the Portuguese Civil Code applies without further complication. If, however, the driver acts on behalf of another person (in the interest of another person) – as an agent, auxiliary, or employee, in the sense of Article 500 – the impression of simplicity resulting from Article 483(1) is blurred both by Article 500 and by Article 503(3).

Article 483(1) requires fault – and Article 503(3) presumes fault of every single driver acting on behalf of another person as an agent, auxiliary or employee:

> Whoever drives a vehicle on behalf of another person shall be liable for the damage he causes, unless he proves that he had no fault. If, however, he drives the vehicle outside the scope of his or her functions as agent, auxiliary, or employee, he shall be liable pursuant to paragraph 1.

It follows from Article 503(3) that the auxiliary is to be held liable for fault-based liability, and the principal is to be held liable for no-fault, strict liability.

In the case of no-fault, objective liability, the duty to compensate is to be imposed on whoever meets the two requirements in Article 503(1).

In the first place, Article 503(1) requires the defendant to be in possession of the vehicle. In Portuguese, it reads '*direcção efectiva do veículo*', and the closest translation for '*direcção efectiva*' probably is *actual and effective control* of the vehicle.

The defendant is deemed to be in possession of the vehicle whenever he has actual and effective control. It follows from the broad definition of *actual and effective control* that the plaintiff may claim compensation from both the driver and the owner – both of them will be liable, for both of them have *actual and effective control.*

Second, Article 503(1) requires the defendant to use the vehicle in his own interest.

The requirement aims at excluding whoever drives the vehicle on behalf of another person – as an agent, auxiliary, or employee.

The meaning of both requirements is to be updated by considering the relationship between tort law and insurance law. In keeping with Article 15(2) of Decree-Law No. 291/2007 of 21 August 2007, compulsory insurance is to cover liability even if the vehicle has been stolen. It has been authoritatively argued that Article 15(2) of Decree-Law No. 291/2007 requires an alternative reading of Article 503(1) of the Civil Code. In the event the vehicle has been stolen, neither the first nor the second requirement are to apply.[515]

515. *See* J. Calvão da Silva, '[Anotação ao] acórdão [do Supremo Tribunal de Justiça] de 13 de Fevereiro de 2003', 134 *Revista de Legislação e de Jurisprudência* (2001) 192–202.

II. Requirements Regarding the Plaintiff: (Who Is Entitled to Claim Compensation?)

82. If there is fault on the part of the driver, Articles 495 and 496(2) and (3) apply.

In all cases of bodily injury, the person responsible is to pay compensation to the injured party to those who render assistance to the injured party, as well as to those who may have contributed to the treatment or assistance of the victim.[516] In some particular cases of bodily injury where the victim dies, the person responsible is to pay compensation to a spouse who is not legally separated from the persons and assets and to the children or other descendants; failing the latter, to the parents or other ascendants; and, finally, to the brothers and sisters or nephews and nieces representing them.[517]

If, however, there is no fault on the part of the driver, the general principles and rules on fault-based, subjective liability are to be confronted to particular, specific rules on no-fault, objective, strict liability, enshrined in Article 504 of the Portuguese Civil Code:

1. Third parties and transported passengers shall benefit from liability for damage caused by vehicles.
2. In the case of contract-based transport, liability shall only cover the damage suffered by the transported persons themselves and the things they transport.
3. In the case of gratuitous transport, liability shall only cover the bodily injury of the transported passengers.
4. All clauses that exclude the carrier's liability for accidents injuring the transported person, or limit his or her liability, shall be void.

The concepts of 'third parties' and 'transported passengers' require further elaboration. The concept of *transported persons* refers exclusively to persons *inside the vehicle* (apart from the driver). The concept of *third parties* or *third persons* refers almost exclusively to persons *outside the vehicle*. It is commonly accepted that it also comprehends *persons inside the vehicle* involved in the vehicle's activity – *persons involved in the vehicle's activity*, such as ticket inspectors, should not be subject to the restrictive rules on damages sustained by transported persons.

In what concerns liability for damages caused to third parties, in the sense of Article 504, the extent of the duty to compensate is subject to no particular restriction.

In what concerns liability for damages caused to the transported persons, or passengers, the extent of the duty to compensate depends on two things.

First, it depends on whether the transport is contract-based or not. The concept of *gratuitous transport* in paragraph (3) is to comprehend cases where there is no contract at all. Second, in the event the transport is contract-based, liability depends on

516. *See* Portuguese Civil Code, Art. 495(2).
517. *See* Portuguese Civil Code, Art. 496(2). Article 496(3) makes it clear that the position of married and non-married persons, living in a de facto union, is to be equated.

the nature of the contract. Paragraph (2) applies exclusively to cases where there is an onerous contract, and paragraph (3) applies both to cases where there is no contract at all and to cases where there is a gratuitous contract between the parties.

If the case falls within the scope of paragraph (2), 'liability [under Article 503] shall only cover the damage suffered by the transported persons themselves and the things they transport'; if the case falls within the scope of paragraph (3), liability shall only cover the damage of the transported passengers themselves. It is submitted that the term 'damage suffered by the transported persons themselves', as well as the term 'damage of the transported passengers themselves', aim at excluding damage to the persons referred to in Article 495 and in Article 496(2) and (3) of the Portuguese Civil Code.

III. On the Connection Between *Danger* and *Damage*

83. In the case of fault-based, subjective liability, there must be a connection between damage and the unlawfulness of the defendant's conduct. The defendant is only to be held liable for damage resulting from the infringement of his duty.

In the case of no-fault, objective liability, there must be a connection between damage and a particular, specific source of danger. The defendant is only to be held liable for damage resulting from that particular, specific danger – from that particular, specific risk – underlying that particular, specific rule on no-fault, objective liability.

Article 503(1) of the Portuguese Civil Code explicitly refers to the connection between damage and danger by invoking the concept of damage inherent to the vehicle's own danger – 'whoever is in possession of a road vehicle and uses it in his own interest […] shall be held liable for damage inherent to the vehicle's own danger'. The concept of the vehicle's own danger comprehends at least three types of danger. It comprehends danger inherent to the vehicle itself, danger inherent to the road where the vehicle circulates, and danger inherent to the driver (such as the risk of a heart attack).

Furthermore, Article 503(1) is to be read in connection with Article 505:

> Safeguarding the provisions of Article 570, the liability determined by Article 503 (1) shall be excluded only when the accident is imputable to the injured party himself or herself or a third party, or when it results from force majeure unrelated with the vehicle's functioning.

The concept of force majeure unrelated to the vehicle's functioning results from the coordination between Article 505 and Article 509(2) on liability for facilities used for transmitting or delivering electricity or gas. In accordance with Article 509(2), '[f]orce majeure is any external cause independent of the functioning and use of the thing'.

It follows from the systematic relationship between Article 505 and Article 509(2) that force majeure is to be limited to external causes; moreover, it follows from the systematic relationship between Article 505 and Article 509(2) that force majeure is to be limited to causes independent of the functioning and use of the vehicle.

The concept of an *accident imputable to the injured party* requires further development.

In keeping with the general principle on contributory negligence enshrined in Article 570, whenever the injured party contributed to the existence or extension of damage, courts have a discretionary power: 'it is for the court to determine on the basis of the degree of fault of both parties and the consequences resulting from it, whether the compensation should be awarded in its entirety, reduced, or excluded'.[518] Contributory negligence of the injured party would lead to an apportionment of liability.

In keeping with the particular, specific rule on contributory negligence enshrined in Article 505, whenever the injured party contributed to the existence or extension of damage so that the accident is imputable to him, courts have no discretionary power at all. Compensation should always be excluded. Contributory negligence would never lead to an apportionment of liability – it would always lead to the exclusion of all liability.

It is submitted that the result of such an interpretation is far from sensible. If the danger inherent to the vehicle concurred with the damage, Article 503(1) should apply. The owner of the vehicle should be held liable – whether fully or partially would be an open question.

Therefore, it has been suggested that the concept of an *accident imputable to the injured party* should be interpreted restrictively. *Accident imputable to the injured party* should mean accident *exclusively* imputable to the injured party.[519]

It can be argued that Article 505 merely specifies the requirements in Article 503(1).

If it could be assumed that the behaviour of the injured party was the *only cause* of the accident, the rule in Article 505 should apply. Contributory negligence should lead to the exclusion of all liability. If, however, it could not be assumed that the behaviour of the injured party was the *only cause* of the accident, the rule in Article 505 should be replaced by the rule in Article 570. Contributory negligence should lead to an apportionment of liability.

The wording of Article 505 strongly favours such a restrictive interpretation – in fact, Article 505 explicitly says: 'safeguarding the provisions of Article 570'.

Finally, it is submitted that the concepts of accident imputable to the injured party and accident imputable to a third party should be interpreted coherently. If accident imputable to the injured party means accident exclusively imputable to the injured party, then accident imputable to a third party should mean exclusively imputable to a third party.

518. *See* Portuguese Civil Code, Art. 570(1).
519. *See* J.C. Brandão Proença, *A conduta do lesado como pressuposto e critério de imputação do dano extracontratual*, 811–826.

IV. Liability in Cases of Traffic Collisions (under Article 506 of the Portuguese Civil Code)

84. Article 506 of the Portuguese Civil Code applies to traffic collisions:

> If a collision of two vehicles results in damage regarding both or one of them, and none of the drivers is at fault, liability shall be shared as a proportion of each vehicles risk contribution to damage. If the damage is caused only by one vehicle and none of the two drivers is at fault, only the person liable for such damage is obliged to pay compensation.
>
> When in doubt, the contribution of each vehicle shall be considered equal, as equal shall be considered the contribution of each driver's fault to the damage.

The concept of 'damage regarding both or one of them', that is, damage regarding both of the vehicles or one of the vehicles, requires an extensive interpretation.

The criteria in Article 506 should apply to all damages. It should apply to damages regarding the vehicles, to damages regarding things and to damages regarding persons. It should comprehend, for instance, damages to the transported persons and to third parties.

In the event that there are only two vehicles involved in the accident, the principles and rules in Article 506 require the judge to distinguish at least six situations:

In the first place, it may happen that the fault of both drivers has been proved – that both of them are liable under Article 483(1) of the Portuguese Civil Code.

Second, it may happen that the fault of one of the drivers has been proved, according to the general rule in Article 487(1), and that fault of the other is presumed.

As in the first situation, both of them are liable under Article 483. The difference lies in the fact that one's fault has been proved and the other has not. One of them is to be held liable, for his fault has been proved, and the other is to be held liable, although his fault has not been proved, for it is presumed. That will be the case, for instance, if one of the persons involved in the collision drives the vehicle on his own and the other drives the vehicle on behalf of another person, namely, as his agent, auxiliary or employee.[520]

Third, it may happen that the fault of both drivers is presumed.

As in the first and the second situations, both of them are liable under Article 483. The difference lies in the fact that none's fault has been proved. That will be the case, for instance, if both of the persons involved drive the vehicle on behalf of another person.

Fourth, it may happen that there is fault on the part of one of the drivers, that fault being proved, and there is no fault at all on the part of the other.

While the former is liable under Article 483, the latter is liable under Article 503. Fault-based, subjective liability applies to the former, and strict liability applies to the latter.

---

520. *See* Portuguese Civil Code, Art. 503(3).

Fifth, it may happen that it is deemed to be a fault on the part of one of the drivers, that fault being presumed, and there is no fault on the part of the other.

Whereas the former still is liable under Article 483, in conjunction with any of the provisions establishing a presumption of fault – such as Article 503(3) – the latter is liable under Article 503, for he is at no fault at all. Fault-based liability still applies to the former, and no-fault, strict liability still applies to the latter.

Sixth, it may well happen that there is no fault on the part of any driver – In spite of the fact that none of them is at fault, both of them are to be held liable.

In the first hypothesis, Article 570 applies in connection with Article 506(2).

Article 570(1) refers to contributory negligence as a ground for apportionment of damages. 'If any faulty conduct of the injured party has contributed either to the occurrence of the damage or to its aggravation, the court shall determine, on the basis of comparison of the gravity of each party's fault, as well as on the basis of their consequences, whether compensation is to be fully awarded [to the injured party], fixed equitably at an amount lower than that of damage, or fully excluded.'

Article 506(2) further states a criterion as to the 'comparison of the gravity of each party's fault, as well as on the basis of their consequences': 'When in doubt, […] the contribution of each driver's fault to the damage [shall be considered equal].'

In the second hypothesis, there is a doubt on whether Article 570(2) applies.

In keeping with Article 570(2), if liability is merely based on a presumption of fault, contributory negligence on the part of the injured party completely excludes the liability of the defendant. In the case of a collision between a vehicle driven by someone acting on his own and a vehicle driven by someone acting on behalf of another person, the first driver would be liable for all damage and the second would be liable for no damage at all.

It has been argued that the result is unfair. Article 570(2) should be interpreted so as to apply to cases where the defendant demonstrates that the conduct of the driver whose fault has been proved is the only exclusive cause of the damage.

If this is the case – if there is *exclusive* causation – Article 570(2) applies. The driver whose fault has been proved shall be held liable for all damage. If this is not the case, however – if there is *concurrent, cumulative* causation – Article 570(1) should apply. The driver whose fault has been proved may or may not be liable for all damage. In fact, Article 570(1) may lead to an apportionment of damages.[521]

In the third hypothesis – that is, in the case of presumed fault of both drivers (for instance, for both vehicles are driven by agents, auxiliaries, or employees, in the course of their employment) – Article 570(1) applies in connection with Article 506(2).[522]

In the fourth and fifth hypothesis – that is, in the case of fault on the part of one of the drivers and no fault on the part of the other – Article 505 applies in connection with Article 570.

521. *See* J.C. Brandão Proença, *A conduta do lesado como pressuposto e critério de imputação do dano extracontratual*, 742 ff.

522. In that case, the relative, rebuttable presumption in Art. 506(2) practically transforms itself in an absolute, irrefutable presumption. For the liability of both drivers is based on a mere presumption of fault, it is practically impossible to demonstrate that the contribution of each driver's fault to the accident was different (unequal).

If the wording of Article 505 were to be interpreted declaratively, i.e., according to its ordinary meaning, the driver whose fault had been proven or merely presumed would be held liable for all damage and the driver whose fault had neither been proven nor presumed would be held liable for no damage at all. The accident would be imputable to the injured party himself or herself.

The result of such an interpretation is subject to criticism – especially in cases where fault on the part of one of the drivers is merely presumed.[523]

In the event of a vehicle driven by someone acting on his own collides with a vehicle driven by someone acting on behalf of another person, and none's fault has been proved, the driver acting on behalf of another person would be liable for all damage.[524]

Therefore, it is submitted that Article 505 is to be interpreted restrictively, so as to apply only to causes of exclusive causation. If the accident has been caused by the driver who is at fault or who is deemed to be at fault, as a result of a presumption – *and by that driver only* – Article 505 should apply. Liability of the driver who is at no fault at all should be excluded – he should be exempted from liability. If the accident has been caused by both drivers, Article 570 should apply. Liability of the driver who is at no fault should not be excluded – none of the drivers should be exempted from liability.[525]

Finally, in the sixth hypothesis – that is, in the case of no-fault of both drivers – Article 506 establishes three criteria:

> If the accident has been caused only by one of the vehicles, only the owner of such vehicle is obliged to make compensation; if the damage has been caused by both vehicles, liability shall be shared as a proportion of each vehicle's risk contribution to damage;[526] if the damage has been caused by both vehicles, and each vehicle's contribution to damage could not be established, liability shall be shared on equal parts (on a fifty-fifty basis).[527]

523. *See* J. Sousa Ribeiro, 'O ónus da prova da culpa na responsabilidade civil por acidentes de viação', in: *Boletim da Faculdade de Direito* [da Universidade de Coimbra] – *Estudos em homenagem ao Professor Doutor José Joaquim Teixeira Ribeiro*, vol. II – *Iuridica)*, 1980, 413–542; M. Graça Trigo, 'Das presunções de culpa no regime da responsabilidade civil por acidentes de viação', in: *Cadernos de direito privado* No. 32 (2010) 22–44; M. Graça Trigo, 'Das presunções de culpa no regime da responsabilidade civil por acidentes de viação', in: *Cadernos de direito privado* No. 32 (2010) 22–44; M. Graça Trigo, *Responsabilidade civil. Temas especiais*, 23–40.
524. Article 503(3) establishes a presumption of fault: 'Whoever drives a vehicle on behalf of another person shall be liable for the damage he causes, unless he proves that he had no fault.' For such a presumption has not been rebutted, the driver acting on behalf of another person would be liable for all damage.
525. *See* J.C. Brandão Proença, *A conduta do lesado como pressuposto e critério de imputação do dano extracontratual*, 811–827.
526. *See* Portuguese Civil Code, Art. 506(1).
527. *See* Portuguese Civil Code, Art. 506(2).

V. Ceilings for No-Fault, Strict Liability in the Case Traffic Accidents (under Article 508 of the Portuguese Civil Code)

85. Finally, whereas a fault-based, subjective liability is subject to no limits, no-fault, strict liability is subject to Article 508 – therefore, it is to be limited by ceilings.

In keeping with Article 508, there should be a perfect match between the minimum amounts covered by compulsory insurance and the ceilings of no-fault, strict liability.

Chapter 2. Product Liability

86. Directive 1985/374/EEC of 25 July 1985, on the approximation of the laws, regulations and administrative provisions of the Member States concerning liability for defective products, has been implemented in Portugal by Decree-Law No. 383/89 of 6 November 1989, as amended by Decree-Law No. 131/2001 of 21 April 2001.[528,529]

§1. General Principle

87. In accordance with the Court of Justice of the European Union (CJEU's) case law, the directive 'seeks to achieve, in matters regulated by it, complete harmonization of the laws, regulations, and administrative provisions of the Member States'.[530] In spite of the fact that complete harmonization leaves little room for Member States innovation, Decree-Law goes further than Directive 1985/374/EEC.[531] Article 1 of Directive 1985/374/EEC holds the producer liable for any damage caused by a defect in his product. Article 1 of Decree-Law No. 383/89 holds the producer liable, *irrespective of fault*, for any damage caused by a defect in the

---

528. For a comprehensive analysis of products liability under European and Portuguese law, *see* J. Calvão da Silva, *Responsabilidade civil do produtor* (Coimbra: Livraria Almedina 1990) and J. Calvão da Silva, *Compra e venda de coisas defeituosas. Conformidade e segurança* 5th edition (Coimbra: Livraria Almedina 2008) especially at 183–222.
529. For a short presentation of products liability under Portuguese law, *see,* for instance, A. Mota Pinto/J.P. Castro Mendes, 'Chapter 11 – Portugal', in: Ch.D. Varner/B.W. Pratt (eds), *The Product Regulation and Liability Review* (London: Law Business Research 2014) 111–115; A. Mota Pinto/J.P. Castro Menedes, 'Chapter 15 – Portugal', in: Ch.D. Varner/B.W. Pratt (eds), *The Product Regulation and Liability Review*, 2nd edition (London: Law Business Research 2015) 166–171; A. Lickfold de Novaes e Silva/P. Pires Fernandes, 'Chapter 14 – Portugal', in: Ch.D. Varner/B.W. Pratt (eds), *The Product Regulation and Liability Review*, 3rd edition (London: Law Business Research 2016) 155–165; A. Lickfold de Novaes e Silva/P. Pires Fernandes, 'Chapter 16 – Portugal', in: Ch.D. Varner/B.W. Pratt (eds), *The Product Regulation and Liability Review*, 4th edition (London: Law Business Research 2017) 169–178; A. Guerreiro/J. Matos Viana, 'Chapter 37 – Portugal', in: *The International Comparative Legal Guide to Product Liability 2007* (London: Global Legal Group 2007) 261–267; M. Morgado/J. Pimentel, 'Portugal', in: H.L. Kaplan/G.L. Fowler/S. Castley (eds), *Product Liability 2015* (London: Law Business Research 2015) 90–94; M. Barrocas, 'Product Liability and Safety in Portugal: Overview', available at https://uk.practicallaw.thomsonreuters.com/w-012–7174?transitionType=Default&contextData=(sc.Default)&firstPage=true&bhcp=1. – The English-speaking reader with an interest in product liability under Portuguese law should be advised to consult the *Product Liability Database* at the British Institute of International and Comparative Law Website, available at https://www.biicl.org/plf/portugal/, with both on overview of Decree-Law No. 383/89 of 6 Nov. 1989, and rather up-to-date references to the case law of the upper courts.
530. *See, for example,* Court of Justice of the European Union (CJEU), judgment of 25 Apr. 2002 in Case C-183/00 (González Sánchez); judgment of 25 Apr. 2002 in Case C-52/00 (*Commission v. France*); judgment of 25 Apr. 2002 in Case C-154/00 (*Commission v. Greece*); judgment of 10 Jan. 2006 in Case C-402/03 (Skov Æg); judgment of 3 Feb. 2012, in Case C-495/10 (Dutrueux and Caisse primaire d'assurance maladie du Jura), judgment of 20 Nov. 2014, in Case C-310/13 (Novo Nordisk Pharma).
531. *See* M.S. Shapo, 'Comparing Products Liability: Concepts in European and American Law', 26 *Cornell International Law Journal* (1993) 279–330, at 289 (footnote 57).

product he has put on the market. In referring to the title of a famous article by W.L. Prosser,[532] Professor Calvão da Silva explained that '[t]he reason for this explicit sanctioning of the [strict liability] principle is to erase all doubt about the 'fall of the citadel' and to emphasize the strict liability of the producer to the consumer'.[533]

The difference between European and Portuguese law causes no problem at all, for '[t]he policy heart of the directive [...] lies in its imposition of strict liability'.[534]

In the preamble of Directive 1985/374/EEC, Recital (2) reads that 'liability without fault on the part of the producer is the sole means of adequately solving the problem, peculiar to our age of increasing technicality, of a fair apportionment of the risks inherent in modern technological production', and Article 1 of Decree-Law No. 383/89 appropriately implemented the directive conforming to its purpose and scope.

§2. Elements of Product Liability

88. Articles 2, 3 and 4 of Decree-Law No. 383/89 define *producer*, *product* and *defect*. Article 2 defines *producer* in terms that correspond to Article 3 of Directive 1985/374/EEC. Paragraph (1) reads that '[p]roducer is the manufacturer of a finished product, the producer of any raw material or the manufacturer of a component part and any person who, by putting his name, trade mark or other distinguishing feature on the product presents himself as its producer'. Paragraph (2) reads that producer is also: (a) any person who imports into the Community a product for sale, hire, leasing or any form of distribution in the course of his business and (b) supplier of the product whose producer or importer cannot be identified, unless he informs the injured person, in writing and within a reasonable time, of the identity of the producer or of the person who supplied him with the product. Whereas Article 2 defines *producer*, Article 3 of Decree-Law No. 383/89, as amended by Decree-Law No. 131/2001, defines *product* in terms that correspond to Article 2 of Directive 1985/374/EEC, as amended by Directive 1999/34/EC, of 10 May 1999: '[P]roduct means all movables, even if incorporated into another movable or into an immovable.'

Finally, whereas Articles 2 and 3 define *producer* and *product*, Article 4 defines *defect* in terms that correspond to Article 6 of the directive:

1. A product is defective when it does not provide the safety which a person is entitled to expect, taking all circumstances into account, namely its presentation, the use to which it could reasonably be expected that the product would be put and the time when the product was put into circulation.
2. A product shall not be considered defective for the sole reason that a better product is subsequently put into circulation.

---

532. W.L. Prosser, 'The Assault upon the Citadel (Strict Liability to the Consumer)', 69 *The Yale Law Journal* (1960) 1099–1146.
533. *See* J. Calvão da Silva, 'Implementation of the EEC Product Liability Directive in Portugal', *European Consumer Law Journal* (1992) 36–40, at 36.
534. M.S. Shapo, 'Comparing Products Liability: Concepts in European and American Law', at 225.

It has been consistently pointed out that the concept of defect relevant to the law of contracts – relevant, for instance, to the law of sales – is distinct from the concept of defect relevant to the law of torts. In the law of contracts, as, for example, in the law of sales, the judge is to assess whether the product is defective by referring to the purpose of the buyer or if no particular purpose of the buyer could be determined by referring to the general purpose for which goods of the same type are normally used. The product is to be considered defective when it is not fit either for the particular purpose of the buyer or go the general purpose for which goods of the same type are normally used.[535] In the law of torts, the judge is to assess whether the product is defective by referring to safety. The product is to be considered defective when it does not provide the safety which a person is entitled to expect. It follows that Decree-Law No. 383/89 is to be interpreted in conjunction with product safety regulations. In particular, it is to be interpreted in conjunction with Decree-Law No. 69/2005 of 17 March 2005, aimed at implementing Directive 2001/95/EC of 3 December 2001, on general product safety.[536]

In spite of the fact that there is a difference between both concepts of defect, it has been argued that the current dual regime should be replaced with a single, unified regime.[537] It is submitted that the construction of such a single, unified regime of liability for defects would probably be easier in Portugal than, for instance, in Germany, for Portuguese law on consumer sales allows direct claims of consumers against producers.[538]

Within the general concept of the defect under Directive 1985/374/EEC and Decree-Law No. 383/89, there is a distinction to be established between: (i) manufacturing defects, (ii) design defects, and (iii) instructions and warning defects.[539]

In what concerns manufacturing defects, there is some consensus as to the nature of product liability – liability for manufacturing defects [under Decree-Law No. 383/89] is no-fault, strict liability. In what concerns design defect, there is no consensus at all, for Decree-Law No. 383/89 adopts the so-called *state of the art* defence:

> The producer shall not be liable [...] if he proves that the state of scientific and technical knowledge at the time when he put the product into circulation was not such as to enable the existence of the defect to be discovered.[540]

535. *See* Art. 913 of the Civil Code, as well as Art. 2 of Decree-Law No. 67/2003 of 8 Apr. 2003, aimed at implementing Directive 1999/44/EC, of 20 May 1999.
536. *See* J. Calvão da Silva, *Compra e venda de coisas defeituosas. Conformidade e segurança* 183 ff.
537. *See* J. Calvão da Silva, *Compra e venda de coisas defeituosas. Conformidade e segurança 223* ff.
538. *See* Decree-Law No. 67/2003 of 8 Apr. 2003, as amended by Decree-Law No. 84/2008 of 21 May 2008, Art. 6.
539. *See*, for a distinction between the three types of defects under Portuguese law, J. Calvão da Silva, *Responsabilidade civil do produtor*, 655–663; L. Menezes Leitão, L. Menezes Leitão, *Direito das obrigações*, I. – *Introdução. Da constituição das obrigações,* 388–394; for a comparison between American and European law, N.M. Pinto Oliveira, 'Le défaut dans la responsabilité civile du fait des produits – rapport anglo-américain', in: *La responsabilité du fait des produits défectueux* (Paris: IJRS Editions 2013) 221–238.
540. Decree-Law No. 383/89 of 6 Nov. 1989, Art. 5(e).

In fact, Article 5 of the decree-law corresponds to Article 7 of the directive, and Portugal did not make use of the possibility to 'provide in this legislation that the producer shall be liable even if he proves that the state of scientific and technical knowledge at the time when he put the product into circulation was not such as to enable the existence of a defect to be discovered'.[541] Professors Menezes Cordeiro and Menezes Leitão argued that Article 5(e) of Decree-Law No. 383/89 renders product for design defects similar to fault-based liability, albeit modified with a presumption of fault.[542] Professor Calvão da Silva argued that the criteria for assessing *fault, negligence*, and for assessing the *state of the art* are fundamentally different. The concept of fault, as defined by Article 487(2) of the Civil Code, refers to the standard of an *average, normal person*. If it were to be applied to product liability, it would refer to the standard of an *average, normal producer*. The concept of state of the art, as defined both by Directive 1985/374/EEC and by Decree-Law No. 383/89, refers to the standard of an *ideal person*, clearly *above average*. The *ideal producer* presupposed both by the directive and by the decree-law is to be up-to-date with the 'state of the scientific and technical knowledge at the time when he put the product into circulation' and may not argue that an *average, normal producer* would not be up-to-date to that state of the art. Therefore, liability for design defects under Decree-Law No. 383/89 clearly goes beyond fault-based, subjective liability; it goes beyond subjective liability for presumed fault – liability for design defects [under Decree-Law No. 383/89] is no-fault, strict liability.[543]

Article 8 of Decree-Law No. 383/89 refers to the types of damages relevant to product liability. In the first place, it refers to damages caused by or by personal injuries.[544] Second, it refers to damages to any item of property other than the defective product itself, provided that the item of property is of a type ordinarily intended for private use or consumption and was used by the injured person mainly for his own private use or consumption.[545] Article 9 of Decree-Law No. 383/89 refers to the threshold of EUR 500 for damages to the property.[546] In keeping with Article 4 of Directive 1985/374/EEC, the injured person is to prove the damage, the defect, and the causal relationship between defect and damage.[547] Therefore, Directive 1985/374/EEC 'clearly include[s] causation as an element'.[548] In spite of the fact, Article 4 strongly suggests that causation is a matter regulated by the directive so

541. *See* Directive 1985/374/EEC, of 25 Jul. 1985, Art. 15(1)(b).
542. *See* A. Menezes Cordeiro, *Tratado de direito civil português*, vol. II – *Direito das obrigações*, III. – *Gestão de negócios. Enriquecimento sem causa. Responsabilidade civil,* 689, and L. Menezes Leitão, *Direito das obrigações*, I. – *Introdução. Da constituição das obrigações,* 393.
543. *See* J. Calvão da Silva, *Responsabilidade civil do produtor*, 503–524; N.M. Pinto Oliveira, 'Responsabilidade objectiva', in: *Cadernos de direito privado,* special issue – *II Seminário dos Cadernos de Direito Privado* (2012) 107–121.
544. *See* Directive 1985/374/EEC, of 25 Jul. 1985, Art. 9(a).
545. *See* Directive 1985/374/EEC, of 25 Jul. 1985, Art. 9(b), (i) and (ii).
546. *See* Directive 1985/374/EEC, of 25 Jul. 1985, Art. 9(b).
547. *See* Directive 1985/374/EEC, of 25 Jul. 1985, Art. 4.
548. *See, for example*, S. Lenze, 'German Product Liability Law: Between European Directives, American Restatements and Common Sense', in: D. Fairgrieve (ed.), *Product Liability in Comparative Perspective* (Cambridge: Cambridge University Press 2005)100–125, at 116.

that '[i]n theory, courts should […] apply common rules on causation',[549] and there are no European criteria for causation. 'By and large, causation is determined under the general principles governing the issue in private law, which may vary among jurisdictions.'[550] It follows that causation is to be assessed in a two-step approach, the first referring to causation-in-fact and the second step to adequacy.

Contrary to Article 4 of Directive 1985/374/EEC, Decree-Law No. 383/89 contains no particular, specific provision requiring the injured person to prove the defect, the damage and the causal relationship between defect and damage. It is submitted that no particular, specific provision was required, for Article 4 of Directive 1985/374/EEC states the general principles and rules on the burden of proof set forth by Article 342 of the Civil Code.

§3. Compensation of Damage Caused by Defective Products: Contributory Fault – Plurality of Tortfeasors

89. In what concerns contributory negligence of either the injured person or of a third party, Article 7(1) of Decree-Law No. 383/89 fully matches Article 8(2) of Directive 1985/374/EEC, for it establishes that '[t]he liability of the producer may be reduced or disallowed when, having regard to all the circumstances, the damage is caused both by a defect in the product and by the fault of the injured person', and Article 7(2) of Decree-Law No. 383/89 fully matches Article 8(1) of Directive 1985/374/EEC, for it establishes that 'the liability of the producer shall not be reduced when the damage is caused both by a defect in product and by the act or omission of a third party'. In conforming to the directive, Article 7 of Decree-Law No. 383/89 deviates, however, from consolidated principles and rules of Portuguese law on strict liability, such as from the principles and rules in Article 505 of the Civil Code on strict liability for traffic accidents.[551]

In what concerns plurality of tortfeasors, Article 6 of Decree-Law No. 383/89 conforms both to Article 5 of Directive 1985/374/EEC and to Articles 497 and 507 of the Civil Code.

Paragraph (1) of Article 6 of Decree-Law No. 383/89 reads that '[w]here two or more persons are liable for the same damage, they shall be liable jointly and severally'. Paragraph (2) holds that recourse among producers is to be determined by

549. S. Lenze, 'German Product Liability Law: Between European Directives, American Restatements and Common Sense', at 116.

550. M. Reimann, 'Liability for Defective Products at the Beginning of the Twenty-First Century: Emergence of a Worldwide Standard?' 51 *The American Journal of Comparative Law* (2003) 751–838, at 772; *see also, for example*, M. Tulibacka, *Product Liability Law in Transition. A Central European Perspective* (Furnham: Ashgate 2009) 83–84, stressing that 'it is difficult to pinpoint exactly […] which issues belong to causal considerations and which are part of other elements or requirements of liability' [such as the scope of the duty, the scope of the rule, or even fault].

551. In accordance with Art. 505 of the Civil Code, on strict liability for traffic accidents, the fact that damage is caused by acts or omissions of either the injured person or a third party automatically disallows strict liability.

taking into account all circumstances, especially the risk created by each person, the degree of each person's fault and the degree of each person's contribution to the damage.[552]

In the case of doubt, each person's creation of risk, each person's degree of fault, as well as each person's contribution to the damage shall be presumed to be equal.[553]

Finally, as *time limits for the exercise of subjective rights*, it should be stressed that, in Portugal, there are two types of time limits to the exercise of subjective rights – *prescrição* and *caducidade*. The Portuguese word *prescrição* can be translated into English as *prescription,* and *caducidade* as *expiration, forfeiture* or *limitation.*[554] Article 11 of Decree-Law No. 383/89 implements the limitation period of three years in Article 10 of Directive 1985/374/EEC by referring to the concept of *prescription*[555] and Article 12 of Decree-Law No. 383/89 implements the extinction period of ten years in Article 11 of Directive 1985/374/EEC by referring to the concept of *forfeiture* – '[t]he [injured person's] right to compensation expires in three years, counting from the date on which the producer put into circulation the actual product which caused the damage, unless the injured person has in the meantime instituted proceedings against the producer'.

---

552. This is in line with Arts 497(2), 506(2) and 507 of the Civil Code.
553. This is in line with Art. 497(2) and in Art. 506(2) of the Civil Code.
554. The criterion for distinguishing the two types of time limits results from Art. 298(2) of the Civil Code. It is purely formal: 'Whenever a right is supposed to be exercised within a time limit, set either by the law of by contract, the rules on forfeiture shall apply, unless the relevant statute makes express reference to prescription.' In general, individual, subjective rights are subject to a prescription period and, in special cases, where either the law or the contract set a specific time limit, subjective rights will be subject to forfeiture.
555. *See* Decree-Law No. 383/89 of 6 Nov. 1989: '[t]he [injured person's] right to compensation prescribes in three years, counting from the day on which the plaintiff became aware, or should reasonably have become aware, of the damage, the defect and the identity of the producer'.

Chapter 3. Liability for Service

90. In Portugal, there are no specific provisions on the liability for service. In spite of the fact that there are a few general principles and rules on the contract for the provision of services,[556] there are no specific rules on liability for services.

Article 1154 of the Civil Code defines contracts for the provision of services as contracts 'whereby one of the parties undertakes to provide the other party with a given result from his or her intellectual or manual work'; Article 1155 distinguishes three types of contracts for the provision of services – mandate, deposit and contracts to produce a work – and Article 1156 determines that the provisions on mandate 'shall be extended, with the necessary adaptations, to the types of the contract for the provision of services that are not specially governed by law'. It follows from the fact there are no specific rules on liability for services that the general rules on contractual and non-contractual, tortious liability apply.

It could be argued that the provisions in the Civil Code are supplemented by the Consumer Protection Act (*Lei de Defesa do Consumidor*), approved by Law No. 24/96 of 31 July 1996. In fact, Article 12(1) of the Consumer Protection Act (*Lei de Defesa do Consumidor*) reads that both sellers of goods and providers of services are to be held liable for both pecuniary and non-pecuniary losses arising from defective products or services.

In the absence of particular, specific provisions on the conditions and effects of liability, Article 12(1) of the Consumer Protection Act is, however, interpreted as referring to Articles 798 and 799 of the Civil Code.[557] Therefore, specific provisions on liability for services can only be found in relation to specific services, such as in the case of services provided by medical practitioners, legal practitioners, builders, architects and engineers, accountants and statutory auditors. In contrast to Article 4:202 of the Principles of European Tort Law, which provides for a general principle of enterprise liability,[558] it should be emphasized that both the general and the specific provisions on liability for service refer to contractual liability and to contractual liability only.[559] 'Thus, Portuguese law only offers less protection than the proposed Enterprise Liability of the Principles to third parties who suffer damage arising from a service.'[560]

---

556. *See* Portuguese Civil Code, Arts 1154 to 1156.
557. *See*, for instance, J. Morais Carvalho, *Manual de direito do consumo* (Coimbra: Livraria Almedina 2013) 215–216.
558. In accordance with Art. 4:202 of the Principles of European Tort Law, '[a] person pursuing a lasting enterprise for economic or professional purposes who uses auxiliaries or technical equipment is liable for any harm caused by a defect of such enterprise or of its output unless he proves that he has conformed to the required standard of conduct'.
559. *See*, for instance, A.G. Dias Pereira, 'Portuguese Tort Law: A Comparison with the Principles of European Tort Law', at 637: 'Concerning liability for services, the parties to a contract are protected by the contract law regime, which also provides an inversion of the burden of proof (Art. 799 (1) CC).'
560. *See*, for instance, A.G. Dias Pereira, 'Portuguese Tort Law: A Comparison with the Principles of European Tort Law', at 637.

Chapter 4. Environmental Liability

91. Law No. 19/2014 of 14 April 2014 establishes the basis of environmental policy.

Article 3 of Law No. 19/2014 states two general principles on environmental liability: the so-called principle of liability (*princípio da responsabilidade*) and the so-called principle of recovery or restoration (*princípio da recuperação*). In accordance with the so-called *principle of liability*, anyone who threatens or damages the environment, whether directly or indirectly, acting intentionally or negligently, shall be held liable for the damage he causes.[561] In accordance with the so-called *principle of recovery*, anyone who causes environmental damage shall restore the affected environment to its prior condition.[562]

The principles in Law No. 14/2014 inspire Decree-Law No. 147/2008 of 29 July 2008[563] on environmental liability.[564] In examining the provisions in Decree-Law No. 147/2008, the concepts of environmental damage and ecological damage are to be strictly distinguished. Environmental damage (*dano ambiental*) results from injury to concrete, individual rights and interests. Ecological damage (*dano ecológico*) does not – it results from damage to the ecosystem. For damage to qualify as purely ecological, no concrete, individual rights and interests are to be affected.[565] It follows that there is a difference between European and Portuguese legislation: European directives, such as Directive 2004/35/EC of 21 April 2004 and Directive 2006/21/EC of 15 March 2006, concentrate on ecological damage, and Decree-Law No. 147/2008 focuses both on ecological and environmental damage.

Article 8 of Decree-Law No. 147/2008 confirms the general principles of fault-based, subjective liability in Article 483 of the Civil Code: '[w]hoever, whether by wilful misconduct (dolus) or by negligence infringes rights or interests of another person by means of an offence to environmental components must compensate the injured party for damage arising from such violation'. Article 7 goes beyond general principles, for it affirms no-fault, strict liability, for dangerous activities to environmental components.

It reads that, '[w]hoever, in exercising an economic activity referred to in annex iii to the present decree-law, infringes rights or interests of another person by means of an offence to environmental components must compensate the injured party for damage arising from such violation, irrespectively of wilful misconduct (*dolus*) or

561. *See* Law No. 19/2014 of 14 Apr. 2014, Art. 3(f).
562. *See* Law No. 19/2014 of 14 Apr. 2014, Art. 3(g).
563. As amended by Decree-Law No. 245/2009 of 22 Sep. 2009, by Decree-Law No. 29–A/2011 of 1 Mar. 2011, by Decree-Law No. 60/2012 of 14 Mar. 2014, and by Decree-Law No. 13/2016 of 9 Mar. 2016.
564. For a short presentation of Decree-Law No. 147/2008 of 29 Jul. 2008, *see* A.G. Dias Pereira, 'Portugal', in: H. Koziol/B.C. Steininger (eds), *European Tort Law 2008* (Wien/New York: Springer 2009) 527–540, at 529.
565. *See* L.M. Menezes Leitão, 'A responsabilidade civil por danos causados ao ambiente', in: C. Amado Gomes/T. Antunes (eds), *Actas do colóquio A responsabilidade civil por dano ambiental* (Lisboa: Instituto de Ciências Jurídico-Políticas da Faculdade de Direito da Universidade de Lisboa 2010) 21–41, available at: http://www.icjp.pt.

negligence', and the list in Annex iii basically comprehends all dangerous economic activities. Furthermore, whoever exercises any of the dangerous economic activities referred to in Annex iii is to obtain financial guarantees in order to ensure the payment of the damages.[566]

The particular principle of no-fault, strict liability for environmental damage is supplemented by specific rules on causation. It has been pointed out that '[t]here is a relaxation of the rules concerning causation in order to accept proof that the damage was probably caused by a certain behaviour'.[567] While the general principles and rules on tort law require causation-in-fact to be assessed under the *conditio sine qua non*, 'but-for test', the specific principles and rules on tort law for environmental damage do not, whereas Article 563 of the Portuguese Civil Code requires a two-step approach to causation,[568] Article 5 of Decree-Law No. 147/2008 does not. In the first place, causation, in fact, for environmental damage is to be established by assessing the *probability* of the injuring, wrongful event being the cause of actual damage.[569] Second, the judge shall take into account all circumstances of the case. Third, among the circumstances of the case, the judge shall take into account: (i) 'the degree of danger and risk', (ii) the 'normality' or 'abnormality' of the injuring, wrongful event, (iii) the practical 'feasibility' or 'unfeasibility' of going forward with scientific evidence as to the causal process, as well as (iv) the defendant's compliance, or non-compliance with protective duties (e.g., statutory protective duties). It is submitted that whenever protective duties are infringed, the defendant is to bear the burden of proving – and, therefore, the risk of failing to prove – that there is no causal relationship whatsoever between damage and infringement.

In accordance with the general principles in Article 497 of the Civil Code, '[w]here two or more persons are liable [for environmental damage], they shall be liable jointly and severally',[570] and that liability extends to the directors of legal entities.[571]

566. *See* Decree-Law No. 147/2008 of 29 Jul. 2008, Art. 22(1).
567. *See* A.G. Dias Pereira, 'Portugal', at 529.
568. In the first step, the judge is to assess whether the injuring event is a *condition* of the damages sustained by the victim. In the second step, after it passed the *conditio sine qua non* or 'but-for test', the judge is to assess whether the injuring event is an *adequate* or *appropriate* condition.
569. In accordance with the text of Art. 5 of Decree-Law No. 147/2008, it would be possible to go a step further and to affirm that causation-in-fact is to be established by assessing the *probability* of the injuring, wrongful event being *appropriate* to cause actual damage (*see* A. Perestrelo de Oliveira, 'A prova do nexo de causalidade na lei da responsabilidade civil ambiental', at 180). It seems, however, that with such a step we would go much too far.
570. *See* Decree-Law No. 147/2008 of 29 Jul. 2008, Art. 4(1).
571. *See* Decree-Law No. 147/2008 of 29 Jul. 2008, Art. 4(1).

Part IV. Defences and Exception Clauses

Chapter 1. Limitation of Action (Suspension and Interruption)

92. The ordinary period of limitation of action is twenty years, as established in Article 309, but Article 498 consecrates a special three years' period of limitation of action for the right to compensation. The rationale behind this shortening lies in the growing over time difficulties in demonstrating the necessary facts or in gathering accurate witness testimony.[572] Notwithstanding, the ordinary period keeps running and can ultimately limit liability proceedings. However, these terms can be extended when the wrongful act simultaneously constitutes a criminal act by the endeavour of the accordant criminal law limitation of action period – 498(3), 'if the wrongful act simultaneously constitutes a criminal act for which the law establishes a longer period of prescription, the latter applies'.

It is counted starting when the injured party knows of his right, as stated by Article 498(1), '(…) calculated from the date the injured party knew of his right, even if he was ignorant of the liable person and the full extent of the damage'. Only the ordinary period of limitation starts with the wrongful action. Consequently, there should be no waiting time in order to assemble more facts or to trace the identity solely/or of all the jointly liable. It was the legislator's understanding that the beginning of the limitation period should not depend on the negligence or laxness of the wronged party to assemble those essential facts.[573] Despite that, if the identity of the liable person is unknown by a force majeure motive or wilful misconduct by the wrongdoer, the three-year period can be suspended while the aggrieved party cannot exercise his/her right, as established in Article 321(1) and (2).[574]

The same period of limitation (three years) stands, according to Article 498(2), for the right to regress claims with respect to a co-debtor in joint liability.

If the injured party can resort to any action in rem or an unjust enrichment claim, the three-year period does not apply to those since it is merely applicable for tort claims.

572. J. Antunes Varela, *Das obrigações em geral*, I, 625.

573. F.A. Pires de Lima/J.M. Antunes Varela (/ M.H. Mesquita), *Código Civil anotado*, vol. I, 3.ª ed., 437.

574. F.A. Pires de Lima/J.M. Antunes Varela (/ M.H. Mesquita), *Código Civil anotado*, vol. I, 3.ª ed., 438.

Chapter 2. Grounds of Justification

93. The Portuguese law enshrines ways of justifying wrongfulness, the so-called *defences*, such as self-defence, necessity and consent. Different authors find different meanings for justification, such as an exclusion of the wrongfulness link between the action and the damage, *ex vi,* the transfer of risk to the injurer; a tolerance by the legal system; or a real authorization of action.

By the exclusion of wrongfulness, any justification results in the preclusion of consequential self-defence.

§1. Consent

94. Consent is a unilateral legal act which results in the exclusion of wrongfulness.[575] It is enshrined in Article 340 in its express, tacit, and presumed forms. Paragraph (1) consecrates that 'the act that infringes the rights of another is lawful if the injured party consents in the injury', which concerns consent given expressly or tacitly if the law does not state otherwise. It can only be presumed (3) if it cannot be effectively obtained if it is the injured party's interest to consent and it is compatible with its presumable will.

In order to consent, the person must have the legal capacity to act and when dealing with some specialized matters, all the information necessary to understand the reach and implications of the consent (as in, e.g., medical interventions).[576]

There will be no exclusion of wrongfulness if consent is regarded as being contrary to a legal prohibition or to good morals, Article 340(2), and, if concerning personality rights, additionally to the principles of public order (Article 81(1)). Good morals are commonly associated with good faith and honest behaviour that, being socially and geographically changeable, can only be asserted within each concrete context.[577] Nowadays, it cannot be used to impose a certain moral or religious standard. Rather, it is defined according to the injury's severity. Therefore, an injury will be regarded as wrongful – despite the giving of consent – if it is regarded as irreversible and serious harm.[578] Living donor transplants are an acknowledged exception to this criterion.[579]

The frontier between the exclusion of wrongfulness in general and with respect to a personality right implicates that consent for the latter is always revocable – even if it carries a need to compensate the other party, as stated by Article 81(2).

---

575. R. Capelo de Sousa, *O Direito Geral de Personalidade*, 2011, 411–412.
576. M. Miranda Barbosa, *Lições de Responsabilidade Civil*, 2017, 212.
577. R. Capelo de Sousa, *O Direito Geral de Personalidade*, 2011, 411, note 1039.
578. Elaborated by the criminal law doctrine, *see*, J. Figueiredo Dias, *Direito Penal – parte geral*, 2.ª ed., 2012, 481–483.
579. *See*, A. Dias Pereira, *O Consentimento Informado na Relação Médico-Paciente*, 2004, 144–146.

§2. Necessity

95. The justification by *necessity*, as established by Article 339, upholds the exclusion of wrongfulness with respect to the destruction of property of others when it allows the removal of 'an evidently higher present danger, both for the wrongdoer or a third party'. Hence, it encompasses not only a way of protecting one's property but also of others. The justification occurs even if the source of danger originates from the one who now seeks to act with the exclusion of wrongfulness. Nevertheless, Article 339(2) anchors an example of civil liability without the requirement of wrongfulness, conveying a sense of commutative justice, stating that 'there is nevertheless an obligation to compensate if the danger was created solely by the wrongdoer'. The same paragraph also refers to the court's possibility to equitably fixate a compensation and '(…) condemn not only the wrongdoer, but also those who profited from the wrongful act or contributed to its cause', when other circumstances occur, such as a third party or a fortuitous act.[580]

§3. Self-Help and Self-Defence

96. Contrary to a clause of *necessity*, self-defence is a reaction to someone else's action.[581] Article 337(1) states that 'the act intended to remove any present and unlawful aggression against the person or property of the doer or of a third party, is justified as long as it is not possible to be done by normal means and if the caused detriment is not greater than the one meant to be avoided'. This implicates a judgment of proportionality and a weighting of harm, but the differentiating notes consist of the fact that the subsequent harmed interest belongs to the primary aggressor and that those actions were wrongful.[582] If, instead, the harm is done to a third party's property or personal being, the otherwise justified action will be wrongful – with the only exception of possibly abiding by the requirements of justification by *necessity*.

As for the need for an evaluation of fault, the doctrine divides itself. Antunes Varela sees no need for a consideration of fault and, therefore, allows self-defence against someone incapable of fault;[583] Pessoa Jorge, by contrast, considers it a requirement.[584]

Another discussion concerns the possibility of self-defence against aggression carried out by an animal. Considering that the primary action must be wrongful and that an animal is, in itself, incapable of acting within a normative concept of wrongfulness, it seems that harm perpetrated by an animal cannot be opposed with self-defence (remaining, for some, the possibility of *necessity*). Notwithstanding, if the

580. *See* F.A. Pires de Lima/J.M. Antunes Varela (/ M.H. Mesquita), *Código Civil anotado*, vol. I, 3.ª ed., 301.
581. Or omission, which is the minority argument of Pessoa Jorge, *see* F. Pessoa Jorge, *Ensaio sobre os pressupostos da responsabilidade civil*, 233, note 203.
582. F. Pessoa Jorge, *Ensaio sobre os pressupostos da responsabilidade civil*, 227–228.
583. J. Antunes Varela, *Das Obrigações em Geral, I*, 556.
584. F. Pessoa Jorge, *Ensaio sobre os pressupostos da responsabilidade civil*, 235–239.

animal is merely an instrument and the action is true of an individual and played through an animal, the general rules apply, and self-defence can be enforced.[585]

By the feature of being present aggression, the legislator intended to rule out not only past and future injuries but also summon a normative concept of urgency to act in a specific moment – it must be impending harm.[586]

The possibility of running away cannot be used as an argument to exclude the justification of wrongfulness since that is constructed as being a dishonourable route which the aggrieved party is not obliged to take[587] and a form to avoid the *survival of the fittest* system.

In the case of faultless turmoil or fear, the act is still considered justified even if there is an overuse of self-defence (Article 337(2)). This does not include intended excessive behaviours, which will be classified as wrongful.

I. Self-Help

97. Self-help is a deviant derogation of the coercive power's monopoly exercise by the State, defined in Article 336, along with Article 1 of the Civil Procedure Code.

According to Article 336(1), 'it is lawful to resort to force, within the needs to avert the injury, in order to attain or ensure a personal right whenever self-help is indispensable, given the impossibility to timely call in upon the State's coercive power and avoid that damage'. Therefore, in order to invoke a self-help justification, there is a need for an acknowledged basis for action, an urgency to act in due course without regular legal instruments, the suitability of employed resources and, finally, impair a superior interest than the safeguarded one. If this last requisite is not fulfilled, Article 336(3) states that 'self-help can be wrongful when it impairs interest's superior to the ones it intends to uphold'.

According to Article 226(2), 'self-help can comprise appropriation, destruction or deterioration of an object, as well as eliminating irregular opposition to exercising rights or any other analogue situation'. Similar settings can, *inter alia*, span to personal detention of the wrongdoer and his immediate entrust to an authority.[588]

585. *See*, M. Miranda Barbosa, *Lições de Responsabilidade Civil*, 210.
586. F. Pessoa Jorge, *Ensaio sobre os pressupostos da responsabilidade civil*, 233.
587. F. Pessoa Jorge, *Ensaio sobre os pressupostos da responsabilidade civil*, 240.
588. J. Antunes Varela, *Das Obrigações em Geral, I*, 555, note 1.

Chapter 3. Contributory Fault

98. The topic of victim's exclusive or contributory fault should be analysed on two levels, in line with the Civil Code, depending on each case circumstance. Article 570 pertains to the injured party's fault in general terms and Article 505 to the concurrence of fault and risk.

§1. Victim's Fault in General Terms

99. Article 570 establishes that 'when the action of the wrongdoer concurs with a culpable action from the wronged party to the existence or aggravation of its damages, the court determines, attending to both parties' faults severity and accordant consequences, if full, reduced, or any compensation at all should be awarded'.

One main inference is that any account of the fault must underlie the injured party's actions for them to be significant, be it negligence or wilful misconduct. If invoked, it becomes a requisite to be proven, either effectively or via a presumption of fault in general terms. Nevertheless, Article 572 establishes that, even if it is not invoked, the Court can ascertain the injured party's exclusive or contributory fault. Also, its relevance depends on the possibility of being truly identified as a cause for the damage, according to Article 563.[589]

From its number (2) results another important consequence. It states that 'If the liability is solely based in a presumption of fault, and the law does not state otherwise, the concurrence of the injured party's fault excludes the right to compensation.' In this case, contrary to the previous studies, the concurrence of the victim's fault leads immediately to the rejection of any compensation. Thus, the legislator recognizes that a mere presumption is not enough to meet the standard of right to compensation if, simultaneously, there was the victim's contributory fault. One way of circumventing this outcome is for the injured, albeit the existence of a legal presumption, to prove the defendant's fault effectively.

Brandão Proença dedicated his PhD dissertation to a meticulous analysis of this subject and emphasizes that from it, by the consideration of the victim's fault, emerges a *principle of self-responsibility*, which cannot be mistaken for a concern in protecting one's interests from oneself. Consequently, Brandão Proença does not fathom the victim's fault as a liability in its true sense, by the lack of otherness, but as bearing of consequences for one's actions.[590]

§2. The Confrontation Between Risk and Fault

100. Article 503 establishes liability regardless of fault for vehicle holders, stating in its (1) that 'Whoever has actual command of any road circulating vehicle and

---

589. *See* Part V, Causation. F.A. Pires de Lima/J.M. Antunes Varela (/ M.H. Mesquita), *Código Civil anotado*, V. I, 511.

590. J.C. Brandão Proença, *A conduta do lesado como pressuposto e critério de imputação do dano extracontratual*, Almedina, 2007, 104.

deploys it their own interest, even if by intermediary of an agent, is liable for damages that arise from the vehicle's own risks, even if it wasn't circulating.' However, it is followed by Article 505, whose epigraph is the *exclusion of liability*. It states that 'Notwithstanding Article 570, the liability fixed by Article 503(1) is only excluded when the accident is attributable to the injured or third party, or when it is caused by force majeure unrelated to the vehicle's functioning.'

The difference between the scope of Articles 505 and 570 is that the former only contends with risk liability for the vehicle's holder, i.e., one party's responsibility is blind to a fault and grounded in other's principles,[591] and the latter assumes that both parties' faults are considered, i.e., the tortfeasor is necessarily liable by the fault or presumption of fault. That being said, the understanding of this Article's interpretation has been changing, and a Supreme Court of Justice decision from 2007 is commonly identified as a hallmark for the switch in case law and legal opinions.

The traditional legal doctrine argued that any contributory fault by the injured party (e.g., being run over by a car while jaywalking) encompasses a breach of a causal link and, therefore, should exclude liability for risk to the vehicle's holder. That was the vision of Antunes Varela, one of the Civil Code's fathers, and therefore, he interpreted Article 505 as an exclusion of liability norm, following the settled case law on Assento no. 1/1933.[592] Varela, based on the premise that the vehicle's holder liability (503) was grounded in the intrinsic risk of a vehicle,[593] saw the interference of an action by the injured party as a basis for its exoneration.[594] Consequently, Varela argues that the Article's reference to 'attributability' does not signify a true requirement of fault but only a causal link between the damage and the harmed person's action. As a result, the author indicates that the outcome of Article 505 still stands even if the victim is incapable of fault.[595]

Calvão da Silva, however, defended that Article 505 should be read as follows: 'regardless of the concurrence of the victim's fault, the vehicle's holder liability for risk is only to be excluded when the accident is solely attributed to the injured or third party, or when it is caused by force majeure unrelated to the vehicle's functioning'. The distinction to the letter of the law (above-cited) is that Calvão da Silva interprets this norm in a restrictive manner, therefore diminishing its scope by seeing as relevant only the victim's actions, which portray the exclusive causal origin for the damage. Admitting that not all actions attributed to the injured party are appropriate to serve as the causal link between the actions of the vehicle's holder (perpetrated through the vehicle), it now allows for concurrence between the fault of the victim and the vehicle's own risks.[596] At the same time, the author also expands the scope of Article 570 since now it encompasses not only the coexistence

591. *See*, Road and Traffic Accidents.
592. http://www.dgsi.pt/jstj.nsf/954f0ce6ad9dd8b980256b5f003fa814/ba357c2f5b28a765802568fc0039f757?OpenDocument&Highlight=0,047139.
593. Which created special duties of care, not only for the holder but for the community in general and notably to pedestrians. *See*, J.M. Antunes Varela, *Das Obrigações em Geral*, 675.
594. J.M. Antunes Varela, *Das Obrigações em Geral*, 675.
595. J.M. Antunes Varela, *Das Obrigações em Geral*, 679.
596. J. Calvão da Silva, *Acidente de viação: concorrência do risco com a culpa do lesado (art. 505.º); limites máximos da responsabilidade objectiva (508.º) e montantes mínimos obrigatórios do seguro; indemnização e juros de mora (566.º n.º 2 e 805.º n.3)*, RLJ, 134, p. 115.

of fault by both parties but also cases where there is the concurrence of risk and of victim's fault, but where the latter is not the exclusive cause of the damage.

The author gives other examples where the exclusion of liability requires sole causal attribution to the injured party: as Article 13(2), Decree-Law No. 321/89, 25 September:

> The owner or operator of an aircraft is not liable for the caused damages, if the accident is solely attributed to the injured party.

And, among others, Article 43, Decree-Law No. 329/95, 9 December:

> The owner and the commander of a recreational craft are jointly liable, regardless of fault, for the compensation of damages caused to a third party's craft, except if the accident is solely attributed to the latter.

Encouraged by those examples, Calvão da Silva claims a new interpretation of Article 505, appealing to a principle of solidarity and distributive justice, as well as to Article 9 of the Civil Code, which consecrates, among others, a principle of interpretation according to the legal systems' harmony and unity, stating that, (1) 'Interpretation should not reduce itself to the letter of the law, but also reconstruct the circumstances in which the law was made and the specific conditions of the time when it is applicated, taking into consideration the harmony of the legal system.'[597] Coincidently, the new Law pertaining to the liability of public authorities, Law No. 67/2007 of 31 December, also enshrines in its Article 11 a norm that allows the concurrence of risk and victim's fault:

> The State and other legal persons governed by public law are liable for its activities, property or administrative services resulting damages, except if proven to had happen an event of force majeure or the concurrence of the injured parties' fault, case in which the Court can, attending all the circumstances, reduce or exclude any due compensation.

In the author's view, the caveat at the beginning of Article 505 – 'Notwithstanding Article 570 (…)' – is the basis for his thesis since it allows a direct reference to Article 570 where a ponderation of contribution is to be made.

Other authors advocate for the same result – allowing the concurrence – but use different ways – e.g., Vaz Serra and Pereira Coelho claim the existence of an analogy with Article 570, and Brandão Proença favours the stance of similarity between this circumstance and Article 570.[598]

---

597. J. Calvão da Silva, *Acidente de viação: concorrência do risco com a culpa do lesado (art. 505.º); limites máximos da responsabilidade objectiva (508.º) e montantes mínimos obrigatórios do seguro; indemnização e juros de mora (566.º n.º 2 e 805.º n.3)*, RLJ, 134, p. 118.
598. *See*, J. Calvão da Silva, *Concorrência entre risco do veículo e facto do lesado: o virar de página?*, RLJ, ano 137, n.º 3946, 2007, p. 51.

The Portuguese Supreme Court of Justice upheld Calvão da Silva's position in a decision from 4 October 2007,[599] and since then, that has been recognized as the opinion of the majority.

Moreover, this understanding of Articles 505 and 570 seems to be in accordance with the EU Directives on Motor Insurance, also invoked by the Portuguese Supreme Court of Justice, which seeks to give the victims high standard protection, and with the CJEU case law. Notably, in the case law Candolin,[600] where the Court established that:

> It is only in exceptional circumstances that the amount of the victim's compensation may be limited on the basis of an assessment of his particular case.

Albeit the European case law, Calvão da Silva maintains that the possibility of excluding compensation still stands, not only as a reduction. The main requisite is that it cannot be based on any abstract norm but only on a concrete assessment of the victim's behaviour while keeping in mind the necessary exceptionality of this exclusion.[601]

599. *See*, http://www.dgsi.pt/jstj.nsf/954f0ce6ad9dd8b980256b5f003fa814/7a828815800c8d758025754a004f9abb?OpenDocument.
600. Case 537/03, available at http://curia.europa.eu/juris/showPdf.jsf;jsessionid=9ea7d2dc30dd3dc48fb7645641c1b619ff3b3d54128c.e34KaxiLc3qMb40Rch0SaxyOa3v0?text=&docid=59869&pageIndex=0&doclang=EN&mode=lst&dir=&occ=first&part=1&cid=271996.
601. *See*, J. Calvão da Silva, *Concorrência entre risco do veículo e facto do lesado: o virar de página?*, RLJ, ano 137, n.º 3946, 2007, pp. 60–61.

Chapter 4. Exemption Clauses

101. Article 809 establishes, as a general rule, that any clause intending to serve as a renunciation of the creditors' rights is void. However, this norm, as is the common legal opinion, is only applicable to contractual liability, attending its systematic framework and teleology.[602] Therefore, the majority of authors, moving away from Article 809, argue the feasibility of a deal to exclude liability with respect to non-contractual liability. The preparatory works of the Civil Code, drafted in this subject by Vaz Serra, dictated that, in regard to contractual liability, exemption clauses would be valid if they did not cross public order principles and if the action did not carry wilful misconduct. And, subsequently, another article extended this norm to non-contractual liability. However, after the First Ministerial Review, the latter was eliminated, which could lead to the conclusion of any agreement of this sort being void beyond contractual law. Yet, Pessoa Jorge perceives this as a mere result of unnecessity, i.e., the legislator recognized the validity of agreements of this ilk and saw no need to state that expressly.[603]

By nature, it cannot entail a previous contract between two (or more) known parties, since a non-contractual liability presupposes a link between two (or more) previous strangers in terms of the liability relationship. It emerges from the wrongful act against an absolute right (*erga omnes*), which could lead to being objectively impossible to predetermine the injured party. Nevertheless, Pinto Monteiro argues that it does not constitute an impediment; it just makes its usage rarer.[604] The author reasons that the typical situation where an agreement like this could be done would involve some kind of proximity relationship, the best example being a neighbourhood relationship, for which it can be a useful tool.[605] Another possible example is advanced by Pessoa Jorge, referencing the joint takeover of dangerous endeavours or even the reciprocal exclusion of possible liability when it is foreseeable to happen.[606]

Some authors suggest that agreements like this cannot be made because civil liability is a concern of public order. However, that argument is topped with the possibility of disposing of some rights within the boundaries of public order – as seen in regard to consent.[607] Also, estranged from the umbrella of Article 809, its bedrock is found in the private autonomy principle and in Article 405(1) of the Civil Code, which states that 'Within the confines of the law, parties can freely set the content of contracts, conclude different contracts than those provided by this Code

---

602. A. Pinto Monteiro, *Claúsulas limitativas e de exclusão da responsabilidade civil,* Almedina, 2011, p. 406.
603. F. Pessoa Jorge, *A limitação convencional da responsabilidade civil*, BMJ n.º 281, 1979, pp. 27–28.
604. A. Pinto Monteiro, *Claúsulas limitativas e de exclusão da responsabilidade civil,* Almedina, 2011, pp. 392–393.
605. A. Pinto Monteiro, *Claúsulas limitativas e de exclusão da responsabilidade civil,* Almedina, 2011, pp. 393–395.
606. F. Pessoa Jorge, *A limitação convencional da responsabilidade civil*, BMJ n.º 281, 1979, p. 21.
607. A. Pinto Monteiro, *Claúsulas limitativas e de exclusão da responsabilidade civil,* Almedina, 2011, p. 409.

or add to them any convenient clauses', and is also limited by a principle of public order by the ring-fencing within the law's limits.[608]

It can be asked if an arrangement like this would not shift the liability's nature, but Pinto Monteiro advocates otherwise, excluding also any liability concurrence. In that regard, Pessoa Jorge also advocates that 'the single circumstance of making an agreement on civil liability does not imply that that is necessarily a contractual liability: being covered by a contract does not make it contractual, only, as we have said, the fact that the infringed obligation emerges from a contract'.[609] Also, because of that, it cannot be rigorously called a clause, if there is not any contract, but rather an agreement. And, being an agreement, it requires at least to the parties in the contract, not being enough to wave responsibility a simple warning or sign.[610]

608. F. Pessoa Jorge, *A limitação convencional da responsabilidade civil*, BMJ n.º 281, 1979, p. 28.
609. F. Pessoa Jorge, *A limitação convencional da responsabilidade civil*, BMJ n.º 281, 1979, p. 20.
610. A. Pinto Monteiro, *Claúsulas limitativas e de exclusão da responsabilidade civil,* Almedina, 2011, pp. 400–401.

Part V. Causation

§1. On the Requirement of Causation

102. Article 563 of the Portuguese Civil Code states a general principle as to causation:

> The duty to compensate only extends to damages the victim probably would not have sustained, were it not for the injuring event.

In keeping with the dominant doctrine, Article 563 requires a two-step approach to causation.

§2. Factual Causation

103. In the first step, the judge is to assess whether the injuring event is a *condition* of the damages sustained by the victim.

All injuring events that contributed to the damaging result pass the *condition sine qua non* test. It is not necessary that the injuring event caused the damage on its own. It is sufficient that the injuring event contributed to the damage[611] – i.e., it is sufficient that the injuring event is one of the conditions of the damage (among others).[612]

§3. Legal Causation: The Adequacy Requirement

104. In the second step, after the injuring event passes the *conditio sine qua non* or 'but-for test', the judge is to assess whether the injuring event is an *adequate* or *appropriate* condition. The adverb 'probably' in Article 563 clearly refers to the adequacy test.[613]

611. *See, for example*, M. Andrade, *Teoria geral das obrigações*, at 356–357; F.M. Pereira Coelho, *Obrigações. Obrigações. Sumários das lições ao curso de 1966/1967* (Coimbra 1967) 169–171; J.M. Antunes Varela, *Das obrigações em geral* I, at 894–895; J. Ribeiro de Faria, *Direito das obrigações* II (Coimbra: Livraria Almedina 1999) at 506.
612. J.M. Antunes Varela, *Das obrigações em geral* I, at 895.
613. *See, for example*, F.M. Pereira Coelho, 'O nexo de causalidade na responsabilidade civil', 9 (1951) *Suplemento ao Boletim da Faculdade de Direito* [da Universidade de Coimbra] 65–242; M. Andrade, *Teoria geral das obrigações* 3rd edition (Coimbra: Livraria Almedina 1966) 355–367;

In general, in abstract terms, the fact (= the damaging event) must be adequate/appropriate to the damaging result. In assessing whether the fact (= the damaging event) is appropriate, the judge is to take into account only the circumstances the agent/the tortfeasor knew or that an experienced observer should have known.[614]

That is to say that the damaging result must be foreseeable – or, at the very least, that the damaging result must not be completely unforeseeable.[615]

In applying the adequacy test, two criteria have been adopted by Portuguese scholars and judges – adequacy may be described either negatively or positively.

In keeping with the negative formulation of adequacy – which seems to have been borrowed from Enneccerus – a *conditio sine qua non* is not to be considered the *cause* to the damaging result if such a *conditio*, for its very nature, is normally indifferent to that type of damaging result. In such cases – where the *conditio sine qua non* does not normally *increase*, nor even *modify*, the risk of that type of damaging event – the *conditio* would not be the *cause* of the damaging result, in the legal sense of the word *cause*.

In keeping with the positive formulation of adequacy – which seems to have been borrowed from von Kries and, especially, from Traeger – a *conditio sine qua non* is to be considered a *cause* of the damaging result if, and only if, such a *conditio*, for its very nature, normally increases the risk of that type of damaging result.[616]

F.M. Pereira Coelho, *Obrigações. Obrigações. Sumários das lições ao curso de 1966/1967* (Coimbra 1967) 162–165; J.M. Antunes Varela, *Das obrigações em geral* I, at 881–901; I. Galvão Telles, *Direito das obrigações* 7th edition (Coimbra: Coimbra Editora 1997) 397–410; M.J. de Almeida Costa, *Direito das obrigações* 12th edition (Coimbra: Livraria Almedina 2008) 760–767; F. Pessoa Jorge, *Ensaio sobre os pressupostos da responsabilidade civil* 2nd edition (Coimbra: Livraria Almedina 1999) 388–413; J. Ribeiro de Faria, *Direito das obrigações* II (Coimbra: Livraria Almedina 1999) 496–508; L. Menezes Leitão, *Direito das obrigações*, I. – *Introdução. Da constituição das obrigações* 12th edition (Coimbra: Livraria Almedina 2015) 346–350; P.R. Martinez, *Direito das obrigações* 3rd edition (Lisboa: AAFDL 2011) 128–131; E. Santos Júnior, *Direito das obrigações I* (Lisboa: AAFDL 2010) 347–352; N.M. Pinto Oliveira, *Princípios de direito dos contratos* (Coimbra: Coimbra Editora 2011) 640–668; *see*, however, A. Menezes Cordeiro, *Tratado de direito civil português*, II. – *Direito das obrigações*, III. – *Gestão de negócios. Enriquecimento sem causa. Responsabilidade civil*, at 531–550 – suggesting that adequate causation should be replaced by 'normative causation': In assessing causation, the judge should refer to the protective scope of the rules.

614. *See*, for example, M. Andrade, *Teoria geral das obrigações*, 3rd edition (Coimbra: Livraria Almedina 1966) 357; F.M. Pereira Coelho, *Obrigações. Obrigações. Sumários das lições ao curso de 1966/1967* (Coimbra 1967) 165; J.M. Antunes Varela, *Das obrigações em geral*, I, 10th edition (Coimbra: Livraria Almedina 2000) 891–893; N.M. Pinto Oliveira, *Princípios de direito dos contratos* (Coimbra: Coimbra Editora 2011) 648–649.

615. *See, for example*, M. Andrade, *Teoria geral das obrigações*, 355–356; F.M. Pereira Coelho, *Obrigações. Obrigações. Sumários das lições ao curso de 1966/1967*, 162–165; J.M. Antunes Varela, *Das obrigações em geral* I, 887–891; I. Galvão Telles, *Direito das obrigações*, 404–410; F. Pessoa Jorge, *Ensaio sobre os pressupostos da responsabilidade civil*, 392–398; M.J. de Almeida Costa, *Direito das obrigações*, 763–766; J. Ribeiro de Faria, *Direito das obrigações* I, 500–506; N.M. Pinto Oliveira, *Princípios de direito dos contratos*, 644–649.

616. *See*, for example, M. Andrade, *Teoria geral das obrigações*, at 355–356 (fn. 4), F.M. Pereira Coelho, *Obrigações. Obrigações. Sumários das lições ao curso de 1966/1967*, at 162–163; J.M. Antunes Varela, *Das obrigações em geral* I, at 887–891; J. Ribeiro de Faria, *Direito das obrigações* I, at 500–506; N.M. Pinto Oliveira, *Princípios de direito dos contratos*, at 649–651.

It has been argued that both formulations have different scopes of application. The *negative formulation* of adequacy should apply to fault-based, subjective liability. The *positive formulation* of adequacy should apply to no-fault, objective or strict liability.

§4. Deviations to the General Requirements on Causation

I. Alternative and Cumulative Causation

105. In Portugal, alternative causation is controversial, for, in accordance with the *conditio sine qua non* test, the victim should be left without compensation.

In Germany, the Civil Code provides for a deviation to the *conditio sine qua non* test in cases of alternative causation.[617] In Portugal, the Civil Code does not so provide for any deviation at all – in the absence of a rule similar to § 830(1) of the German Civil Code, the victim would bear the risk of failing to identify the wrongdoer.[618]

Professor Calvão da Silva proposed a particular, specific solution in the field of product liability. In cases where the producers belonging to the group of potential tortfeasors are determined – the problems stemming from the fact that the actual tortfeasor, whose defective product causes the damage, is not – three solutions were to be considered: no liability, total liability (= joint and several liability of all potential tortfeasors), and partial liability (such as market-share liability).[619] In keeping with the principles and rules of the Portuguese system, only the first and the second solutions would stand – partial liability should be ruled out.[620]

The problem then would come at determining whether the situation of alternative causation is regulated in the Portuguese Civil Code – namely, in Article 563.

Professor Calvão da Silva argued that it is not – in the particular, specific situation of product liability, alternative causation should be considered a gap ('*lacuna*'). In filling the gap, the judge should follow two rules on the burden of proof. In the first place, the plaintiff would bear the onus of proving that the defendants belong to the group of potential wrongdoers[621] and the defendants would bear the onus of proving that they do not – for example, that they did not distribute the

617. German Civil Code, § 830(1): 'If several persons have caused damage by an unlawful act committed in common, each is responsible for the damage. The same rule applies if it cannot be discovered which of several participants has actually caused the damage.'
618. *See, for example*, F.M. Pereira Coelho, *O problema da causa virtual na responsabilidade civil*, 2nd edition (Coimbra: Livraria Almedina 1998) 24 (fn. 2), and, for a recent restatement of the no-liability rule, A. Menezes Cordeiro, *Tratado de direito civil português*, I. – *Direito das obrigações*, III. – *Gestão de negócios. Enriquecimento sem causa. Responsabilidade civil* (Coimbra: Livraria Almedina 2010) 739–740.
619. *See* J. Calvão da Silva, *Responsabilidade civil do produtor* (Coimbra: Livraria Almedina 1990) 581–583.
620. J. Calvão da Silva, *Responsabilidade civil do produtor*, at 581–581.
621. J. Calvão da Silva, *Responsabilidade civil do produtor*, at 582.

defective product at the relevant time and place.[622] If the defendants failed to do so, they would be held joint and severally liable.[623]

It is submitted that Portuguese courts would apply the total liability rule in cases of alternative causation in the particular, specific sector of tort liability for defective products.

In spite of the fact that the doctrine is divided,[624] the Portuguese Supreme Court's judgment of 19 May 2015 applied total liability to a case where no tort liability for defective products was at stake. In cases of alternative causation, the *conditio sine qua non* test would apply with qualification and with qualification only.[625]

It is therefore submitted, albeit with a doubt, that Portuguese courts would apply the total liability rule to all cases of concurrent, alternative and cumulative causation.

In external relations, all members of the group of potential tortfeasors would be held joint and severally liable.[626] In internal relations, liability would be apportioned, taking into account the degree of fault of each tortfeasor and his contribution to damage.[627]

In the case of product liability, the criterion of each tortfeasor's contribution to damage would probably lead to an apportionment taking into account market shares.

Contrary to alternative causation, in Portugal, cumulative causation is not at all controversial:[628] all tortfeasors are to be held joint and severally liable.

II. Hypothetical, Potential, or Virtual Causation

106. Article 566(2) of the Portuguese Civil Code strictly adheres to the so-called difference theory.[629] The judge is to assess damages by comparing the actual state of the victim's assets with the hypothetical state of his assets in the absence of the damaging event.

In keeping with the difference theory, as laid down in Article 566(2) of the Portuguese Civil Code, hypothetical, potential or virtual causes would be relevant.[630]

---

622. J. Calvão da Silva, *Responsabilidade civil do produtor*, at 582–583.
623. J. Calvão da Silva, *Responsabilidade civil do produtor*, at 586–587.
624. *See*, *for example*, P. Mota Pinto, *Interesse contratual positivo e interesse contratual negativo* I (Coimbra: Coimbra Editora 2008) 653–654 and 687–688.
625. *See* Portuguese Supreme Court, judgment of 19 May 2015 (Júlio Gomes).
626. Portuguese Civil Code, Art. 497(1).
627. Portuguese Civil Code, Art. 497(2).
628. For a definition of cumulative causation, *see* F.M. Pereira Coelho, *O problema da causa virtual na responsabilidade civil* 2nd edition (Coimbra: Livraria Almedina 1998) 24 (fn. 5); J.M. Antunes Varela, *Das obrigações em geral* I 10th edition (Coimbra: Livraria Almedina 2000) 923 (fn. 1); A. Menezes Cordeiro, *Tratado de direito civil português*, I. – *Direito das obrigações*, III. – *Gestão de negócios. Enriquecimento sem causa. Responsabilidade civil* (Coimbra: Livraria Almedina 2010) 739.
629. For an explanation of the so-called difference theory, *see* H. Koziol, *Basic Questions of Tort Law from a Germanic Perspective*, 123–124.
630. *See* F. Pessoa Jorge, *Ensaio sobre os pressupostos da responsabilidade civil*, 2nd edition (Coimbra: Livraria Almedina 1999) 416–418.

There is, however, a difference between the statutory rule, as enshrined in Article 566(2) of the Civil Code, and the doctrinal rule, recognized by the courts.

It is assumed that tort law aims at compensation, deterrence (prevention), and punishment.[631] In the case of hypothetical or potential causation, damages would be justified on the preventive and/or punitive functions of tort law.[632]

Furthermore, Articles 491, 492 and 493(1) of the Portuguese Civil Code seem to confirm the irrelevance of hypothetical, potential or virtual causation.[633]

In Article 491, as well as in Articles 492 and 493(1), the legislator attributed relevance to hypothetical, potential or virtual causes. Article 491 applies to damages caused by incompetent persons, allowing persons under a statutory or contractual duty to supervise the incompetent wrongdoer to escape liability by proving that 'damages would have occurred even if their conduct conformed to such a duty [to supervise]'. Article 492 applies to damages caused by buildings and Article 493(1) applies to damages caused by animals, as well as by movable and immovable things, allowing owners of buildings of movable and immovable things to escape liability by proving that damages would have occurred even if their conduct conformed to all relevant statutory and contractual duties.

631. *See, for example*, J.M. Antunes Varela, *Das obrigações em geral*, I, 10th edition (Coimbra: Livraria Almedina 2000) 542–544; A. Menezes Cordeiro, *Tratado de direito civil português*, I. – *Direito das obrigações*, III. – *Gestão de negócios. Enriquecimento sem causa. Responsabilidade civil* (Coimbra: Livraria Almedina 2010) 419–422; J.F. Sinde Monteiro 'Rudimentos da responsabilidade civil' (2005) *Revista da Faculdade de Direito da Universidade do Porto* 349–380, at 353–358; M. Carneiro da Frada, *Direito civil, Responsabilidade civil. O método do caso* (Coimbra: Livraria Almedina 2006) 64–72. Whether deterrence (prevention) and punishment are different, or not, may remain an open question.

632. *See*, however, A. Menezes Cordeiro, *Tratado de direito civil português*, I. – *Direito das obrigações*, III. – *Gestão de negócios. Enriquecimento sem causa. Responsabilidade civil*, at 740–746, suggesting that irrelevance of hypothetical, potential or virtual causes is required by tort law's compensatory function; 'otherwise, there will be many damages without compensation'.

633. *See, for example*, F.M. Pereira Coelho, *O problema da causa virtual na responsabilidade civil*, 6–13 and 210–221; M. Andrade, *Teoria geral das obrigações*, 369–373; F.M. Pereira Coelho, *Obrigações. Obrigações. Sumários das lições ao curso de 1966/1967*, 184–185; J.M. Antunes Varela, *Das obrigações em geral* I, 931–933; M.J. de Almeida Costa, *Direito das obrigações*, 767–770; I. Galvão Telles, *Direito das obrigações*, 410–422; J. Ribeiro de Faria, *Direito das obrigações* II, 477–478 and 494–495; L. Menezes Leitão, *Direito das obrigações*, I. – *Introdução. Da constituição das obrigações*, 350–351; P.R. Martinez, *Direito das obrigações* 3rd edition (Lisboa: AAFDL 2011) 131–135; E. Santos Júnior, *Direito das obrigações I* (Lisboa: AAFDL 2010) 352–354; J.F. Sinde Monteiro, *Responsabilidade por conselhos, recomendações ou informações*, 289–291; J.C. Brandão Proença, *A conduta do lesado como pressuposto e critério de imputação do dano extracontratual* (Coimbra: Livraria Almedina 1997) 431–437; M. Carneiro da Frada, *Teoria da confiança e responsabilidade civil* (Coimbra: Livraria Almedina 2004) 325–327; J.C. Brandão Proença, *Direito das obrigações. Relatório sobre o programa, o conteúdo e os métodos de ensino da disciplina* (Porto: Universidade Católica 2007) 209–210; A.G. Dias Pereira, 'Portuguese Tort Law: A Comparison with the Principles of European Tort Law', 634.

It would follow from the circumstance that, in all cases under scrutiny, liability is aggravated, that the rules in Articles 491, 492 and 493(1) would be exceptional.[634,635]

In spite of the fact that both arguments have been called into question,[636] it does not seem that Portuguese case law came to change or even that Portuguese scholarly writings came to recognize any need to modify previously held positions.[637]

It is submitted that the rule is the irrelevance of hypothetical, potential or virtual causation. It is, however, further submitted that the effects of the rule on the irrelevance of hypothetical, potential or virtual causation are to be read in conjunction with the principle in Article 494 of the Portuguese Civil Code, allowing the judge to fix compensation at an amount lower than that corresponding to the damage caused, provided that the degree of fault of the wrongdoer, the financial situation of the wrongdoer and of the injured party, as well as the other circumstances of the case so justify.[638] In fact, hypothetical, potential or virtual causation would be among the 'other circumstances of the case'.[639]

III. Liability for Lost Chances

107. In Portugal, as everywhere else, liability for lost chances is a highly controversial issue.

634. *See*, for instance, A.G. Dias Pereira, 'Portuguese Tort Law: A Comparison with the Principles of European Tort Law', at 634: 'in these cases, there are presumptions of liability (or, for other reasons, an aggravated liability) and the legislator tries to compensate that hard regime giving the possibility to escape liability by proving that such damage would have occurred for a different reason, that is, the damages would have occurred even if the wrongdoer had not breached any duty of care'.
635. *See*, however, P. Mota Pinto, *Interesse contratual negativo e interesse contratual positivo* I (Coimbra: Coimbra Editora 2008) 614–710; N.M. Pinto Oliveira, *Princípios de direito dos contratos* (Coimbra: Coimbra Editora 2011) 701–711, suggesting that Arts 491, 492 and 493(1) of the Portuguese Civil Code are irrelevant to the problem of hypothetical, potential or virtual causation, for they refer to lawful alternative conduct.
636. P. Mota Pinto, *Interesse contratual negativo e interesse contratual positivo* I and II (Coimbra: Coimbra Editora 2008).
637. *See*, for instance, A. Menezes Cordeiro, *Tratado de direito civil português*, I. – *Direito das obrigações*, III. – *Gestão de negócios. Enriquecimento sem causa. Responsabilidade civil*, at 745–746; L. Menezes Leitão, *Direito das obrigações*, I. – *Introdução. Da constituição das obrigações* at 350–351; P.R. Martinez, *Direito das obrigações*, at 132–133; E. Santos Júnior, *Direito das obrigações I*, at 353–354; N.M. Pinto Oliveira, *Princípios de direito dos contratos*, at 705–711.
638. *See* A.G. Dias Pereira, 'Portuguese Tort Law: A Comparison with the Principles of European Tort Law', at 647. In M. Bussani/V.V. Palmer (eds), *Pure Economic Loss in Europe* (Cambridge: Cambridge University Press 2003) xxxv, the translation of Art. 494 of the Portuguese Civil Code reads as follows: 'If the liability is based upon negligence compensation may be equitably settled at a lesser amount so as to correspond to the damage caused, as long as the degree of culpability of the agent, his financial conditions and those of the injured party and other circumstances justify it.'
639. *See*, for instance, F.M. Pereira Coelho, *O problema da causa virtual na responsabilidade civil*, at 10–11; J.C. Brandão Proença, *A conduta do lesado como pressuposto e critério de imputação do dano extracontratual*, at 431–437.

In the first place, it is not clear whether it relates to the theory of causation[640] or to the theory of damages.[641] Even though the doctrine is divided, the Portuguese Supreme Court seems to consider lost chances as autonomous damages.[642]

Second, the criteria for distinguishing cases of relevant and irrelevant chances are far from consensual. Whereas some of the most influential scholarly writings clearly reject compensation for lost chances,[643] some others accept it, albeit with a few qualifications.

In order to distinguish relevant from irrelevant chances, two criteria have been suggested.

It has been argued that the problem of lost chances should be resolved by taking into account the scope of the duty which has been infringed or violated.

In contractual liability, lost chances should be compensated, for the scope of the contractual duties which have been infringed or violated would precisely be the one of preserving or even enhancing the chances of achieving a positive result; in non-contractual, tortious liability, lost chances would not, and should not, be compensated.[644]

The argument is, however, rather doubtful. In fact, under Portuguese law, the differences between contractual and non-contractual, tortious liability do not apply to the effects of both liabilities (= to the duty to compensate). For Article 563 of the Portuguese Civil Code is among the principles and rules relating to the duty to compensate; it applies both to the duty to compensate emerging from contracts and from

---

640. *See, for example*, J. Gomes, 'Em torno do dano da perda de chance – algumas reflexões', in J. Figueiredo Dias/J.J. Gomes Canotilho/J. Faria Costa (eds), *Ars judicandi. Estudos em homenagem ao Prof. Doutor António Castanheira Neves*, II – *Direito privado* (Coimbra: Faculdade de Direito da Universidade de Coimbra/Coimbra Editora 2008) 289–327; P. Mota Pinto, *Interesse contratual positivo e interesse contratual negativo* II (Coimbra: Coimbra Editora 2008) 1106; J. Gomes, 'Ainda sobre a figura do dano da perda de oportunidade ou perda de chance', in (2012) *Cadernos de direito privado*, special edition – *II Seminário dos Cadernos de Direito Privado. Responsabilidade civil* 17–29.

641. *See, for example*, J.F. Sinde Monteiro, *Responsabilidade por conselhos, recomendações ou informações* 291–300; M. Carneiro da Frada, *Direito civil. Responsabilidade civil. O método do caso* 103–106; R. Teixeira Pedro, *A responsabilidade civil do médico. Reflexões sobre a perda de chance e a tutela do doente lesado* Coimbra: Centro de Direito Biomédico da Faculdade de Direito da Universidade de Coimbra/Coimbra Editora 2009); R. Cardona Ferreira, *Indemnização do interesse contratual positivo e perda de* chance *(em especial, na contratação pública)* (Coimbra: Coimbra Editora 2011) 264–271; M. Carneiro da Frada, 'Danos societários e governação de sociedades *(corporate governance)*', in *Cadernos de direito privado*, special edition – *II Seminário dos Cadernos de Direito Privado. Responsabilidade civil* (2012), 31–44; R. Cardona Ferreira, 'A perda de chance – análise comparativa e perspetivas de ordenação sistemática', in (2012) 144 *O Direito* 28–57; R. Cardona Ferreira, 'The Loss of Chance in Civil Law Countries: A Comparative and Critical Analysis', 20 *Maastricht Journal of European and Comparative Law* 53–74 (2013).

642. *See*, for three recent examples, the judgments of the Portuguese Supreme Court of 1 Jul. 2014 (Fonseca Ramos), 30 Apr. 2014 (M. Pizarro Beleza), 5 May 2015 (Silva Salazar) and judgment No. 2/2022 of 26 Jan. 2022 (Ana Paula Boularot); suggesting, however, that the loss of a chance is a problem of causation, *see* the judgment of the Portuguese Supreme Court of 9 Dec. 2014 (S. Póvoas).

643. P. Mota Pinto, *Interesse contratual positivo e interesse contratual negativo* II, at 1106.

644. M. Carneiro da Frada, *Direito civil. Responsabilidade civil. O método do caso* (Coimbra: Livraria Almedina 2006) 104.

torts.[645] It is not at all clear why liability for the loss of a chance should be an exception to the equal treatment of the causation requirement, both in contract and in tort law.

Furthermore, the argument failed to convince the Portuguese Supreme Court.[646]

It has also been suggested that the relevant criterion of causation should be made more flexible, so as to allow compensation in every single case where the probability of achieving the positive result, the chance of which has been lost, exceeds 50%.[647]

In refusing both criteria, the Portuguese Supreme Court held different, disparate standards for assessing whether lost chances were to be compensated.

In a first group of judgments, it is required that the positive result, the chance of which has been lost, is 'highly expectable'[648] or 'highly probable'.[649,650] In a second group of judgments, it is required that the positive result is 'probable'. Finally, in a third group of judgment, it is only required that the chance is 'consistent',[651] 'real'[652] or 'serious'.[653]

It is submitted that, for an event to have a 'consistent' or a 'serious' probability of passing, the 50% threshold is much too high. In fact, 'consistent', 'real' or 'serious' probability seems to be something less than 'preponderant' probability.

In 2022, the Supreme Court of Justice n. 2/2022, in a plenary decision (in a judgment standardizing jurisprudence), stated that: 'The damage resulting from the loss of procedural chance, the basis of the obligation to compensate, must be consistent and serious, with the burden of proving such consistency and seriousness falling on the injured party.'

645. J. Gomes, 'Ainda sobre a figura do dano da perda de oportunidade ou perda de chance', at 20.
646. *See, for example*, the judgment of the Portuguese Supreme Court of 30 Sep. 2014 (M. Mendes), according to which the loss of a chance is to be compensated both in contract and in tort.
647. J. Gomes, 'Ainda sobre a figura do dano da perda de oportunidade ou perda de chance', at 20.
648. *See* the judgment of the Portuguese Supreme Court of 30 Sep. 2014 (M. Mendes).
649. *See* the judgment of the Portuguese Supreme Court of 30 Apr. 2015 (M. Pizarro Beleza) 5 May 2015 (Silva Salazar).
650. It is submitted that, for an event to have a 'high probability' of passing, the 50% standard in much too low.
651. *See* the judgments of the Portuguese Supreme Court of 14 Mar. 2013 (M. Pizarro Beleza) and 1 Jul. 2014 (Fonseca Ramos) and 30 Sep. 2014 (M. Mendes).
652. *See* the judgments of the Portuguese Supreme Court of 14 Mar. 2013 (M. Pizarro Beleza), 6 Mar. 2014 (Pinto de Almeida), 1 Jul. 2014 (Fonseca Ramos), of 30 Sep. 2014 (M. Mendes) and 5 May 2015 (Silva Salazar).
653. *See* the judgment of the Portuguese Supreme Court of 5 May 2015 (Silva Salazar).

Part VI. Remedies

Chapter 1. General Principles

108. Remedies are mainly regulated in Article 562 and following, within Section VIII – obligation to compensate – of Chapter III – obligation's categories – of the second book of the Civil Code, concerning the Law of Obligations. The system is complex but can be outlined by appealing to three fundamental principles: its primarily reparatory scope; the preference for restitution in kind; and the granting of full compensation.

§1. Scope Primarily Reparatory

109. Article 562 establishes the general and basilar principle that the scope of the law of torts is to repair the caused damage by putting the injured party in the hypothetical present situation that would exist if the damage had not occurred – it reads 'the person who is bound to make compensation must restore the situation which would exist if the circumstance making him liable to compensate had not occurred'. It prioritizes a compensatory function rather than a repressive or punitive one.[654] The same derives from the central role played by the damage in triggering the tort law system.[655]

§2. Preference for Restitution In Kind

110. In line with the reparation principle of restoring the present hypothetical situation, Article 566(1) lays down the legislator's preference for natural reparation, i.e., in kind, over its pecuniary equivalent – it reads, 'Compensation shall be calculated in monetary terms if natural restoration is not possible, would not fully repair the damage or would be excessively onerous to the debtor.' Therefore, pecuniary compensations should only be made if in kind reparation cannot be reached and the Article in analysis foresees three circumstances where that could happen: by reason of impossibility; because of reparation in kind not allowing full compensation; or, lastly, for it being excessively costly for the liable party.

654. *See*, Functions of tort law, and, for all, F. Pessoa Jorge, *Ensaio sobre os pressupostos da responsabilidade civil*, 1968, 52.
655. *See*, Remedies. *See*, M. Miranda Barbosa, *Lições de Responsabilidade Civil,* Principia, 2017, 45.

Restitution in kind can be impossible as a natural consequence of the damage's nature, as is the case with non-pecuniary damages and non-interchangeable assets. With respect to non-pecuniary damages, albeit the wrongdoer can undertake other forms of mitigation that do not constitute a pecuniary compensation, such as a public disclaimer, they are not characterized as restitution in kind.[656] Non-interchangeable assets, by nature, cannot be replaced by something equivalent in quantity or quality.

As a second circumstance where restitution in kind would not be preferable, the legislator cites its inability to grant full compensation. That would be the case when the mere substitution or fixing of the harmed asset would not be enough to address all the assessed damages, which can be present or future, and in both cases, either emergent or loss of profit.[657]

Lastly, the law balances both parties' interests, allowing a pecuniary compensation, even if restitution in kind is possible and fully compensates the injured party, but, nonetheless, is unduly painful for the wrongdoer in contrast to the benefits it brings to the aggrieved party.[658]

Being the primary method of compensation, the injured party has the right to decline pecuniary compensation if restitution in kind is attainable, even if that is not the wrongdoer's preference.[659]

§3. Granting Full Compensation of Damages

111. Article 564 gives ground for the guiding principle of full compensation by establishing that: (1) 'The obligation to pay compensation covers not only damage caused but also benefits that the injured person failed to obtain as a consequence of the injury', and adding in (2) 'In calculating compensation, the court may consider future damage, provided that it is foreseeable; if it is not determinable, the calculation of the corresponding compensation shall be postponed to a later decision'.

That being said, the tortfeasor must compensate not only for the emergent damage but also loss of profit. Also, as stated in its (2), foreseeable future damage is to be compensated.

Another echo of the intention to fully compensate the injured party is in the general clause of Article 483,[660] which refers indistinctly to the caused damage, and in the generous norm anchored in Article 496, which allows for the compensation of all proven non-pecuniary damages if they are regarded as serious.[661]

656. *See*, A. Menezes Cordeiro, *Tratado de Direito Civil Português*, V. II, T. III, Almedina, 2010, 725.
657. *See*, Remedies.
658. F.A. Pires de Lima/J.M. Antunes Varela (/ M.H. Mesquita), *Código Civil anotado*, vol. I, 2.ª ed., 506.
659. F. Pessoa Jorge, *Ensaio sobre os pressupostos da responsabilidade civil*, 1968, 421.
660. *See*, Unlawfullness.
661. *See*, Non-pecuniary damages.

Chapter 2. Kinds of Damages

112. The Portuguese Civil Code contains no statutory definition of the general concept of a damage (similar, for instance, to the definition in § 1293 of the Austrian Civil Code[662]). Therefore, the general concept of damage is to be defined by the doctrine – damage is to consist of 'material or immaterial harm to a legally protected interest'.[663]

§1. Individual and Collective Damage

113. Normally, compensation is assessed and awarded for individual damages as a result of being a private law matter and, therefore, requiring the injured party's procedural initiative which shapes the entire claim. That derives primarily from the consecrated forms of unlawfulness in the Article 483 general clause[664] since each protected legal interest is regarded as a personal interest and the legal protection is awarded to each specific individual. The same act can generate multiple damages, whether on one or several individuals, but, nevertheless, each of those affected must take legal action on its own and prove (if needed) its respective damage.

Sometimes, however, compensation is awarded, by law, to a group of people, as seen in regard to the non-pecuniary loss suffered by persons having a close relationship with the victim of a *fatal* injury.[665]

The main example of what can be described as collective damages comes from Law No. 83/95, 31 August 1995, concerning The Right to Procedural Participation and Popular Action, anchored in Article 52 of the Constitution. This law aims to the protection of diffuse interests, illustrated in its Article 1(2) as public health, environment, quality of life, consumer goods and services, cultural heritage and the public sphere. Article 2 recognizes the right to popular action to 'any citizen with full exercise of his/her civil and political rights, as well as to associations and foundations which aim to protect those diffuse interests, regardless of any direct interest in the litigation'. A diffuse interest is not to be mistaken with an individual or with a collective interest. It entails the refraction of the unitary interests of a global community in each individual.[666]

---

662. § 1293 of the Austrian Civil Code reads as follows: 'Damage is any harm that has been inflicted on someone to his patrimony, rights or his person. This is distinguished from loss of profit, which someone is entitled to expect in the normal course of events' (for the translation of § 1293 of the Austrian Civil Code, *see* H. Koziol, *Basic Questions of Tort Law from a Germanic Perspective*, 109).
663. *See* Art. 2:101 of the Principles of European Tort Law and the corresponding commentary by H. Koziol, 'Title II. General Conditions of Liability – Chapter 2. Damage – Article 2:101. Recoverable Damage', in European Group on Tort Law, *Principles of European Tort Law. Text and Commentary* (Wien/New York: Springer 2005) 27–29.
664. *See*, Unlawfulness.
665. *See*, to pecuniary damages in case of death or personal injury.
666. J.J. Gomes Canotilho e Vital Moreira, *Constituição da República Portuguesa Anotada*, p. 698.

In regard to civil liability, its Article 22(1) states that 'the liability for, with wilful misconduct, violating the interests enshrined in Article 1, imposes on the wrongdoer the duty to compensate for the caused damages'. Adding, (2) and (3), respectively, that 'the compensation for the violation of interests with non-identifiable holders is to be fixated globally' and that 'the holders of identifiable interests have the right to a corresponding compensation established in civil liability's general terms'. With concern to Article 22(2), Figueiredo Dias argues that the global amounts fixated for non-identifiable holders should have the same fate as time-barred credits, as established by Article 22(5) – being allocated to the payment of legal fees and legal assistance, and, furthermore, eventually to the promotion of akin natural reparation strategies.[667]

According to Article 12, a popular civil action follows any procedural form available on the Civil Procedure Code, and via Article 15, any interest holder has the right to be excluded from the popular action – *opting out* –after being informed, normally by public notice, as prescribed by the same article. If the interest holder does not exercise his/her right of opting out, risks the popular action's decision being applicable to him/her and the matter becoming indisputable.

In spite of this procedural mechanism for collective action at national level, the opportunity to transpose Directive (EU) 2020/1828 of the European Parliament and of the Council of 25 November 2020, on representative actions for the protection of the collective interests of consumers has been taken to establish a specific national collective action regime for the protection of consumers' rights and interests – enshrined on Decree-Law No. 114-A/2023 of 5 December 2023.

The aim is for this system to be applicable whenever there are infringements of the provisions of national and EU law identified in Annex I of the Directive or of any other consumer protection legislation, insofar as it is in force in the Portuguese legal system, which harm or are likely to harm the collective interests of consumers. However, the rules on popular actions provided for in the popular action law are applicable in everything that is not provided for in this decree-law.

§2. Direct and Indirect

I. As a Matter of Causal Link

114. Article 563 establishes the adequacy criterion, which can include not only direct but also indirect damage.[668]

II. As a Matter of Right to Compensation

115. As a general rule, the civil liability system aims to compensate the directly injured party, i.e., the holder of the legal right or protected legal interest, not any

667. J.E. Figueiredo Dias, *Os efeitos da sentença na Lei de Acção Popular, in CEDOUA magazine*, year 11, 1999, p. 58.

668. *See* the Part V on Causation.

third party eventually affected.[669] That stems not only from the unlawfulness clauses of Article 483 and 334 but also from the understanding of causation as enshrined in Article 563 – 'The obligation of compensation only exists in relation to damage that the injured person probably would not have suffered if it was not for the injury' – demonstrating that the injured party, and its protected rights, plays a central role. That is a natural outcome of the pure economic loss not being compensated under the first unlawfulness clause of Article 483.[670] Still, some exceptions are made where the Civil Code allows for compensation for indirect damage.

Article 495 concerns compensations to third parties when an injury leads to death or causes bodily harm, stating in: (1) that 'When an injury leads to death, the person responsible shall be obliged to pay compensation for the costs incurred in seeking to save the injured party, and all other expenses, not excluding funeral expenses', and adding in (2) that 'In any such case, and in all other instances of bodily injury, those who render assistance to the injured party have a right to compensation, as well as hospitals, doctors or other persons or entities who may have contributed to the treatment or assistance of the victim.' Thus, the Civil Code recognizes exceptionally that a person who could not seek otherwise any compensation through Article 483 can, thereby, be compensated for their *objective* damages. The same also occurs with respect to its (3), which sets forth the 'The right to compensation shall also be available to those entitled to require maintenance (alimony) from the injured party and to those to whom the injured party paid maintenance in fulfilment of a natural obligation.'[671]

With regard to non-pecuniary damage, Article 496(2) establishes that 'When the victim's death occurs, the right to compensation for non-pecuniary damages belongs *en bloc* to the spouse, if there's no legal separation, and to the victim's children or other descendants; in absence of those, it belongs to the victim's parents or other ascendants; lastly, it belongs to the brothers or nephews representing the victim.'[672] Adding, (3) says that 'If the victim had a non-marital partnership, the right to compensation of the number above [(2)] belongs, firstly, en bloc, to the partner and to the victim's children or other descendants.'

Recently, *via* an amendment to the Civil Code with regard to the status of animals under the law,[673] Article 493A was added. It reads as follows:

669. J.M. Antunes Varela, *Das Obrigações em Geral*, pp. 620–621.
670. *See*, pure economic loss.
671. Which includes not only present maintenance obligations, either legal or natural, but also future ones as long as they are foreseeable. *See*, J.M. Antunes Varela, *Das Obrigações em Geral*, p. 624.
672. In the recent judgment of the Portuguese Supreme Court of 15 Dec. 2022 delivered by Justice João Cura Mariano was discussed the possibility of compensating the parents of a 2–year-old-girl who was attacked by a dog for indirect non-pecuniary damages. The Court concluded that, giving the type of aggression suffered, the child's age, the area of the body affected, the characteristics of the most serious injuries suffered and the marked permanent aesthetic damage caused, there was an enormous emotional impact on the child's parents that allows the application of the updated reading of the provisionais of Arts 483(1) and 496(1) of the Civil Code stated in the judgment of the Portuguese Supreme Court of 22 May 2014 (No. 6/2014).
673. Law No. 8/2017 of 3 Mar. 2017.

1. In case of bodily harm to an animal, the liable person has to compensate the animal's owner or the individuals or entities who render assistance to the injured animal for their expenses with treatment, irrespectively of due compensation in general terms.
2. The compensation defined in the previous number, is due even if the expenses surpass the animal's pecuniary value.
3. In case the of, in consequence of the injury, occurring the death, deprival of an organ or limb, or a serious and permanent damage of the locomotion capacity of a domestic animal, its owner has the right, in line with Article 496(1), to a suitable compensation for sorrow and moral grievance, equitably determined by the Court.

Article 493A is, therefore, similar to Article 495, admitting compensation to people who render assistance, even if the animal does not belong to them, representing another example of compensation for indirect damages.

§3. Pecuniary and Non-pecuniary Losses

116. Even though the Portuguese Civil Code contains no statutory definition of the concept of damage, it establishes a distinction between pecuniary and non-pecuniary loss.

On the one hand, the economic, pecuniary loss shall be defined positively. It consists of a diminution of the victim's patrimony.[674] The concept of a diminution is, however, to be interpreted in a comprehensive sense, for, in keeping with Article 564(1) of the Portuguese Civil Code, economic, pecuniary loss comprehends loss of profits.[675]

On the other hand, the non-economic, non-pecuniary loss shall be defined negatively, and only negatively – it does not consist of a diminution of the victim's patrimony.

Whereas pecuniary losses can; non-pecuniary losses cannot be monetized:

In the case of pecuniary losses, the principle is that the judge is to award damages that correspond exactly to the amount of the loss; in the case of non-pecuniary loss, the principle that the judge is to award damages that correspond to the amount of the loss cannot be followed – the judge is to award equitable damages to the victim.

It should be mentioned that there is a discussion as to the scope of Article 496(1):

674. *See*, for a similar definition of pecuniary loss, Art. 10:201 of the Principles of European Tort Law: 'Recoverable pecuniary damage is a diminution of the victim's patrimony caused by the damaging event' [for a commentary, U. Magnus, 'Title VI. Remedies – Chapter 10. Damages – Section 2. Pecuniary Damage – Article 10:201. Nature and Determination of Pecuniary Damage', in European Group on Tort Law, *Principles of European Tort Law. Text and Commentary* (Wien/New York: Springer 2005) 161–164].

675. *See*, for a similar definition of pecuniary loss, Art. VI – 2:101, para. (4), sub-para. (a) of the (Draft) Common Frame of Reference: 'economic loss includes loss of income or profit, burdens incurred and a reduction in the value of property'.

> For the determination of compensation, regard must be had to non-pecuniary damage that, due to its seriousness, deserves protection by the law.[676]

It has been pointed out that the formal, external structure of the Civil Code suggests that Article 496(1) is to apply to non-contractual, tortious liability – and to non-contractual, tortious liability only.[677] It has also been pointed out that allowing the creditor to claim compensation for non-pecuniary damage would unduly complicate the functioning of the legal system.

In fact, creditors would be tempted to claim compensation for the inconvenience of asking the debtor to perform, for the anxiety of not knowing whether the debtor would perform or not, and for the inconvenience of having to depose a claim.[678] In favouring such a temptation, the system would fail to perform its function of keeping the floodgates shut.[679]

In spite of the powerful arguments against compensation for non-pecuniary loss, it is submitted that Article 496 of the Portuguese Civil Code is to apply, at least by analogical reasoning, to contractual liability.[680]

---

676. For the translation of Art. 496(1), *see* A.G. Dias Pereira, 'Portuguese Tort Law: A Comparison with the Principles of European Tort Law' in H. Koziol/B.C. Steininger (eds), *European Tort Law 2004* (Wien/New York: Springer 2005) 623, at 643.
677. In spite of the fact Art. 496(1) of the Portuguese Civil Code clearly applies to all cases of non-contractual, tortious liability, there are still quite a few cases where the appropriateness of compensating the plaintiffs for non-pecuniary losses is called into question. That is the case, *for example*, of non-pecuniary losses arising from occupation of property. In a recent judgment of the Portuguese Supreme Court, of 21 Jun. 2012, the case was as follows: A and B, urban property owners of building X, filed a provisional injunction against C and D for restitution of possession of a plot of land near X, which had always been part of the building and had been used continuously and without interruption for more than twenty or thirty years by the claimants to grow vegetables for their own consumption. This situation was never opposed or challenged by anyone, and the claimants were recognized as owners of that land. However, C and D took over the plot on 29 Jul. 2006, leaving only a small strip of land in front of the claimants' house. As a result, A and B felt dispossessed, and emotionally distressed until restitution in court by the injunction of 22 Sep. 2006. In the main action, A and B requested that C and D be ordered to recognize them as owners of urban property X, which included the aforementioned plot. They also requested that C and D be ordered to pay EUR 2,500 as compensation for the non-pecuniary damage they had suffered. Both the trial court, as well as the court of appeal partially upheld the action, recognizing that A and B were the legitimate owners of the building which is located on land occupied by C and D. However, they dismissed the claim for damages. The Supreme Court considered that the difficulties the claimants experienced during the occupation of their land (about two months) cannot be considered normal when there are conflicts of ownership, as the court of appeal had concluded. It is not part of everyday life for an owner to have to bear the occupation of his or her property and to be forced to go to court for the previous situation to be restored. It was, in the words of the Supreme Court, an abnormal situation, which caused serious inconvenience and suffering to the claimants' who, therefore, deserve the protection of the law under Art. 496(1) CC, which prescribes the right to compensation for non-pecuniary losses that are serious and deserve the protection of the law. As for the actual amount of compensation sought, EUR 2,500, the Supreme Court held that it appeared reasonable.
678. *See* F.A. Pires de Lima/J.M. Antunes Varela (/ M.H. Mesquita), *Código Civil anotado*, vol. I, 4th edition (Coimbra: Combra Editora 1986) 502.
679. *See* the title of Jaap Spier's book – *The Limits of Liability. Keeping the Floodgates Shut* (The Hague/London/Boston: Kluwer Law International 1996).
680. *See*, *for example*, I. Galvão Telles, *Direito das obrigações*, 378–387; R. de Alarcão, *Direito das obrigações*, 210; M.J. Almeida Costa, *Direito das obrigações*, 603–605; L. Menezes Leitão,

In the first place, there are areas of the law where all, or almost all, contractual liability is to be a liability for non-pecuniary loss. Second, Article 496(1) of the Civil Code provides for a reasonable, sensible criterion so as to determine whether the non-pecuniary loss is to be compensated.

In fact, Article 496 of the Civil Code does not read, sic et simpliciter: 'For the determination of compensation, regard must be had to non-pecuniary damage.' It reads rather differently: 'regard must be had to non-pecuniary damage that, due to its seriousness, deserves protection by the law'.

The judge has to draw a line between damage that deserves protection by the law and damage that does not. Furthermore, the judge has to draw such a line by referring to the damage's seriousness.[681] It all comes down to determining whether non-pecuniary damage deserves protection by the law. Irrespectively of the fact liability is to be qualified as contractual or non-contractual, tortious, it all comes down to assessing the damage's seriousness. While serious damage is to be taken into due account, non-serious damage is not.[682]

§4. Pure Economic Loss

There is no right to maintain any patrimonial integrity under Portuguese Law and, therefore, pure economic loss is not to be compensated.[683]

§5. Actual and Future Damage (Lost Profits)

117. Article 564 relates to compensation assessment and consecrates both actual and future damage, respectively, in its (1) and (2). The first one states that 'The duty to compensate encompasses not only the emergent damage, but also lost profit in consequence of the caused harm.' The latter states that 'in the compensation's determination, the Court can take into account future damages, if they are predicable; if future damage is not determinable at that moment, they can be ascertained in a subsequent judgment'.

In the same way, both actual and future damage can encompass emergent damage and/or loss of profit. Consequently, loss of profit is not to be confounded with

---

Direito das obrigações, vol. I – *Introdução. Da constituição das obrigações*, 340; J. de Figueiredo Dias/J.F. Sinde Monteiro, 'Responsabilidade médica em Portugal', in: 332 *Boletim do Ministério da Justiça* (1984) 21–79 (41); A. Pinto Monteiro, *Cláusulas limitativas e de exclusão da responsabilidade civil* (Coimbra: Livraria Almedina 2011, reprint) 84–89, footnote 164; A. Pinto Monteiro, *Cláusula penal e indemnização* (Coimbra: Livraria Almedina 1990) 31–34, footnote 77; J.F. Sinde Monteiro, 'Rudimentos da responsabilidade civil', 352; N.M. Pinto Oliveira, *Princípios de direito dos contratos*, 636–639.

681. *See, for example*, M.M. Veloso Gomes, 'Danos não patrimoniais', in: *Comemorações dos 35 anos do Código Civil e dos 25 anos da Reforma de 1977*, vol. III – *Direito das obrigações* (Coimbra: Coimbra Editora 2007) 495–559, especially at 501–508.

682. *See* A. Pinto Monteiro, *Cláusulas limitativas e de exclusão da responsabilidade civil* 84–89, footnote 164; A. Pinto Monteiro, *Cláusula penal e indemnização*, 31–34, footnote 77; N.M. Pinto Oliveira, *Princípios de direito dos contratos*, 639.

683. *See*, in regard to the requirement of unlawfulness – liability for one's own acts.

future damage. Emergent damage is understood as the changing of a current advantageous situation and loss of profit as the benefits that would be earned were it not the harm caused. Future damage, on the other hand, is the development and evolution of the actual damage. For that reason, Article 563(2) *in fine* states that they will only be assessed and measured if they are predictable. If not, the law allows the Court to decide on that specific matter when it becomes possible.

There are, although, a few exceptions provided by law where loss of profit will not be compensated, mainly in contract law. Article 899, regarding sales contracts, states that 'the seller must compensate the buyer with bona fides, even if any wilful misconduct or fault underlie his/her actions; but, if that is the case, the compensation entangles only emergent damage that are not expenditure on luxuries'. A similar solution is enshrined in Article 909, pertaining to simple error.

§6. Other Costs (Costs of Assessing Damage and Liability; Costs in Obtaining Judicial or Extra Judicial Payment)

118. All the legal costs of the Portuguese judicial system are set on Rules on Procedural Costs, approved by the Decree-Law No. 34/2008, 26 February 2008. The Code of Civil Procedure (CPC) regulates all the costs that a civil liability action can enmesh, from the triggering of the judicial system (justice fee) to the expenses with the process incurred by the parties. Article 446(1) of the Civil Procedure Code states that 'The decision in which any main actions, incidents or appeals are judged must condemn the party who motivated the action's costs, or, in the case of neither parties winning the action, the person who benefited from the proceedings.' And (2) clarifies that 'Motivating the action's cost is understood as being the defeated party, which can be defined also in a certain proportion.' Adding (3) that 'If the sentencing is in favour of joint liability, the solidarity is extended to the costs.'

Article 447(2), (3) and (4) make clear the meaning of each of those items. The justice fee is, as said, the cost of triggering the system and relies on the complexity of each case and the value of the claim. By process' expenses, it is to be understood as all the costs of conducting proceedings (e.g., asking for expertise examinations), be it by party's request or judge's order. Each party pays for the respective asked proceedings, in line with 447C, except if they are ordered by the Court, in which case, they are to be paid by the benefited party. Finally, expenses incurred by the parties are spending related to the judicial process which, otherwise, the party would not have been subjected to.

An exceptional sanctioning fee can be imposed if, in keeping with Article 447B, the Court finds the claim to be overtly unfounded and resulting from a lack of caution and diligence.

Some people are exempt from paying procedural costs, as established in Article 4 of the Rules on Procedural Costs, such as Public Prosecutors when they carry out their duties; any person if it is a Popular Action; judges and their representatives in legal actions related to their positions; minors when in the trial for the application of tutelary measures, among several others.

The credit for costs is, according to Article 37 of the Rules on Procedural Costs, time-barred after five years.

§7. Mitigation of Damages

119. As we have seen with respect to the victim's exclusive or contributory fault, Article 570 alludes not only to the emergence of the damage but also to its aggravation by the victim's behaviour, which could change the duty to compensate.

The Portuguese legislator introduced in 1967 the limitation of compensation in cases of mere fault (Article 494): 'Where liability is based on mere fault, compensation may be fixed equitably to an amount *lower* than that corresponding to the damage caused, provided that the degree of fault of the wrongdoer, the financial situation of the wrongdoer and of the injured party as well as the other circumstances of the case so justify.' A similar rule is to be found, among other legal systems, in Swiss law or in the very recent Article 944 of the Brazilian Civil Code (which entered into force in 2003).[684] In the case of negligence, the court might decide the defendant is not liable for full compensation. The degree of fault, the economic situation of both the defendant and the victim and other circumstances of the case are the criteria the court shall take into consideration. Pointed out as a 'spectacular turning point' in the Portuguese Civil Code, the idea to shape compensation according to the degree of fault in case of non-intentional fault was warmly welcomed by private lawyers. Before the Code, supplementary statutes imposed that solution, but it was not a general rule. Still, the provision should not be seen as an automatic right of the defendant. Full compensation is the scope of liability, according to Article 562 CC. Deviations from that basic rule in the law of damages must be applied with a reserve and must be justified. The prevailing opinion in Portugal undermined the field of application of the moderation 'clause', discarding the same solution in contractual liability[685] and in cases of strict liability.[686]

---

684. *See* A. Pereira, 'Brazil', H. Koziol/B.C. Steininger (*supra* n. 24), 458. André Tunc, *La Responsabilité Civile* (1981), 73: 'la diminution des dommages-intérêts quand la partie responsible est un individu et non une organisation est tout-à-fait courante dans nombreux pays socialistes, y compris la Chine, ainsi qu'au Portugal. Elle est couramment acceptée pour les dommages causes par un malade mental, et elle est maintenant prise sérieusement en consideration ou meme partiellement introduite en Allemagne, aux Pays-Bas et en Scandinavie.' In fact the new Dutch Civil Code (BW – *Burgerlijk Wetboek*) introduced in Art. 6:109 such a provision (*see* Ewoud Hondius/Cees van Dam, Niederlande, in: Christian von Bar, *Deliktsrecht in Europa* (1994) 20).

685. *See* Pinto Monteiro (*supra* n. 125), 95, fn. 182. *See also* STJ [2003] CJ-STJ, 17 Jun. 2003: the Court did not apply Art. 494 CPC, not because there was contractual liability, but because the agent had acted with gross negligence.

686. Accepting it instead Antunes Varela, Rasgos inovadores do código civil português de 1966, [1972] BFD, 100–104. *See*: Sinde Monteiro/M. Veloso (*supra* n. 372).

Chapter 3. Assessment and Compensation of Damages

120. Article 562 of the Portuguese Civil Code states the general principle on the content and the effects of the duty to compensate:

> The person who is bound to make compensation must restore the situation which would exist if the circumstance making him liable to compensate had not occurred.

It follows from the general principle in Article 562 that full compensation is the scope of liability. Furthermore, it follows from the general principle in Article 562: (i) that compensation shall comprehend pecuniary and non-pecuniary losses;[687] (ii) that compensation for non-pecuniary loss shall comprehend lost profits;[688] and (iii) that compensation for non-pecuniary loss shall comprehend the present and future damage.[689]

Article 564(1) refers to lost profits: 'The duty to compensate includes not only the loss that was caused but also the benefits/the profits the victim did not obtain because of the injury.' The term 'the loss that was caused' refers to *damnum emergens* and the term 'the benefits/the profits the victim did not obtain because of the injury' refers to lost profits (to the so-called *lucrum cessans*). Article 584(2) refers to future damage: 'In calculating indemnity, court may look to the coming damage as long as it is predictable; if it is not determinable, calculation of the corresponding indemnity shall be made later.'[690]

In what concerns compensation for pecuniary loss, Articles 562 and 566(1) establish the principle that compensation in kind (*in natura*) is to be preferred to monetary compensation. As a rule, the duty to compensate generally obliges the defendant to restore the actual situation which would exist if no damage had occurred – as an exception, applying only in cases foreseen by Article 566, it obliges the defendant to restore the economic situation that would exist, by paying a sum of money to the plaintiff.

Article 566(1) establishes that monetary compensation should only be awarded in three circumstances: if compensation in kind is impossible; if compensation in kind is insufficient, as it does not completely eliminate the damage; if compensation in kind is excessively burdensome. In spite of the legal, theoretical priority of compensation in kind (*in natura*), it is submitted that monetary compensation is the practical rule.

It is to be assessed *in concreto* by taking into account the value the damaged goods have for the plaintiff (for the victim), and it is to be assessed following the *difference theory*:

687. *See* Portuguese Civil Code, Art. 496(1).
688. *See* Portuguese Civil Code, Art. 564(1).
689. *See* Portuguese Civil Code, Art. 564(2).
690. For a different translation, *see* Ch. von Bar/U. Drobnig (eds), *The Interaction of Contract Law and Tort and Property Law in Europe. A Comparative Study,* 72: 'the courts while determining the damage can consider future damage, as far as it is foreseeable; if it is not foreseeable, the determination of the corresponding damages is reserved for a later decision'.

> Whenever damages [for pecuniary loss] are to be awarded in money, they shall correspond to the difference between the actual situation of the defendant's assets, at the most recent date that could be taken into account by the court, and the hypothetical situation of the defendant's assets in the absence of damaging event.[691,692]

In spite of the fact that the principles and rules in Articles 562 and 566(1) and (2) of the Portuguese Civil Code seem to exclude any discretionary power of the judge, Portuguese civil law allows two types of limitations on duty to compensate.

On the one hand, Articles 570 to 572 contain a particular, specific clause on the reduction of compensation. It allows for a discretionary reduction of the amount of damages in cases of contributory negligence. On the other hand, Article 494 contains a general clause on the reduction of compensation for negligence-based liability.

In accordance with Article 570, whenever the injured party contributes to the existence or extension of damage, the judge has the discretionary power to determine, on the basis of the degree of fault of both parties and the consequences resulting from it, whether the compensation should be awarded in its entirety, reduced, or excluded.[693]

Article 572 clarifies that contributory negligence shall be taken into account ex officio.

In keeping with Article 494, 'where liability is based on mere fault',[694] the judge has the discretionary power to fix compensation 'at an amount lower than that corresponding to the damage caused'. In doing so, he is to consider the degree of fault, the economic situation of both the defendant and the plaintiff, as well as the circumstances of the case.

Even if there is no such a thing as a right of the defendant, let alone an *automatic right* of the defendant, to have a reduction made in the compensation, Article 494 softens the black letter rules in Articles 562 to 572. It allows the judge to deviate from the principle of full compensation, whenever full compensation would be manifestly unjust.

It has been pointed out that the idea to shape compensation according to the degree of fault was a 'spectacular turning point' in the Portuguese Civil Code and, indeed, in comparative terms, the existence of a general clause, allowing the judge

---

691. *See* Portuguese Civil Code, Art. 566(2).
692. For a thorough critique of the so-called *difference theory, see* P. Mota Pinto, *Interesse contratual negativo e interesse contratual positivo*, vol. I (Coimbra: Coimbra Editora 2008), especially at 552 ff.
693. Article 571 of the Portuguese Civil Code equates contributory negligence of the injured party to contributory negligence of his auxiliaries, employees and legal representatives.
694. As Professors von Bar and Drobnig point out, '[t]he possibility of reducing the amount of compensation is limited to cases of negligence. If the defendant has acted deliberately, a reduction of the compensation is generally excluded, if further circumstances of a particular case are not involved' [*see* Ch. von Bar/U. Drobnig (eds), *The Interaction of Contract Law and Tort and Property Law in Europe. A Comparative Study,* 153].

to fix compensation taking into account the circumstances of the case, is an exception. There are, however, similar rules in the Swiss Code of Obligations[695] and in the Dutch Civil Code,[696] as well as in the new Brazilian Civil Code (which entered into force in 2003).[697]

In what concerns compensation for non-pecuniary loss, the judge is to refer to Article 496(1) and (3), as well as to Article 494 of the Portuguese Civil Code.

Article 496(1) requires the judge to fix compensation according to equity, and Article 496(3) requires the judge to consider the factors enumerated in Article 494.

Furthermore, the rules in Articles 494 and 496 are to be read in connection with the general principles on interpretation and application of statutes in Articles 8 to 10.

Article 8(3) reads that the judge is to consider all cases deserving a similar treatment for the purpose of uniformly applying and interpreting the law.[698] It follows from Article 8(3), as well as from Article 13 of the Portuguese Constitution that 'in assessing damages (..) similar sums should be awarded for objectively similar losses'. It is submitted that case law conforms to the principles in the Constitution and the Civil Code. Courts fix the amount of damages for the non-pecuniary loss by referring to previous judgments.

§1. Objective Versus Subjective

121. With regard to pecuniary damage, authors normally make a doctrinal distinction between the damage *in natura*, named real damage, and its monetary representation, called calculation damage. Still, they do not intend to be opposites but complementary to each other.

With regard to the calculation determination, both an objective and a subjective angle are possible. The first one measures the damage by the immediate loss caused by the tortfeasor's action (e.g., the sole cost of the damaged property, the cost of the hospital bill), whereas the second considers the patrimonial impact on the injured person, notably the impacted interest or set of interests.

Article 556(2) states the need to compare the injured person's patrimonial situation at the most recent date before the damage, with the situation that would exist if there had been no damage – and, therefore, consecrates a plea to the calculation damage perspective and a subjective criterion.

The damage is not regarded as the mere loss of the market value of the damaged goods or immediate expenses but rather for damaged asset's worth for its owner,

695. *See* Swiss Code of Obligations, Arts 43 and 44.
696. *See* Dutch Civil Code, Art. 6:109 [on the Dutch provision, *see* E. Hondius/C. van Dam, 'Niederlande', in: Ch. Von Bar (ed.), *Deliktsrecht in Europa* (Köln: Carl Heymans Verlag 1994) 20].
697. *See* Brazilian Civil Code, Art. 944.
698. On the importance of Art. 8(3) of the Portuguese Civil Code for the law of torts, *see* J.M. Pires da Rosa, 'Cálculo da indemnização pelos danos não patrimoniais', and João Luís Marques Bernardo, 'A indemnização pela perda do direito à vida', both in: Centro de Estudos Judiciários, *O dano na responsabilidade civil* (Lisboa: Centro de Estudos Judiciários 2014), 45–62 and 73–84 (available at: http://www.cej.mj.pt/cej/recursos/ebooks/civil/O_Dano_Responsabilidade_Civil.pdf).

highlighting its role within the whole estate and relying on the interest of the injured person (e.g., the destruction of a car can have significantly different impacts on different people).

In keeping with Article 564, as seen, only with a viewpoint like this could grant full compensation, with the consideration of loss profit and *compensatio lucri cum damno*. Also, in contrast, an objective assessment allows merely to determine the *status quo ante*, not the hypothetical situation of the wronged party.

It should not be mistaken for a measurement of affection. A subjective criterion, as described, is not speculative but economic, since the main goals of compensation are the damage's reparation and the recreation of the hypothetical situation.

Although the law references the patrimonial situation of the injured party, that does not amount to an endorsement over an objective assessment. The grasp over the concept of the estate does not necessarily point to a predetermined pecuniary value, but rather a 'range of rights with pecuniary value that belong to one person or several people'.

With regard to non-pecuniary damage, by nature, the assessment cannot be labelled as either objective or subjective in link with the attributed significance since the involved interests are immeasurable.

§2. Concrete Versus Abstract

122. In line with the previous observations, the assessment of damage envisioned as subjective is also classified as concrete rather than abstract. Calvão da Silva, Pereira Coelho and Almeida Costa use the terms concrete/subjective and abstract/objective interchangeably. Antunes Varela favours the dichotomy of concrete/abstract while referencing the same thing.[699]

§3. Methods of Assessing Damages

123. As described above, if possible, reparation in kind should be made by giving the injured party something identical, in quantity and quality, to the damaged good. However, if that is not the case, an equivalent pecuniary compensation is due, and the law enshrines pathways to attain the compensation's amount.

Article 566(2) lays, 'Unless otherwise provided, compensation in money is measured by the difference between the patrimonial situation of the injured person at the most recent date that can be assessed by the court and the situation that would exist if there had been no damage.' It enshrines as a method of assessing pecuniary damages the so-called *difference theory*. As for the moment when these two patrimonial situations should be considered, Pereira Coelho lays out four possibilities:

1. First, it could be deemed relevant to contrast the injured party's patrimonial situation at the time of the assessment with the one before the wrongful action occurred.

699. *See*, J.M. Antunes Varela, *Das Obrigações em Geral*, 907.

2. A second option would be to take into consideration the patrimonial situation right before the wrongful action and the one immediately after it.
3. Third, to consider the situation of the injured party's estate promptly before the action and compare it to the one that hypothetically would exist at the assessment moment if any damage was caused.
4. Lastly, to weigh the patrimonial situation at the present moment (while assessing damages) and the one that would exist at the same time but assuming the wrongful action had never occurred.

The author sustains that Article 566(2) anchors the fourth option since it is the only one which balances two present patrimonial situations – one real and one hypothetical. The first option would represent an attempt to remake the *status quo ante*, which consequently does not leave room for loss of profits. The second ignores, in addition to loss of profits, all the original damage's repercussions that we accept as a normal outcome of the adequacy theory of causality. The third one completely disregards the damage in itself. Only by bearing in mind the present hypothetical situation can, in link with the fourth option, the difference made by the wrongful action be fully compensated.[700]

Article 564(1) imposes the consideration of not only emergent damage but also loss of profit, and 564(2) adds the regard of predicable future damage. Present and future damage which cannot be determined at the moment of sentencing, are to be judged later on, albeit a guilty verdict at the moment.

Article 569 exempts the injured party from claiming an exact value of damages and allows those who did to claim modification during the course of legal proceedings, if more or higher damages are uncovered.

Article 566(3) foresees the incapability to assess, under the general rules, pecuniary damages, stating that, in those cases, 'the Court will judge equitably within the limits that are already proven'. However, it does not exempt the injured party from proving the damages.[701]

The general rules of assessing damages can be surpassed if the parties prearranged the compensation amount with a penalty clause, as permitted by Article 810 of the Civil Code, or if another method or fixed value is imposed by law, as in Article 442(2) and (3), concerning to promissory agreements. They can also be limited by law, as seen with respect to risk liability in Articles 508 and 510,[702] the interference of the victim's fault,[703] or, according to the circumstances of the case, amended interference of other elements such as compensation's limitation by Article 494.[704] With respect to people deemed not to bear any liability, a principle of equity can justify imposing on them a duty to compensate, regardless of their condition, if any liable caregiver can be found, as stated by Article 489(1). Nevertheless, the compensation amount cannot deprive the injurer of the right to maintenance for

700. *See*, F.M. Pereira Coelho, *O problema da causa virtual na responsabilidade civil*, Almedina, 196–198.
701. *See* F.A. Pires de Lima/J.M. Antunes Varela (/ M.H. Mesquita), *Código Civil anotado*, vol. I, 2.ª ed., 508.
702. *See*, road and traffic accidents.
703. *See*, victim's exclusive or contributory fault.
704. *See*, Equitable limitation of damages.

him/herself or to comply with the right to maintenance of others. That can, naturally, lead to an assessed amount of compensation shorter than the caused damages.

Lastly, if any enrichment arises from the wrongful act, it must be deducted from the compensation amount – *compensatio lucri cum damno* – as a natural consequence of the assessment method established in Article 566.[705]

With regard to non-pecuniary damage, Article 496(4), as seen, establishes an equitable method complemented by Article 494's criterions: the level of culpability of the wrongdoer, the economic situation of both parties and other circumstances of the case.[706]

Recently, a demand for a more objective assessment has been defended in cases where many injuries and damages arise.

The more prominent example is Law No. 108/2017 and Resolution of the Council of Ministers No. 4/2018 of 4 January. Following the tragic fires of June and October 2017, last year, we reported the Council of Ministers Resolutions 157-/2017 and 179/2017 for lethal victims and severely injured persons. The ombudswoman decided compensation for ca. 300 cases and awarded in total EUR 31 million for the relatives of deceased persons. The ombudswoman decided to set at EUR 80,000 the damage for loss of life (death damage) and to set the basic value of the damage for suffering before death to EUR 70,000. This value was increased according to the relatives who shared the circumstances that dictated the death and the time of agony of the victim. The basic amount of non-equity damages, intended to compensate the family for the pain of loss, was set as follows: EUR 40,000 in the case of spouse/de facto parents and children. This value was increased when the family member accompanied the victim at the time of the injury event, and a second increase was applied in the case of a minor child whose parents were both killed in the fire or a mother/father who lost a minor child. In the absence of the above, the base value was set at EUR 20,000 for grandparents or siblings who cohabited with the victim and (if they did not) EUR 10,000 for siblings or nephews. In both cases, the increase occurred when the applicant was with the victim at the time of the event, which was higher if it was a minor. As regards pecuniary damage, the terms indicated by the Council were followed. Non-patrimonial damages and, where appropriate, patrimonial damages were paid individually to each applicant.

Concerning *severely injured persons*, a special commission was created and is working at the Coimbra Court of Appeal, working closely with the National Institute of Forensic Medicine and Forensic Sciences, which elaborates the forensic reports on the evaluation of bodily damage. In 2018, this Commission for Evaluation of Compensation Claims evaluated hundreds of claims.

In Portugal, there is no table of compensation established in the legislation applicable to all personal injuries. For efficiency purposes, Law No. 108/2017 states that the permanent functional deficit of physical and physical integrity should be compensated by the table in Annex IV of Ordinance No. 679/2009 of 25 June (motor traffic accidents) with an update of 20%. These are the values for each degree of personal damage:

---

705. A. Menezes Cordeiro, *Tratado de Direito Civil Português,*V. II, T. III, Almedina, 2010, 730.
706. *See*, Non-Pecuniary Damages.

Quantum doloris: Degree 1: EUR 250; Degree 2: EUR 500; Degree 3: EUR 1,000; Degree 4: EUR 500; Degree 5: EUR 5,000; Degree 6: EUR 7,500; Degree 7: EUR 10,000.

Aesthetic damage: Degree 1: 1,000; Degree 2: EUR 2,000; Degree 3: EUR 3,500; Degree 4: EUR 5,500; Degree 5: EUR 8,000; Degree 6: EUR 11,000; Degree 7: EUR 15,000.

Damage of personal fulfilment: Degree 1: EUR 1,000; Degree 2: EUR 2,000; Degree 3: EUR 3,500; Degree 4: EUR 5,500; Degree 5: EUR 8,000; Degree 6: EUR 11,000; Degree 7: EUR 15,000.

Sexual damage: Degree 1: EUR 300; Degree 2: EUR 600; Degree 3: EUR 1,250; Degree 4: EUR 3,125; Degree 5: EUR 6,250; Degree 6: EUR 9,375; Degree 7: EUR 12,500.

§4. Equitable Limitation of Damages

124. As a deviation from the general rules of compensation assessment, Article 496 allows for the equitable limitation of some damages, stating that:

> Where liability is based on mere fault, compensation may be fixed equitably at an amount lower than that corresponding to the damage caused, provided that the degree of fault of the wrongdoer, the financial situation of the wrongdoer and of the injured party, as well as the other circumstances of the case so justify.

The resort to an equity judgment is not the first step, since, as the law clearly says, this norm allows for the limitation of a previously determined amount. On the contrary, when Article 496 refers to Article 494's criteria, the implicated equitable judgment is, in its nature, a primary method of assessing non-pecuniary damages.

An equitable judgment differs from the assessment based on the difference theory because it appeals to the so-called justice for a specific case – an evaluation *ex aequo et bono* – straying from established legal standards but still in keeping with legal principles and within the legal system as a whole. In line with that, Article 4 of the Civil Code enshrines that:

> The Courts can only judge by equity:
> a) When a specific law so indicates;
> b) When all the parties agree, and the legal matter is not unavailable to negotiation;
> c) When the parties have previously stipulated the resort to equity in an arbitration clause.

As legally established, this equitable limitation is not an option when wilful misconduct underlies the action, only when there is a mere fault, i.e., negligence. If there is negligence, likewise, the Court is not bound to invoke this norm; it is a choice as displayed by the formulation 'compensation may be fixed equitably'.

According to Article 494, if the Court opts for the limitation, it must consider the degree of fault of the wrongdoer, the financial situation of the wrongdoer and of the injured party, and other circumstances of the case so justify. Lately, the consideration of the injured party's financial situation has been questioned by the Courts, who argue it is unconstitutional for violating the principle of equality (enshrined in Article 13 of the Constitutional).[707] With regard to the consideration of other circumstances of the case, Maria Manuel indicates the importance of taking into consideration the 'intensity and nature of the harm and the value of the undermined legal interest', as well as the victim's age, the existence of contributory fault and, among others, the forecast for the damage's progression.[708]

§5. Methods of Payment

I. Lump Sum

125. Once the damage's amount is assessed, the liable person has the duty to pay its sum, which is classified as an obligation of instantaneous performance,[709] i.e., lump sum.

II. Annuities

126. Notwithstanding, Article 567 allows for it to be received as annuities, i.e., of income, stating in: (1) that 'Given the continuous nature of the damage, the Court can, if solicited by the wronged party, attribute the compensation, as a whole or in part, in the form of lifelong or transitory annuities, making the necessary arrangements to ensure its payment.' If any circumstances are to change, (2) foresees the possibility of asking the Court for the modification of the annuity's terms.

This is especially helpful when the damage impacts the injured party's ability to work or increases daily needs and expenses.[710] The Court cannot impose a duty to compensate in these terms by its own recreation since it must stem from the aggrieved person's will and petition[711] – a legislative option questioned by some authors, such as Sinde Monteiro.[712]

707. Decisions from the Portuguese Supreme Court such as the ones from 11 Jan. 2007, 7 Feb. 2008 and 24 Apr. 2013. *See*, F. Albuquerque Matos, Reparação por danos não patrimoniais: inconstitucionalidade da relevância da situação económica do lesado (artigos 496 (3) e 494 do Código Civil), RLJ, A. 143, 3984, 2014, 203–207.

708. M.M. Veloso, *Danos não patrimoniais*, in: *Comemorações dos 35 anos do Código Civil e dos 25 anos da Reforma de 1977*, vol. III – *Direito das obrigações* (Coimbra: Coimbra Editora 2007) 542–543.

709. J.M. Antunes Varela, *Das Obrigações em Geral*, 941 and M.J. Almeida Costa, *Direito das Obrigações*, Almedina, 2013, 776.

710. M.J. Almeida Costa, *Direito das Obrigações*, Almedina, 2013, 776.

711. F.A. Pires de Lima/J.M. Antunes Varela (/ M.H. Mesquita), *Código Civil anotado*, vol. I, 2.ª ed., 509.

712. J. Sinde Monteiro, *Rudimentos da Responsabilidade Civil*, RFDUP, A. II, 2005, 379.

III. Others

A. Restitution In Kind

127. As a general principle, the legislator prefers restitution in kind since pecuniary compensation is presented in Article 566(1) as a mere substitute. That is in direct link with the principle of reconstituting the hypothetical situation, consecrated in Article 562, which serves as an orienting goal for civil liability. Through restitution in kind, the relevant damage perspective is the so-called real damage rather than the calculation of damage pertinent to pecuniary compensation.[713] It can be made, e.g., by giving the injured party something equal, in quantity and quality, to the damaged good or by repairing the caused harm.[714]

B. Provisional Compensation

128. Article 565 prescribes a solution for the reported circumstances in which, despite the wrongdoer being already sentenced, the present damage is still not fully determined. The Court can, under this norm, impose on the liable party a provisional duty to compensate based on the facts already proven. Antunes Varela argues that it is not a mechanism to be used with future damages,[715] but other authors, such as Almeida Costa, disagree.[716]

713. *See*, M.J. Almeida Costa, *Direito das Obrigações*, Almedina, 2013, 771.
714. J.M. Antunes Varela, *Das Obrigações em Geral*, 904.
715. F.A. Pires de Lima/J.M. Antunes Varela (/ M.H. Mesquita), *Código Civil anotado*, vol. I, 2.ª ed., 505.
716. *See*, M.J. Almeida Costa, *Direito das Obrigações*, Almedina, 2013, 773.

Chapter 4. Personal Injury and Death

129. When personal injury or death occurs, the protected rights are covered under the general principle of Article 483. The right to life and the right to bodily integrity are the most protected interests under the law and harming them can originate pecuniary and non-pecuniary damages.

§1. Pecuniary Losses

130. As in every other harmed interest, Articles 483 and 562 provide the basis for full compensation, including actual and future damage, be it emergent or loss of profit.

As we saw with respect to indirect damage, the Portuguese Civil Code has a special provision for compensating third parties when personal injury or death occurs.

The first part of Article 495(1) gives ground for compensating the economic loss of those who intervene to help the injured person who ultimately dies – 'the person responsible shall be obliged to pay compensation for the costs incurred in seeking to save the injured party' –and the second part empathizes the need to full compensation of the injured party and its relative, covering 'all other expenses, not excluding funeral expenses'. When the injury does not result in death, still, Article 495(2) grants compensation to those who render assistance, as well as 'hospitals, doctors or other persons or entities who may have contributed to the treatment or assistance of the victim'. Also, as seen, Article 495(3) gives the right to compensation not only for those who are legally entitled to require maintenance from the injured party but also for those who received it as a fulfilment of a natural obligation.

With regard to the injured party, and in keeping with the full compensation principle, all proven damages are to be compensated, including emergent damages and loss of profit, present and future damages. If necessary, Article 567 gives ground for compensation in the form of annuities, either lifelong or provisional, if the registered damages have an ongoing nature.[717]

With respect to road accidents, Decree-Law No. 291/2007, 21 August 2007, partially transposed the EU Directive 2005/14/EC of the European Parliament and the Council, relating to insurance against civil liability in respect of the use of motor vehicles. In its Article 38, the Decree-Law imposes on insurance companies the duty to make a reasonable proposal to the insured, which relies on the suggestion tables approved in Ordinance No. 377/2008, 26 May 2008 and updated by Ordinance No. 679/2009, 25 June 2009. The Ordinance has five annexes, each concerning a different type of compensation and with different calculation methods. Annex I relates to non-pecuniary damages; II to the successor's compensations for non-pecuniary damages in the case of death; III to future damage; IV to compensation due to bodily and psychological damage; and, lastly, V concerns reasonable proposals for

717. A. Prata (Coord.), *Código Civil Anotado*, V. I, Almedina, 2017, p. 729.

compensating expenses and loss income. Likewise, according to these norms, pecuniary damages are to be fully compensated, since Annex V references emergent damage, loss of profit, as well as future damage.

The usage of these tables with suggestions of compensation values is regarded as useful in mass torts, as well as in creating a starting point for negotiations and making compensations more predictable.[718]

§2. Non-pecuniary Losses

131. Article 496(1) of the Portuguese Civil Code is an apparently simple norm that states:

> For the determination of compensation, regard must be had to non-pecuniary damage which, due to its seriousness, deserves protection of the law.

Therefore, it is up to the courts to decide on what 'deserves the protection of the law'.

It follows from the text in Article 496(1) that it does not exclude, for instance, the possibility of awarding non-pecuniary damage in cases of destruction of a *thing,* such as a family treasure or souvenir. It should be stressed, at any rate, that Portuguese courts have been very conscious and careful in deciding what 'deserves the protection of the law'.

I. Non-pecuniary Losses for Personal Injury in General

132. In order to understand the internal and external structure of the Portuguese Civil Code as to non-pecuniary losses, it is necessary to refer to three particular, specific situation: (i) personal injury, (ii) non-pecuniary loss suffered by persons having a close relationship with the victim of a fatal injury, and (iii) non-pecuniary damage suffered by persons having a close relationship with the victim of a very serious, albeit non-fatal injury.

Article 70 of the Portuguese Civil Code allows the courts to develop a list of personality rights and, consequently, the list of legally relevant losses.

Professor Menezes Cordeiro argues that, whereas 'the 20th Century was the period of the contracts and its refinement, through good faith (Treu und Glauben), the 21st Century can well be the time of the rights of the person … '.[719]

718. *See*, A.G. Dias Pereira, *Direitos dos Pacientes e Responsabilidade Médica,* Coimbra Editora, 2015, 221–223.

719. A. Menezes Cordeiro, 'Os direitos de personalidade na civilística portuguesa', 61 *Revista da Ordem dos Advogados* (2001), 1229–1256, at 1229.

Courts have recognized, for instance, the right to life, the right to a good environment, the right to health, the right to rest and tranquillity; courts have recognized, for instance, the concepts of biological loss[720] and existential loss;[721] furthermore, they have reinforced, for instance, the rights to honour and reputation and the right to privacy.

The approach of the Portuguese Courts as to non-pecuniary loss arising from a personal injury can be illustrated by referring to a few recent examples.

In a judgment of the Portuguese Supreme Court of 21 January 2016, delivered by Justice Lopes do Rego, the plaintiff, a 27-year-old man, suffered *multiple traumas* (including injuries in the pelvis and the thorax, as well as severe traumatic brain injuries), amounting to *psychologically* and *behaviourally* relevant *sequelae*.

The *quantum doloris* was assessed at 5 out of 7, the aesthetic damage was assessed at 2 out of 7, and a permanent functional deficit to his physical and mental integrity was established at 16 points. Furthermore, the victim started suffering from walking claudication and right hip stiffness, limitations which affected his walking, running and all physical activities (including sport and leisure) involving the lower limbs. Finally, the victim started suffering from feelings of sadness, as well as anguish and depression.

Inconveniences and suffering were proven to be irreversible and permanent.

To compensate the non-pecuniary, moral losses of the victim, the first instance fixed the amount of damages at EUR 6,000, the second instance – the Court of Appeal – fixed the amount at EUR 50,000, and the Supreme Court sustained the latter decision.

In a judgment of 17 March 2016, delivered by Justice Belo Morgado, the plaintiff, a 36-year-old woman, suffered a *functional aesthetic injury* consisting of a right foot severe deformity arising from the amputation of the five fingers and the forefoot.

The deformity caused her difficulty in moving and maintaining posture and balance, with consequences at the professional activity and household work levels.

Furthermore, she was left with scars on 18% of her body, a lifelong right foot prosthetic and intense pain in the right foot, the right shoulder, the legs and the back.

Finally, she started experiencing memory alterations, irritation, noise intolerance and lack of joy in living, expressing grief and reluctance to accept what occurred.

To compensate for these damages, the Court of First Instance fixed the amount in EUR 25,000, the Court of Appeal doubled it (EUR 50,000), and the Supreme Court sustained the latter decision. It is worth stressing, the Supreme Court argued, *inter alia*, that 'compensation for moral damage must have a significant reach and not merely a symbolic one'.

In a judgment of 7 April 2016, delivered by Justice Maria da Graça Trigo, the plaintiff, a 22-year-old woman, started suffering from urinary incontinence, with a *quantum doloris* established at 4 on a scale of 7, a permanent functional deficit to

720. *See*, for instance, M. Graça Trigo, 'Adopção do conceito de "dano biológico" pelo direito português', 72 *Revista da Ordem dos Advogados* (2012), 147–178.

721. *See*, for instance, M. Carneiro da Frada, 'Nos 40 anos do Código Civil português: Tutela da personalidade e dano existencial', Themis (2008), 47–68.

her *physical* and *mental* integrity of 8%, aesthetic damage at 3 out of 7 and permanent repercussion in sport and leisure activities at 1 out of 7. In spite of the compatibility of the *sequelae* with the exercise of her usual activity, she was required to apply an additional effort.

Furthermore, the woman started experiencing sadness, anguish, insecurity, nervousness, and sorrow about life – she even started feeling fearful for her life.

To compensate for these losses, the Court of Appeal fixed the amount of EUR 18,000. The Supreme Court overruled that judgment and fixed the amount of damages at EUR 50,000.

In a judgment of 11 May 2022, delivered by Justice Maria Clara Sottomayor, the plaintiff, a 17-year-old-man, who was hospitalized for forty-eight days, underwent four surgeries – three of which in the head area – suffered a *quantum doloris* at 6 out of 7, the aesthetic damage was assessed at 4 out of 7, a permanent repercussion in sports activities at 4 out of 7 and a partial temporary functional deficit of 1984 days.

To compensate for these non-pecuniary damages, the Court of Appeal fixed the amount of EUR 18,500. The Supreme Court overruled the decision and fixed the amount of EUR 60,000.

In a judgment of 21 June 2022, delivered by Justice Isaías Pádua, the plaintiff, a 26-year-old man, suffered several injuries that led to tetraplegia – therefore, he became dependent on assistance from third persons – with a *quantum doloris* established at 7 out of 7 and aesthetics damages at 6 out of 7.

As a result of all the physical suffering, the repercussions and aesthetic damage, the man began to feel fear, sadness, shame, depression and a general loss of expectations for his future life – socially, at work, physically, athletically, sexually and regarding starting a family.

To compensate for all the non-pecuniary damages described, the Court of First Instance fixed the amount of EUR 230,000, the Court of Appeal raised it to EUR 400,000 and, at last, the Supreme Court set the amount of EUR 500,000 as an adequate compensation.

II. Wrongful Birth and Wrongful Life

133. In Portugal, as everywhere else, wrongful birth and wrongful life are heavily discussed. Wrongful birth actions are brought by parents – especially by the mother. Damages for which compensation is sought result from the unwanted birth of a handicapped child. Wrongful life actions are brought by the child (or by the parents, on behalf of their son). Damages for which compensation is sought result from birth itself.[722] While compensation for wrongful birth is widely accepted, compensation for wrongful life is not.

722. *See,* for example, G. de Oliveira, 'O direito do diagnóstico pré-natal', in *Temas de direito da medicina* (Coimbra: Centro de Direito Biomédico/Coimbra Editora 1999) 203–223; F. Araújo, *A procriação assistida e o problema da santidade da vida* (Coimbra: Livraria Almedina 1999) 84–113; A. Pinto Monteiro, 'Direito a não nascer (anotação ao Acórdão do STJ de 19 de Junho de 2001)', (2001) 134 Revista de Legislação e de Jurisprudência 371–384; A.G. Dias Pereira, *Consentimento informado na Relação Médico-Paciente* (Coimbra: Centro de Direito Biomédico) at 375

In order to make things clear, three types of damages should be distinguished. In the first place, the child's mother sustains a pecuniary loss. Second, she sustains non-pecuniary loss resulting from the impairment of her freedom. The child's mother has, or should have, a right to choose between abortion and non-abortion; between killing and letting her unborn, disabled child live. Third, she sustains non-pecuniary loss resulting from the impairment of her integrity. Even if the child's mother decided not to abort, prenatal testing would give her the opportunity to prepare herself for the nervous shock of giving birth to a disabled child.

As to the first and second types of damages, it could make sense for doctors to invoke the exception of an alternative, lawful conduct, arguing that the child's mother would have the child anyway, for that would be the only decision conforming to her ethical, philosophical or religions conviction. As to the third type of damages, it would make no sense at all – the fact that the child's mother would have the child anyway has no relevance at all to the damages resulting from the impairment of her integrity.

The question then relates to pecuniary and non-pecuniary damages resulting from the impairment to the child's mother's right to choose: doctors, in arguing that the child's mother would have the child anyway, invokes the so-called exception of an alternative, lawful conduct (in German, *Rechtmäßiges Alternativverhalten*; in Portuguese, '*comportamento alternativo lícito* or *comportamento hipotético lícito*'). '[T]he issue is whether a perpetrator who has acted wrongfully is liable for the damage caused even if he would have caused the same harm otherwise by lawful conduct.'[723]

In general terms, it is not clear whether arguments relating to an alternative, lawful conduct would be accepted by Portuguese courts.

The Portuguese Civil Code contains no *general rule* on the relevance or irrelevance of the exception of alternative, lawful conduct.

---

ff; A. Menezes Cordeiro, *Tratado de direito civil português, I – Parte geral, III – Pessoas* (Coimbra: Livraria Almedina 2004) 281–289; C.A. da Mota Pinto/A. Pinto Monteiro/P. Mota Pinto, *Teoria geral do direito civil* 4th edition (Coimbra: Coimbra Editora 2005) 217–220; F. Pinto Monteiro, 'Direito à não-existência, direito a não nascer', in: *Comemorações dos 35 anos do Código Civil e dos 25 anos da reforma de 1977*, II – A Parte Geral do Código e a teoria geral do direito civil (Coimbra: Faculdade de Direito da Universidade de Coimbra/Coimbra Editora 2006); M. Carneiro da Frada, 'A protecção juscivil da vida pré-natal. Sobre o estatuto jurídico do embrião' 2008 Direito e justiça 134–155; M. Carneiro da Frada, 'A própria vida como dano? – Dimensões civis e constitucionais de uma questão-limite', D. Leite de Campos/S. de Abreu Chinelatto (eds), *Pessoa humana e direito* (Coimbra: Livraria Almedina 2009) 259–294; P. Mota Pinto, 'Indemnização em caso de "nascimento indevido" e de "vida indevida" ("wrongful birth" e "wrongful life")', *Nos 20 anos do Código das Sociedades Comerciais – Homenagem aos Profs. Doutores A. Ferrer Correia, Orlando de Carvalho e Vasco Lobo Xavier*, vol. III – Vária, (Coimbra: Coimbra Editora 2007) 915–946; M. Nunes Vicente, 'Algumas reflexões sobre as acções de wrongful life: a jurisprudência Perruche' (1009) 4 Lex Medicinae 117–141; V. Lúcia Raposo, 'As wrong actions no início da vida (wrongful conception, wrongful birth e wrongful life) e a responsabilidade médica' (2010) Revista portuguesa do dano corporal 61–99 (61–64); L. Menezes Leitão, 'O dano da vida' (2012) Cadernos de direito privado, special edition – II Seminário dos Cadernos de Direito Privado. Responsabilidade civil 3–16; A.G. Dias Pereira, *Direitos dos pacientes e responsabilidade médica* (Coimbra: Centro de Direito Biomédico/Coimbra Editora 2015) at 250 ff.

723. *See* H. Koziol, *Basic Questions of Tort Law from a Germanic Perspective*, 279.

Articles 491, 492, and 493(1) of the Portuguese Civil Code allow the defendant to escape liability by arguing that the damage would have occurred even if the defendant's conduct conformed to his duties. In spite of the fact, Articles 491, 492 and 493(1) of the Portuguese Civil Code could well be construed as referring to all hypothetical causal procedures; thus, including alternative, lawful conduct,[724] they tend to be interpreted as referring to hypothetical, virtual causation, and to hypothetical, virtual causation only.[725]

Furthermore, Articles 491, 492(1) and (2) and 493(1) of the Portuguese Civil Code apply to rather specific situations. It has been argued that the rules laid down in Articles 491, 492 and 493(1) are exceptional, thus allowing for an *a contrario* argument. If they are exceptional, it is submitted that the general rule should be the opposite.[726]

In the absence of clear statutory rules, case law and scholarly writings could be determinant. The problem is that case law is unclear, for the Portuguese Supreme Court has never applied the exception of alternative, lawful conduct in civil matters, and scholarly writings are far from any consensus.

In older writings, the exception of alternative conduct seems to be interpreted as a special case of hypothetical causation. It follows from the consensus as to the irrelevance of hypothetical, potential causation that the exception of alternative, lawful conduct was likely to be deemed irrelevant. In newer writings,[727] however, the exception of alternative, lawful conduct seems to be interpreted as a distinct, autonomous defence.

As a general rule, alternative, lawful conduct exempts the tortfeasor from liability. Whenever the tortfeasor proves that alternative, lawful conduct would have caused the very same losses to the very same victims, he or she shall not be held liable.

The problem lies in the fact that the scope of such a general, negative rule is to be determined by the scope of the duties that the tortfeasor infringed.[728]

It follows that the defence of alternative, lawful conduct does not apply, for example, where the scope of the duties the tortfeasor infringed was one of guaranteeing the victim space for a free, personal decision.[729] That is to say that the defence of alternative, lawful conduct does not apply, for instance, to cases of wrongful life.

---

724. *See* N.M. Pinto Oliveira, *Princípios de direito dos contratos* (Coimbra: Coimbra Editora 2011) 710–711.
725. *See, for example*, F.M. Pereira Coelho, *Obrigações. Sumários das lições ao curso de 1966/1967* (Coimbra 1967) 184–185; F.M. Pereira Coelho, *O problema da causa virtual na responsabilidade civil*, 2nd edition (Coimbra: Livraria Almedina 1998) 6–13; J.M. Antunes Varela, *Das obrigações em geral I*, at 931–933; M.J. de Almeida Costa, *Direito das obrigações*, at 767–770.
726. F.M. Pereira Coelho, *O problema da causa virtual na responsabilidade civil*, at 7–8; J.M. Antunes Varela, Das obrigações em geral I, at 931–933; M.J. de Almeida Costa, *Direito das obrigações*, at 767–770.
727. *See, for example*, J.F. Sinde Monteiro, *Responsabilidade por conselhos, recomendações ou informações* (Coimbra: Livraria Almedina 1990) 286–291; P. Mota Pinto, *Interesse contratual positivo e interesse contratual negativo II* (Coimbra: Coimbra Editora 2008) 1029–52; N.M. Pinto Oliveira, *Princípios de direito dos contratos*, at 711–716.
728. *See* N.M. Pinto Oliveira, *Princípios de direito dos contratos*, at 716.
729. J.F. Sinde Monteiro, *Responsabilidade por conselhos, recomendações ou informações*, at 289.

In fact, it is submitted that the doctor's duties to disclose and inform aim at guaranteeing the child's mother the right to decide whether to abort or not to abort. The defence of alternative, lawful conduct would not exclude the defendant's liability.

In spite of the fact that the defence would not exclude the doctor's liability for wrongful life, it could have an effect as to the amount of damages. In the case that the doctor was unable to prove that the child's mother would have the child anyway,[730] he or she would be held liable for *all expenses* resulting from the child's birth and upbringing. In the event that the doctor is able to prove so, however, he or she would only be held liable for the additional expenses resulting from the upbringing of a *disabled, handicapped child.*[731]

III. Compensation to Third Parties in Case of Death or Bodily Injury

134. Article 495 of the Portuguese Civil Code reads as follows:

1 – When an injury leads to death, the person responsible shall be obliged to pay compensation for the costs incurred in seeking to save the injured party, and all other expenses, not excluding funeral expenses.

2 – In any such case, and in all other instances of bodily injury, those who render assistance to the injured party [have a right to compensation] as well as hospitals, doctors or other persons or entities who may have contributed to the treatment or assistance of the victim.

3 – The right to compensation shall also be available to those entitled to require maintenance (alimony) from the injured party and to those to whom the injured party paid maintenance in fulfilment of a natural obligation.

4 – In what concerns non-pecuniary loss suffered by persons having a close relationship with the victim Article 495 is to be coordinated with Article 496 (2) to (4).

IV. Non-pecuniary Loss Suffered by Persons Having a Close Relationship with the Victim of a Fatal Injury

135. Until 2010, this topic was debated. The problem was in determining whether Article 496(2) of the Portuguese Civil Code, in referring to 'a spouse who is not legally separated from the persons and assets', was to apply to non-married partners living in a de facto union.[732]

---

730. In keeping with German case law, Portuguese scholarly writings refer to the presumption that the pregnant woman would have adopted an appropriate decision, taking into account all relevant information – *see, for example,* P. Mota Pinto, 'Indemnização em caso de "nascimento indevido" e de "vida indevida" ("wrongful birth" e "wrongful life")', at 931 (fn. 47).

731. *See* P. Mota Pinto, 'Indemnização em caso de 'nascimento indevido' e de 'vida indevida' ('wrongful birth' e 'wrongful life')', at 940.

732. Article 496 of the Portuguese Civil Code read as follows, until its amendment in 2010: '(2) When a victim dies, the right to compensation for non-pecuniary damage shall be available, jointly, to a

The Constitutional Court Judgment No. 275/2002 ruled that Article 496(2) and (3) of the Portuguese Civil Code was unconstitutional, for it infringed Article 36(1) of the Portuguese Constitution.[733]

The Constitutional Court Article 36(1) of the Constitution protects *all kinds of families*. Therefore, the Civil Code should not exclude non-married partners from the right to be compensated.

The judgment of the Constitutional Court was not immediately followed by the Supreme Court of Justice. In a judgment of 4 November 2003, for instance, the Supreme Court of Justice had to deal with the following case: In a collision of vehicles, *A*, a non-married woman living in a de facto union, died in an accident caused by *B*.

The victim had lived for five years with the plaintiff, and they had two children. The courts ordered the insurance company to pay damages to her *children* – they refrained, however, from ordering the insurance company to pay damages to her *partner*.

The Supreme Court argued that the judgment of the Constitutional Court was dramatically conditioned by the facts of the case involving *intentional murder*.

Furthermore, the Supreme Court argued that the legislator might establish distinctions between *legal* and de facto family. Therefore, it applies to Article 496(2) and (3).

The problem has been tackled by Law No. 23/2010 of 30 August 2010.

In the first place, a new paragraph (3) has been added to Article 496, reading that:

> 3. If the victim was living in a de facto union, the right to compensation provided in the previous paragraph shall be available in the first place to the person that lived with the victim together with the children and other descendants.

Second, the old paragraph (3) became the new paragraph (4). Therefore, Article 496 of the Portuguese Civil Code now reads as follows:

> 1. For the determination of compensation, regard must be had to non-pecuniary damage that, due to its seriousness, deserves protection by the law.

---

spouse who is not legally separated from the persons and assets and to the children or other descendants; failing the latter, to the parents or other ascendants; and, finally, to the brothers and sisters or nephews and nieces representing them.'

733. On the decision of the Constitutional Court no. 275/2002, in: Diário da República, II, 24 Jul. 2002, *see* A. Pereira, 'Portugal', in H. Koziol/B. Steininger (eds), *European Tort Law 2002* (Springer: Wien/New York 2003), 346. *A* was condemned as the author of the murder of *B*. The Portuguese Supreme Court held that the tortfeasor was to compensate the victim's relatives. Compensation for pecuniary loss was fixed at EUR 70,000; compensation for non-pecuniary loss sustained by the victim in dying was fixed at EUR 40,000; compensation for non-pecuniary loss sustained by the victim's children was fixed at EUR 15,000 for each child. Furthermore, the Supreme Court held that the tortfeasor was not to compensate the non-married partner. In keeping with Art. 496(2) and (3) of the Civil Code, non-married partners, living in a de facto union, had no right to receive compensation for her own pain and suffering. The non-married partner thus appealed to the Constitutional Court alleging the unconstitutionality of Art. 496(2) and (3) of the Portuguese Civil Code.

2. When a victim dies, the right to compensation for non-pecuniary damage shall be available, jointly, to a spouse who is not legally separated from the persons and assets and to the children or other descendants; failing the latter, to the parents or other ascendants; and, finally, to the brothers and sisters or nephews and nieces representing them.
3. If the victim was living in a de facto union, the right to compensation provided in the previous paragraph shall be available in the first place to the person that lived with the victim together with the children and other descendants.
4. The amount of compensation shall be fixed equitably by the court, having regard in any event to the circumstances mentioned in Article 494; in the event of death, regard may be taken not only of non-pecuniary damage suffered by the victim but also of such damage suffered by the persons entitled to compensation by virtue of the previous paragraphs.

V. On the Distinction Between Losses Sustained by the Victim and Losses Sustained by the Victim's Relatives – I

136. In the case of death, three (possible) losses were thus to be compensated:

In the first place, there could be damages for the loss the victim sustained *before dying*.

Second, there could be damages for the loss the victim sustained *in dying*. That is to say, there could be damages for the *loss of life*.[734]

Third, there could be damages for the loss the victim's relatives sustained.

As to the first two heads of damage, there is a discussion between three theories.

In accordance with the first, there could be no autonomous compensation for the loss the victim sustained in dying. The fact that the law of torts aims at compensating the victim would exclude compensation for the damage the victim sustained in dying.

In fact, compensation for loss of life would be logically impossible.[735]

In accordance with the second theory, there could be compensation both for the loss the victim sustained before dying and for the loss the victim sustained in dying.

Compensation for the loss the victim sustained in dying would be assigned to the victim's relatives. It would be a right of the victim's relatives – it would not be a right of the victim, the relatives acquired by inheritance.

In keeping with the third theory, there could be compensation for both losses.

734. Damages for loss of life are specifically considered under Arts 495 and 496 of the Portuguese Civil Code. The reasoning underlying compensation for the loss of life is as follows: If all personality rights deserve to be protected, namely by means compensation (for non-pecuniary loss), then the most important of all the personality rights, i.e., the right to life, also deserves to be protected, by the same means [*see*, for a comparative approach, H. Koziol, 'Wrongful Death. Basic Questions', in H. Koziol/B. Steininger (eds), *European Tort Law 2006* (Wien/New York: Springer 2007) 33: 'The idea that the destroyed life has an immaterial value and that this value continues in a claim on compensation for non-pecuniary loss does not seem bizarre.'].

735. *See*, for instance, J.M. Antunes Varela, *Das obrigações em geral I*, 608–617.

Compensation for the loss the victim sustained in dying would be assigned to the victim and transferred, on inheritance grounds, to the victim's relatives. It would be a right of the victim, the relatives acquired by inheritance.

The first theory would interpret Article 496 so as to award the victim's relatives two heads on damages. On the one hand, they would be entitled to compensation for the non-pecuniary loss the victim sustained before dying. The grounds for such compensation were to be found in the general principles of inheritance law. On the other hand, they would be entitled to compensation for the non-pecuniary loss they sustained. The grounds for such compensation were to be found in the general principles and rules of tort law.

The second and the third theories would interpret Article 496(2) and (4) so as to award the victim's relatives three heads of damages. The difference between them would be that the second theory conceives compensation for the loss of life as a right of the victim's relatives and the third conceives compensation for the loss of life as a right of the victim to be transferred to the victim's relatives on the grounds of inheritance.[736]

VI. On the Distinction Between Losses Sustained by the Victim and Losses Sustained by the Victim's Relatives – II

137. In a judgment of the Portuguese Supreme Court of 30 April 2015 delivered by Justice Salazar Casanova, the plaintiff, AA, was the mother of a 19-year-old man, BB, who died in a car accident. The victim, a student in his 11th grade, was healthy and lived with his mother and sister. In fact, he maintained a close and affectionate relationship with them, especially because his father had abandoned him at birth. Furthermore, the father was forbidden by the Court of Staryi Sambir (Lviv), Ukraine, from exercising parental authority.

The mother of the victim brought an action against the insurance company, requiring compensation in the amount of EUR 252,000, plus interest at the statutory rate.

Her claim was partially upheld. The court of First Instance and the Court of Appeal awarded the mother the amount of EUR 140,000, corresponding to the sum of EUR 80,000 for non-pecuniary damage suffered by the victim relating to the loss of his life and EUR 60,000 for non-pecuniary damage suffered by the victim's mother.

The Court of Appeal held that the compensation for the loss of life is to be awarded, *de jure proprio*, to the victim's relatives as listed in Article 496(2) of the Portuguese Civil Code (non-pecuniary damage). In the case *sub judice*, as the victim had always lived with his mother, and it was his mother who had 'played the role of father and mother', there was no doubt that only his mother was to be considered in the group of 'parents or other ascendants', defined by the legislator in Article 496(2) of the Portuguese Civil Code.

736. For a presentation of the three theories, *see*, for instance, D. Leite de Campos, 'A indemnização do dano da morte', 50 Boletim da Faculdade de Direito [da Universidade de Coimbra] (1974), 247–297.

The insurance company brought a judicial review before the Supreme Court, claiming that the position taken by the Court of Appeal regarding the interpretation of the literal content of Article 496(2) of the Portuguese Civil Code was incorrect.

It claimed that it could not be assumed that the right to compensation '*is born, directly, in the legal sphere*' of the close relatives referred to in Article 496(2) of the Civil Code. It claimed, further, that the close relatives' right to compensation for the loss of life could not be determined according to a *subjective* criterion based on 'affection and proximity' – it should be determined according to an *objective* criterion. The criteria of *affection* and *proximity* could only apply to the non-pecuniary loss sustained by the victim's relatives.

The Supreme Court of Justice upheld the position of the Court of Appeal, stating that the right to compensation for *non-pecuniary damage* is to be assigned *de jure proprio* and *ex lege.* It would emerge in the 'legal sphere' of the relatives mentioned therein.

Indeed, loss of life could, and should, be considered an 'autonomous fraction' among the non-pecuniary losses suffered by the victim's relatives.

Furthermore, the Supreme Court of Justice upheld that the close relatives' right to compensation should be determined according to a subjective criterion.

Once it was proven that a member of the group 'parents or other ascendants' had not suffered any damage arising from the death of a relative, there would be no legal reason to award him/her 'compensation on this basis'. In other words, 'the assignment of non-pecuniary compensation to the other parent was to be excluded, because it was proven that, within the group, only the mother suffered moral damage'. Therefore, the Supreme Court confirmed the decision of the Court of Appeal and ordered the insurance company to pay the victim's mother the *entire compensation amount* for *non-pecuniary losses.*

The position of the Supreme Court does not seem to be totally correct, especially in regard to the interpretation of Article 496 of the Portuguese Civil Code.

Death damage, corresponding to the suppression of the life of a *victim* – hence, to the injury of *his/her right to life* – should be considered an autonomous head of damages. It should not be included in the global category of non-pecuniary loss sustained by the victim's relatives.

It is submitted that Article 496(2) and (4) of the Portuguese Civil Code distinguishes the loss sustained by the victim and the loss sustained by the victim's relatives.[737]

The loss sustained by the victim is to be assigned to the victim's relatives on the grounds of inheritance law (*de jure hereditario*). The loss sustained by the victim's relatives is to be assigned to the victim's relatives on the grounds of tort law (*de jure proprio*).

---

737. *See* the judgments of the Portuguese Supreme Court of 5 of June 2018 (Salreta Pereira) that fixed the amount of EUR 65,000 for the death damage and EUR 30,000 to compensate for each children's non-pecuniary damage; 12 Feb. 2021 (Abrantes Geraldes) that fixed the death damage compensation of EUR 100,000 and EUR 40,000 for each parent's non-pecuniary damage; 25 Feb. 2021 (Rosa Tching) that fixed the amount of EUR 80,000 for the loss sustained by the victim, EUR 20,000 for the suffering till death and EUR 35,000 as a compensation for the moral damage suffered by his son.

In keeping with the distinction in Article 496(2) and (4) of the Portuguese Civil Code, it is submitted that the requirement of affection and proximity should apply exclusively to the compensation for the loss sustained by the victim's relatives.

The rule should be that compensation for the loss sustained by the victim is not to be subject to restrictions based on affection and proximity. In fact, the right to compensation for the loss sustained by the victim is to be transmitted, *de jure hereditario,* to the individuals listed in Article 496(2) of the Portuguese Civil Code. Exceptions to the rule that the right to compensation for the loss sustained by the victim should not be subject to restrictions based on affection and proximity should apply only in cases where there is no affective, emotional relationship at all between the victim and their relatives.[738]

The case considered by the judgment of the Supreme Court of 30 April 2015 clearly fell within the scope of the exception. It had been established that the father left the victim at birth and that he was legally forbidden from exercising parental authority.

The case thus represents a situation where, exceptionally, the *transmission* of the right to compensate the father for the *death damage* should be *excluded*, and *a fortiori*, where the *compensation* for the *father's own non-pecuniary damage* might be *denied.*

VII. On the Distinction Between Losses Sustained by the Victim and Losses Sustained by the Victim's Relatives – III

138. It follows from the interpretation of Article 496(2) and (4) of the Portuguese Civil Code that close relatives are entitled to two types of compensation for the death damage.

On the one hand, they are entitled to compensation for their own non-pecuniary loss.

On the other hand, they are entitled to compensation for the non-pecuniary losses of the victim.

It is a fact that awarding the relatives a double compensation is controversial.

Professor Koziol, for instance, argues that 'the two solutions – claim of the surviving successor and inheritable claim of the deceased victim – cannot be combined because then relatives would receive double compensation, once for their own grief due to the victim's death and once as an heir of the claim for compensation of the victim's loss of life. Therefore, I feel that the legal system has to decide whether the surviving dependants shall have a claim in their own right or inherit a claim of the deceased victim'.[739]

Even though it is a fact that awarding the relatives a double compensation for non-pecuniary losses is controversial, it is submitted that it is accepted, for it involves neither theoretical nor practical failure. In fact, the reason why there is double compensation is that there is a double loss. First, there is a (non-pecuniary)

---

738. *See* A.G. Dias Pereira, *Direitos dos pacientes e responsabilidade médica* (Coimbra: Coimbra Editora 2015) 160–172.

739. *See* H. Koziol, 'Wrongful Death. Basic Questions', 34.

loss on the part of the victim, which consists of the loss of life, and second, there is a (non-pecuniary) loss on the part of the victim's relatives, which consists of bereavement and grief.

For both losses are different, compensation for both losses is to be different.

In principle, the victims' relatives bear the burden of proving the existence of non-pecuniary, moral loss. In spite of the fact that courts tend to facilitate that proof – even *presuming* that the surviving spouse and the children do suffer from the loss of the deceased – there is a difference between cases where emotional relationships are proved and cases where emotional relationships simply are presumed.

If special emotional relationships (between the deceased and his or her relatives) are proven, the amount of damages tends to be significantly higher.

There is no limitation on the relevant means of proof. Therefore, there is no need to present a medical report, such as a psychiatric report, to prove non-pecuniary, moral loss.

In a judgment of 29 November 2016 delivered by Justice Fonseca Ramos, the victim was a 34-year-old man, married with two children aged 12 and 6, who *drowned* due to the negligent filling of a dam's reservoir. The compensation for the loss the victim sustained in dying was fixed at EUR 70,000. The compensation for the loss the victim sustained before dying was fixed at EUR 15,000. In fact, the victim had a perception of imminent death since there was a time gap between the drowning and the termination of his vital functions. The combined compensation for the loss the victim's relatives sustained was set at EUR 90,000.

Even if a given parcel of the sum is not very high, all together the compensation for non-pecuniary losses is in accordance with European standards.

Finally, there is some debate in the literature concerning the amount of damages to be awarded in case of death (with respect to the specific '*dano da morte*').

On the one hand, it is argued that compensation should be equal for everyone on the ground that, as all lives are equal, compensation for the loss of life should be equal.[740]

On the other hand, it is argued that compensation could be different.

Article 496 refers to the degree of fault of the defendant, to the economic situation of both the plaintiff and the defendant, and to the circumstances of the case.

As the degrees of fault, the economic situations, and circumstances of the case are always different, compensation for the loss of life should be different.[741]

The Portuguese Supreme Court seems to favour the second thesis.

In a judgment of 25 January 2002, for instance, the Supreme Court held that, in establishing the amount of damages for loss of life, *the concrete circumstances of the life of the deceased person are relevant*. The fact that the victim was 24 years old 'with a long life expectancy and a promising future in front of her' was taken into consideration.[742]

740. *See* D. Leite de Campos, 'A vida, a morte e a sua indemnização', Boletim do Ministério da Justiça, 365 (1987), 15, and J.J. Sousa Dinis, 'Dano corporal em acidentes de viação', in: Colectânea de Jurisprudência – Acórdãos do STJ (2001), 7.

741. *See*, for instance, A.G. Dias Pereira, *Direitos dos pacientes e responsabilidade médica*, 171–172.

742. The principles established in the judgment of 25 Jan. 2002 were followed, for instance, in a judgment of 11 Dec. 2008.

VIII. Non-pecuniary Loss Suffered by Persons Having a Close Relationship with the Victim of a Serious Non-fatal Injury

139. In the case of a serious non-fatal injury, the non-pecuniary loss suffered by persons having a close relationship with the victim is only compensated in exceptional circumstances.

In a judgment of the Oporto Court of Appeal of 29 June 2003, the victim of a car accident had suffered serious non-pecuniary losses, including sexual impotence.

The plaintiff, the victim's wife, claimed compensation for non-pecuniary damage consisting of being unable to have sexual intercourse with her husband.

The Court considered that the wife's loss was *direct* damage, arising from the infringement of her right to the free development of her personality within the framework of a family: on the one hand, marriage creates the mutual *duty of cohabitation,* and the *mutual duty of cohabitation* implies rights and duties relating to *regular sexual life;* on the other hand, marriage creates the mutual *duty of fidelity* and the mutual *duty of fidelity* limits the legitimate exercise of the spouses' rights to parenthood and motherhood.

In short, the Court considered that there is a *right to sexual life within marriage* according to the principles and rules relating both to personality rights and to family law.

This line of reasoning was later accepted, for instance, in the judgments of the Portuguese Supreme Court of 26 May 2010 and 16 January 2014.

In the judgment of 26 May 2010, the plaintiff was the wife of the victim of a car accident. The victim, who was born in 1972, was in a coma for eight days, underwent three dramatic operations, and was in a hospital for four months. In spite of all the surgery and treatments he underwent, the victim continually experienced severe pain and suffering, absolute and permanent impotence, as well as incontinence. The victim's wife, who was born in November 1976, claimed compensation for non-pecuniary damage arising from witnessing the pain and suffering of her husband, from being unable to have normal sexual relations with him, from being unable to have more children with him – at least, by natural methods – and for all the anxiety and distress she continually experienced.

The Court of First Instance awarded compensation of EUR 98,674 for pecuniary damage, EUR 150,000 for the non-pecuniary loss sustained by the husband and EUR 20,000 for the non-pecuniary loss sustained by the wife. The court of second instance, the Guimaraes' Court of Appeal, awarded compensation of EUR 54,981 for pecuniary damage – considering that an insurance company had already paid the amount of EUR 85,018 for incapacity to work – a compensation of EUR 200,000 for the non-pecuniary loss sustained by the husband and compensation of EUR 50,000 for the non-pecuniary loss sustained by the wife.

Concerning the damage to the husband, the Supreme Court awarded a higher compensation for pecuniary loss, EUR 153,674 and upheld the compensatory amount of EUR 200,000 for non-pecuniary loss. Concerning the damage to the wife, the Supreme Court upheld the compensatory amount of EUR 50,000. In justifying deviation from the principles and rule in Article 496(3) of the Portuguese Civil Code, the Supreme Court argued that serious injury, albeit non-fatal, harmed the close relatives of the victim.

The judgment of 16 January 2014, aimed at standardizing case law delivered by Justice João Bernardo, affirmed a general rule, according to which persons having a close relationship with the victim of a serious non-fatal injury are entitled to compensation.

The judgment referred to the car accident of a non-qualified worker, who was the victim of a collision between the trash car where he was transported and a circulating vehicle. The victim sustained a serious bodily injury that required hospitalization for several months and was left with severe *sequelae* and permanent disability for work of 80%.

The Supreme Court argued that Articles 483(1) and 496(1) of the Portuguese Civil Code allow for a compensation for the non-pecuniary loss of his wife.

In the first place, considering Article 483(1), it is submitted that serious, non-fatal injury to the victim would entail an infringement of the general right to one's personality of the persons having a close relationship with the victim, such as spouses.

Second, considering Article 496(1), it is submitted that non-pecuniary losses resulting from the infringement of the general right to one's personality of the persons having a close relationship with the victim are so serious that they deserve compensation by the law.

In keeping with the judgment of the Supreme Court, in the exceptional cases where liability may be justified, all persons having a close relationship with the victim may be entitled to compensation – there would be no reason to limit that concept to spouses.[743]

IX. Non-pecuniary Loss Suffered by Persons Having a Close Relationship with a Pet

140. Law No. 8/2017 of 3 March 2017, which entered into force as recently as 1 May 2017, amended the Portuguese Civil Code by adding a new Article 493-A:

> (1) In any case of injury to an animal, the person responsible shall be obliged to pay compensation for the costs incurred in seeking to save the injured animal […].
>
> (2) Compensation [for the costs incurred in seeking to save the injured animal] is due, even if such costs exceedthe pecuniary value of the animal itself.

743. For further developments, *see*, for instance, G. Fontes Cascarejo, *Danos não patrimoniais dos familiares da vítima de lesão corporal grave* (Coimbra: Livraria Almedina 2016). The author argues that serious, non-fatal injury affects family relationships, which end up with close relatives facing 'suffering' and 'anguish'. G. Fontes Cascarejo argues that Art. 70 of the Portuguese Civil Code authorizes the protection of a *subjective right to family relationships* and that the connection between Art. 70 and both Arts 483(1) and 496(1) of the Portuguese Civil Code requires that compensation for non-pecuniary loss is awarded directly to the relatives, as a right of their own, and not as *damages par ricochet*. Finally, the author considers that these damages can be construed by following the lines of the Italian concept of *existential damage*, or perhaps, even by following the lines of the French concept of *préjudice d'accompagnement*.

(3) In the event of injury to a pet, causing either its death, or an amputation of any of its important bodily parts, or a serious hindrance to its ability to move, the owner of the pet is entitled, in accordance to Article 496 (1) of the Portuguese Civil Code, to an appropriate compensation for the pain and moral suffering he or she sustained, to be fixed equitably by the court.

X. Compensation for Non-pecuniary Loss: With a Particular Reference to the Criteria for Compensation of Bodily Injury in Traffic Accidents

141. Decree-Law No. 291/2007 of 21 August 2007 created *tables of bodily harm.* They set the standard according to which the judge is to assess whether the proposal of the insurance companies to compensate the victims of traffic accidents is reasonable.

Tables of bodily harm were regulated by Ordinance (*portaria*) No. 377/2008 of 26 May 2008, amended by Ordinance (*portaria*) No. 679/2009 of 25 June 2009.[744]

In keeping with Ordinance No. 679/2009, proposals for compensation are to refer to the values set in Annexes I to V, from which the following examples are taken:

Loss of life of a person under 25 years of age is to be compensated up to EUR 61,560; loss of life of a person over 75 years of age is to be compensated up to EUR 30,780.

For moral damage of the deceased before death, close relatives are to be awarded from EUR 2,052 (twenty-four hours of suffering before death) to EUR 7,182 (over seventy-two hours of suffering before death). These amounts can be increased depending on pain and suffering and the foreseeability of death. For moral damage of the spouse, he or she is to be awarded compensation up to EUR 25,650. For moral damage of each of the parents of a deceased child, he and she are to be awarded compensation up to EUR 15,390.

In the case of the loss of a foetus, compensation depends on the age of the mother and on the fact that the foetus is their first or second child. In the case that the foetus is their first child, each parent is to be awarded from EUR 7,695 to EUR 12,825; in the event that the foetus is their second child or more, from EUR 2,565 to EUR 7,695. If the mother is over 40 years of age, there can be a majoration of the compensatory sums of up to 50%.

The table for calculation of compensation for violations of physical and psychical integrity takes into consideration the age of the victim and the severity of the damage to physical and psychical integrity. For example, a 20-year-old person with *very severe injuries* (evaluated at 95 points out of 100) would receive EUR 218,500 for bodily injury; a 58-year-old person with medium injuries (40 points out of 100) would receive EUR 36,800.

In the case of pain, the victim is to be awarded a sum from EUR 820 to EUR 5,335 (as an assessment of the *quantum doloris*); in the case of aesthetical damage, the victim is to be awarded a sum from EUR 820 (low *aesthetical damage*) to EUR 10,260 (*severe aesthetical damage*).

744. On Ordinances No. 377/2008 of 26 May 2008 and No. 679/2009 of 25 Jun. 2009, *see,* for instance, M. Graça Trigo, *Responsabilidade civil. Temas especiais*, 82–85.

As to non-pecuniary losses connected with difficulties in the professional life of a person under the age of 30, compensation is to be from EUR 25,000 (medium handicap) to EUR 102,600 (severe handicap); as to non-pecuniary losses connected with difficulties in the professional life of a person between 61 and 70 years of age, it is to be from EUR 10,260 to EUR 41,040.

The table for calculation of future pecuniary loss takes into consideration the following factors: the annual income of the victim (previously declared for tax purposes), the nominal interest rate of financial products, and the number of years for which the income was due.

Even if the injured person does not have the right to this compensation for future pecuniary damage (e.g., if she is a housewife), he/she, in case of (partial) permanent incapacity, has the right to be compensated on the basis of '*danno biologico*', that is, on the basis of the injury to his physical and psychical integrity.

Finally, as to expenses incurred and loss of income caused by incapacity:

Loss of the income declared for tax purposes is to be compensated. The number of days of lost income will be calculated according to the annual income of the victim.

Expenses incurred as a result of the accident, such as accommodation, transportation, and medicines, are to be compensated if they are proven; temporary domestic aid is to be compensated up to EUR 6.16 an hour; adaptation of a vehicle is to be compensated up to EUR 7,695; adaptation of the house is to be compensated up to EUR 30,780.

It should be emphasized that the effect of tables of bodily harm on compensation is subject to three limits. In the first place, they apply only to a particular type of accident – i.e., to traffic accidents; second, they apply only to the proposals for compensation of non-pecuniary loss in traffic accidents; finally, they are not binding to the courts.

In accordance with Article 496(1) of the Portuguese Civil Code, courts have the discretionary power to fix equitable compensation for non-pecuniary losses; furthermore, in keeping with Article 566(3), courts have the discretionary power to fix equitable compensation for pecuniary losses, the exact amount of which is difficult to determine.

In spite of the fact they have no *direct effect*, as they are merely *indicative,* they can be expected to have an indirect influence on the compensation amounts awarded by the courts in all types of accidents – such as in cases of medical malpractice.

Chapter 5. Various Damages (Property)

142. The Portuguese legal system protects property under the general clause of unlawfulness enshrined in Article 483, as seen with respect to unlawfulness.[745]

745. *See*, Unlawfulness – Liability for the infringement of property rights.

Chapter 6. Interference with Collateral Benefits

§1. Insurance

143. The Portuguese Insurance system is mainly regulated by the Decree-Law No. 72/2008, 16 April 2008. Its Article 137 relates to civil liability insurance, stating that '(…) the insurer gives cover to the risk of arising, in the insured's estate, a duty to compensate third parties', adding Article 138(1), '(…) up to the limit of the insured capital per accident, contract validity period or per injured party'.

Article 138(2) clearly recognizes that, except otherwise stipulated, the relevant damage is the same as assessed by general tort rules. By default, 139(1) encompasses all the tort liability triggering events that occur during the contract period, even if the claim for compensation is made after its expiration date.

The obvious interference that an insurance contract, especially a civil liability insurance, has on the tort system is that it adds or changes the implicated parties. Article 140(1) allows for the intervention of the insurer in any legal action that concerns a duty to compensate linked to the undertaken risk. As laid down by Article 140(2), each insurance contract can grant the injured party to take legal action directly against the insurer, either jointly with the insured party or singly. In keeping with Article 140(7), if the insured party either recognizes the aggrieved one's right to compensation or pays it alone and without the consent of the insurer, that cannot be used against the latter.

Article 144 establishes the right to redress in the case of wilful misconduct, i.e., despite initially being the first to respond, afterwards, the insurer has the right to claim the spent value from the insured because of underlying misconduct.

An important aspect of the interference of insurance laws within the law of torts is the existence of motor vehicle compulsory insurance.

In consonance with Article 4 of the Decree-Law No. 291/2007, 21 August 2007, 'Every person who can be civilly liable to repair bodily or material damages caused to third parties by a ground motor vehicle, whose driving requires driving license, as well as by its trailers, and with habitual parking in Portugal, must, for them to circulate, be cover by insurance that encompasses those damages, as laid down by this Decree-Law.' Normally, in line with Article 6(1) of the 291/2007 Decree-Law, the duty to be insured lies upon the vehicle's owner, but it can also be the current holder's responsibility – e.g., be it a usufructuary, a buyer or a lessee. Nevertheless, Article 6(2) exempts those cited above from this obligation if a third party makes an insurance contract with the same object.

Once the liability-triggering event happens, according to Article 34, the insured party has the duty to communicate it to the insurance company with as much information as possible, including witnesses and evidence. It should be done as briefly as possible and, in any case, always within eight days, either of the event or from having knowledge of it. The company has the duty to provide technical expertise in order to determine what happened, as well as to evaluate bodily injuries – in line with Articles 36 and 37. If the final report indicates that the insurance should cover the event, the insurer must make a reasonable proposal of compensation;[746] in the case of an indication not to accept liability, the insurer has the duty to give a well-founded reason.[747]

Article 11(2) states that the insurance enshrined in Article 4 covers all the damages suffered by pedestrians, cyclists and other users of non-motorized vehicles as long as the general rules of civil liability grant them the right to compensation.

The insured capital can also influence the amount of compensation, regardless of the assessed damages, since Article 24 of the Decree-law 291/2007 gives ground to the proportional limitation of compensations if there are several victims and the global compensation amount surpasses the insured capital sum.

Article 27 is dedicated to the right to redress and, as seen above with regard to the Decree-Law No. 72/2008, the insurance company can claim the amount paid if, among others, the liable person acted with wilful misconduct; if the driver is under the influence of alcohol, above the legal limit, or of illegal drugs; if the driver did not have a driving licence, or if the vehicle is abandoned after the event, etc.

§2. Social Security

144. Despite both Social Security and Tort Law having the ability to serve as safety nets for aggrieved parties, their operating mode is different. Tort Law spins around the balance of freedom and personal responsibility, whereas Social Security is enshrined in the Constitution as a universal Social Right coordinated by the State[748] to socialize the answer to misfortune. It is mainly regulated by Law No. 4/2007 of 16 January 2007. The prior is a problem of individual justice, whereas the latter is rooted in collective justice. It is not guided by the same principles as Tort Law, does not aim to restore any hypothetical situation that would presently exist if it were not for some damage, and its intervention does not rely on wrongfulness or fault.[749]

Article 63 of the Constitution of the Portuguese Republic states:

1. Everyone has the right to social security.
2. The state is charged with organizing, coordinating and subsidizing a unified and decentralized social security system, with the participation of the trade unions, other organizations that represent workers and associations that represent the other beneficiaries.
3. The social security system shall protect citizens in illness and old age and when they are disabled, widowed or orphaned, as well as when they are unemployed or in any other situation that entails a lack of or reduction in means of subsistence or the ability to work.

---

746. As we saw with regard to pecuniary damages in case of death or personal injury.
747. Respectively, Arts 38, 39 and 40 of the Decree-Law No. 291/2007.
748. *See*, Art. 94 Law No. 4/2007 16 Jan. 2007.
749. *See*, M.J. Almeida Costa, *Direito das Obrigações*, Almedina, 2013, 552.

4. All periods of work shall, as laid down by law, contribute to the calculation of old age and disability pensions, regardless of the sector of activity in which they were performed.
5. With a view to the pursuit of the social solidarity objectives that are particularly enshrined in this article and in Articles 67(2)(b), 69, 70(1)(e), 71 and 72, the state shall, as laid down by law, support and inspect the activities and modus operandi of private charitable institutions and other not-for-profit institutions that are recognized to be in the public interest.

By law, the Social Security system must be, among other things, universal, i.e., for everyone and global, i.e., encompassing all situations of decrease or loss of livelihoods or ability to work.[750]

Article 26(1) of Law No. 4/2007 establishes as its goals the safeguarding of citizens' basic rights, equal opportunities and the promotion of well-being and social cohesion. Mainly by, adds (2), assuring an existential minimum for economically deprived citizens; poverty and social exclusion prevention and eradication; compensation for family burdens and compensations for burdens with disability and dependency.

The welfare system, according to Article 50, provides substitutive payments to cover for labour income impacted by legally stipulated events, such as those laid in Article 52(1), disease; motherhood, fatherhood and adoption; unemployment; work accident and work-related illnesses; disablement; old age; death. Article 52(2) allows for this list expansion if justified by any new social risks.

These substitutive payments are calculated under Article 62, considering the registered salary and other factors such as the nature of each circumstance, the contribution period, the beneficiary's age and the degree of disability.

With regard to civil liability, Article 70 states that 'If, for the same fact, there is any concurrence between the right to any Social Security payment with the right to compensation arising from the action of a third party, Social Security's entities are subrogated in the injured person's rights up to the threshold of payments that they are required to make.'

750. J.J. Gomes Canotilho e Vital Moreira, *Constituição da República Portuguesa Anotada*, Coimbra Editora, 4.ªed., 2007, 816–818.

Chapter 7. Other Remedies

§1. Restitution (For Unjust Enrichment)

145. Generally, damages are assessed as seen[751] by comparing the present situation with the hypothetically present situation that would exist were it not the wrongful action. That is different from assessing damages from a restitution perspective, i.e., considering the gains the injurer had in connection to the damage. Nevertheless, recently, by the impetus of EU Law, some forms of restitution have been permeating the Portuguese legal system. As an example, the recent EU Directive 2016/943, 8 June 2016,[752] on the 'protection of undisclosed know-how and business information (trade secrets) against their unlawful acquisition, use and disclosure', considers, in its Article 14(2), 'the unfair profits made by the infringer'. The Code of Intellectual Property implemented this Directive and Article 347 provides similar criteria for compensation.[753]

146. The same can be seen in Article 211 of the Code of Copyright and Related Rights (approved by Decree-Law No. 63/85 of 14 March 1985 and amended up to Decree-Law No. 9/2021 of 29 January 2021), which determines that: '2 – When determining the amount of compensation for losses and damages, whether material or non-pecuniary, the court must take into account the profit obtained by the offender, the lost profits and consequential damages suffered by the injured party and the costs incurred by the latter in protecting the right to author or related rights, as well as with the investigation and cessation of conduct harmful to their rights. 3 – To calculate the compensation due to the injured party, the amount of revenue resulting from the illicit conduct of the offender, namely the illegally performed show or shows, must be taken into account.'

§2. Injunctive Relief

147. With regard to personality rights, Article 70(2) of the Civil Code states, 'Regardless of any civil liability, the person threatened or offended may apply to measures adequate to the circumstances of the case to prevent the threat from being realized or to attenuate the effects of an offence already committed', allowing injured parties to ask the Court for some form of injunctive relief.

Keeping with Article 878 and following the Code of Civil Procedure, the law consecrates a special procedure to uphold personality rights. Like Article 70(2) of the

751. *See*, Assessment and Compensation of Damages.
752. Available at: https://eur-lex.europa.eu/legal-content/EN/TXT/PDF/?uri=CELEX:32016L0943&from=PT.
753. Namely in n. 2 and 3: 2 – When determining the amount of compensation for losses and damages, the court must take into account, in particular, the profit obtained by the offender and the resulting damages and lost profits suffered by the injured party and must take into account the costs incurred with protection, investigation and cessation of conduct harmful to your rights. 3 – To calculate the compensation due to the injured party, the amount of revenue resulting from the illicit conduct of the offender must be taken into account.

Civil Code, Article 878 of the Code of Civil Procedure establishes that 'The Court can be petitioned to declare the concrete appropriate measures to avoid the consummation of any unlawful and direct threat to the physical or moral personality of a human being, as well as to mitigate or cease the effects of an already perpetrated offence.'

Being a special procedure, it deviates from the general rules. When the Court reaches a final decision, it will specifically enunciate the behaviours that the defendant must adopt, and Article 879(4) adds that a time period can be set accompanied by a periodic penalty payment for each day of delay or for each breach. Further, Article 879(5) allows, in certain terms, for a provisional and unappealable judgment if the evidence suggests impending and irreversible harm.

Concerning property rights, possessors and owners have various mechanisms to defend their rights.

In terms of possession, Article 1276 of the Civil Code lays down the right to preventive action, i.e., useful for non-consummated dangers, stating that 'If the possessor has a fair fear of being disturbed or dispossessed by others, the author of the threats will be, by request of the threatened party, mandated to abstain from aggravating the situation, under penalty of receiving a fine and being liable for the caused harm.' When the damage already exists, Article 1277 grants the disturbed or dispossessed possessor the right to direct action (referring to Article 336),[754] as well as the right to resort to legal action, where, based on Article 1278(1), the Court can permit provisional possession to the plaintiff while a final decision on the merits is pending. If the dispossessor used violence against the plaintiff, the Court is allowed by Article 1279 to grant provisional possession without a judicial hearing.

As to property rights, Article 1314 also grants the right to direct action (in line with Article 336),[755] and, mainly, in Article 1311, the right to claim ownership, which involves the judicial recognition of the respective right and restitution of property.

A different path is resorting to an interlocutory injunction, which is always an urgent procedure,[756] enshrined in Article 362 and following the Code of Civil Procedure.

Article 362 gives ground for unspecified interlocutory injunctions, stating that 'Whenever somebody has the justified fear of undergoing serious and hardly reparable harm to a personal right caused by others, a claim of an adequate preserving or anticipating injunction, to assure the effectiveness of the protected right, is available.' The claim's success is dependent on the existence of *fumus boni iuris* – reasonable evidence of the existence of the claimed right and the mere likelihood of success[757] – *periculum in mora* – the danger of irreparably aggravating the situation by delaying the necessary measures;[758] and, lastly, a founded interest to take legal action through an instrument of this type.

754. *See*, Self-Help.
755. *See*, Self-Help.
756. *See* Art. 363(1) of the Code of Civil Procedure.
757. *See*, M.F. Carvalho Gonçalves, *Providências Cautelares*, 3.ªed., Almedina, 2017, 178–183.
758. For a more detailed analysis, *see*, M.F. Carvalho Gonçalves, *Providências Cautelares*, 3.ªed., Almedina, 2017, 193–211.

One specifically consecrated interlocutory injunction is the norm within Article 377 and following the Code of Civil Procedure, which contemplates the provisional restitution of possession when violent dispossession occurs. If any violence exists, Article 379 of the Code of Civil Procedure refers to the usage of an unspecified interlocutory injunction (in line, as seen, with Article 362 of the same Code).

Lastly, another specifically consecrated interlocutory injunction is in Article 388 and following the Code of Civil Procedure, and it relates to the granting of a provisional compensation. Article 388(1) states, 'While a legal action grounded in death or bodily injury is pending, the injured parties, as well as third parties with a right to compensation under Article 495 (3) of the Civil Code, can petition for a defined amount, in the form of annuities, as a way of provisional reparation of damages.' According to Article 388(2), the Court will grant it if, as a result of the caused damages, a situation of need is noted or, adds (4), the caused harm jeopardizes the rights to livelihood and to housing. Its intent is clearly to provide an available safety net for some victims and to obviate the disadvantages of a long procedure.[759] This provisional amount is assessed equitably, as established in Article 388(3).

§3. Punitive Damages

148. Albeit prevention and repression play a role within the Portuguese law of torts,[760] punitive damages are not accepted.[761] Article 562 clearly states that the compensation's scope is reparation and that its guideline is the present hypothetical situation were it not the damage.[762]

Nevertheless, the Civil Code has some suspicious norms whose punitive nature can be questioned. Article 1320(2) states that 'However, if there is proof that the animals were allured with fraud or artifice by the shelter's owner, the latter is required to render them to their previous owner or, if restitution is not possible, to pay up to three times more of the animal's value.' Similarly, Article 1552(1) states that 'The owner that, without fair motive, causes an absolute or relative enclave on their own property, can only create a right to servitude if they pay an aggravated compensation', adding (2) that 'the aggravated compensation is fixated, considering the owner's fault, up to twice of the value of a commonly assessed compensation'. Still, some doctrine detects, in norms like the above-cited, a mere scope of prevention.[763]

---

759. *See*, M.F. Carvalho Gonçalves, *Providências Cautelares*, 3.ªed., Almedina, 2017, 296–303.
760. *See*, above, Function of the Law of Torts.
761. *See* P.C. Monteiro Guimarães, *Os danos punitivos e a função punitiva da responsabilidade civil, in* RFDUC, A. XV, T.1, 2001, 160–162.
762. *See*, above, Assessment and Compensation of Damages.
763. *See* M. Miranda Barbosa, *Lições de Responsabilidade Civil,* Principia, 2017, 79–80.

Selected Bibliography

Alarcão, R. (1983). Direito das obrigações (Texto elaborado pelos Drs. J. Sousa Ribeiro, J.F. Sinde Monteiro, Almeno de Sá e J.C. Proença, com base nas lições do Prof. Doutor Rui de Alarcão ao 3.º ano jurídico) (Coimbra).

Albuquerque Matos, F.M. (2011). *Responsabilidade civil por ofensa ao crédito ou ao bom nome* (Coimbra: Livraria Almedina).

Andrade, M. (1966). *Teoria geral das obrigações*, 3rd. ed. (Coimbra: Livraria Almedina).

Almeida Costa, M.J. (2009). *Direito das obrigações*. 12th. ed. (Coimbra. Livraria Almedina).

Antunes Varela, J.M. (2000). *Das obrigações em geral*. Vol. I. 10th. ed. (Coimbra: Livraria Almedina).

Ataíde, R. (2015). Responsabilidade civil por violação de deveres no tráfego (Coimbra: Livraria Almedina).

Brandão Proença, J.C. (1997). A conduta do lesado como pressuposto e critério de imputação do dano extracontratual (Coimbra: Livraria Almedina).

Brandão Proença, J.C. (2017). 'A responsabilidade civil extracontratual nos 50 anos de vigência do Código Civil: um olhar à luz do direito contemporâneo', in: E. Vaz Sequeira/F. Oliveira e Sá (eds), *Edição comemorativa do cinquentenário do Código Civil* (Lisboa: Universidade Católica Editora) 313–388.

Calvão da Silva, J. (1990). *Responsabilidade civil do produtor* (Coimbra: Livraria Almedina).

Carneiro da Frada, M. (2006). *Direito civil. Responsabilidade civil. O método do caso* (Coimbra: Livraria Almedina).

Carneiro da Frada, M. (2004). *Teoria da confiança e responsabilidade civil* (Coimbra: Livraria Almedina).

Carneiro da Frada, M. (2015). *Forjar o direito* (Coimbra: Livraria Almedina).

Dias Pereira, A.G. (2015). *Direitos dos pacientes e responsabilidade médica* (Coimbra: Centro de Direito Biomédico/Coimbra Editora).

Galvão Telles, I. (1997). *Direito das obrigações*, 7th. ed. (Coimbra: Coimbra Editora).

Menezes Cordeiro, A. (1984). *Da boa fé no direito civil*. Vols. I and II (Coimbra: Livraria Almedina).

Menezes Cordeiro, A. (1996). Da responsabilidade civil dos administradores das sociedades comerciais (Lisboa: Lex).

Selected Bibliography

Menezes Cordeiro, A. (2010). Tratado de direito civil português, I. – Direito das obrigações, III. – Gestão de negócios. Enriquecimento sem causa. Responsabilidade civil (Coimbra: Livraria Almedina) = Menezes Cordeiro, A. (2017). Tratado de direito civil, vol. VIII – Direito das obrigações, Getão de negócios. Enriquecimento sem causa. Responsabilidade civil (Coimbra: Livraria Almedina).

Menezes Leitão, L.M. (2018). *Direito das obrigações*, vol. I – *Introdução. Da consttuição das obrigações.* 12th. ed. (Coimbra: Livraria Almedina).

Miranda Barbosa, M. (2013). Do nexo de causalidade ao nexo de imputação: contributo para a compreensão da natureza ninária e personalística do requisito causal ao nível da responsabilidade civil extracontratual. Vols. I and II (Cascais: Principia).

Miranda Barbosa, M. (2014). Responsabilidade civil extracontratual: novas perspetivas em matéria de nexo de causalidade (Cascais: Principia).

Miranda Barbosa, M. (2017). *Lições de responsabilidade civil* (Cascais: Principia).

Mota Pinto, P. (2008). *Interesse contratual negativo e interesse contratual positivo.* Vols. I and II (Coimbra: Coimbra Editora).

Moura Vicente, D. (2001). Da responsabilidade pré-contratual em direito internacional privado (Coimbra: Livraria Almedina).

Pessoa Jorge, F. (1999). *Ensaio sobre os pressupostos da responsabilidade civil* (Coimbra: Livraria Almedina).

Ribeiro de Faria, J. (2000). *Direito das obrigações.* Vols. I and II (Coimbra: Livraria Almedina).

Santos Júnior, E. (2003) Da responsabilidade civil de terceiro por lesão do direito de crédito (Coimbra: Livraria Almedina).

Sinde Monteiro, J.F. (1974). Reparação dos danos em acidentes de trãnsito. Um estudo de direito comparado sobre a substituição da responsabilidade civil por um novo seguro de acidentes de trãnsito (Coimbra).

Sinde Monteiro, J.F. (1983). *Estudos sobre a responsabilidade civil* (Coimbra: Livraria Almedina).

Sinde Monteiro, J.F. (1989). Responsabilidade por conselhos, recomendações ou informações (Coimbra: Livraria Almedina).

Sinde Monteiro, J.F. (2005). 'Rudimentos da responsabilidade civil', in: *Revista da Faculdade de Direito da Universidade do Porto* 2 (2005), 349–390.

Soares Pereira, R. (2017). O nexo de causalidade na responsabilidade delitual. Fundamento e limites do juízo de condicionalidade (Coimbra: Livraria Almedina).

Sousa Antunes, H. (2011). Da inclusão do lucro ilícito entre as consequências da responsabilidade civil extracontratual: a sua legitimação pelo dano (Coimbra: Coimbra Editora).

Trigo, M.G. (2009). *Responsabilidade delitual por facto de terceiro* (Coimbra: Coimbra Editora).

Trigo, M.G. (2015). *Responsabilidade civil. Temas especiais* (Lisboa: Universidade Católica Editora).

Index

The numbers here refer to paragraph numbers.

Index

www.ingramcontent.com/pod-product-compliance
Ingram Content Group UK Ltd.
Pitfield, Milton Keynes, MK11 3LW, UK
UKHW020140290926
15471UKWH00003B/617

9 789403 537498